Two person were in
at Broad   Au

Vehiciles Collid

vehicles col
(SENTINEL P

TRUTH OR CONSEQUENCES

Improbable Adventures,

a Near-Death Experience,

and Unexpected Redemption

in the New Mexico Desert

Newspaper clipping from a report of the crash. Image from *Sierra County Sentinel*.

DANIEL ASA ROSE

TRUTH or CONSEQUENCES

HIGH
ROAD
BOOKS

ALBUQUERQUE

HIGH
ROAD

High Road Books is an imprint of the University of New Mexico Press
© 2023 by Daniel Asa Rose
All rights reserved. Published 2023
Printed in the United States of America

Library of Congress Cataloging-in-Publication Data
Names: Rose, Daniel Asa, author.
Title: Truth or consequences: improbable adventures, a near-death
experience, and unexpected redemption in the New Mexico desert /
Daniel Asa Rose.
Description: Albuquerque: University of New Mexico Press, 2023.
Identifiers: LCCN 2022034475 (print) | LCCN 2022034476 (e-book) |
ISBN 9780826364784 (cloth) | ISBN 9780826364791 (e-pub)
Subjects: LCSH: Rose, Daniel Asa. | Authors—Biography. | Traffic
accident victims—Biography. | Truth or Consequences (N.M.) | LCGFT:
Autobiographies.
Classification: LCC PS3568.O7616 Z46 2023 (print) | LCC PS3568.
O7616 (ebook) | DDC 920–dc23
LC record available at https://lccn.loc.gov/2022034475
LC ebook record available at https://lccn.loc.gov/2022034476

Founded in 1889, the University of New Mexico sits on the traditional
homelands of the Pueblo of Sandia. The original peoples of New Mexico—
Pueblo, Navajo, and Apache—since time immemorial have deep connections to the land and have made significant contributions to the broader
community statewide. We honor the land itself and those who remain
stewards of this land throughout the generations and also acknowledge
our committed relationship to Indigenous peoples. We gratefully recognize
our history.

Epigraph by Sinclair Lewis adapted from *Nobel Lectures, Literature
1901–1967*, edited by Horst Frenz (Amsterdam: Elsevier Publishing
Company, 1969).

Front Cover illustration adapted from photograph by Wirestock on Adobe
Stock. Back Cover Photograph by Isaac Morris
Designed by Isaac Morris
Composed in Barlow, Bookmania, Rosewood

With their rough teasing and their shy idealism,

the Average Citizens of the United States

are the most fascinating and exotic people in the world.

—*Sinclair Lewis*

Whoever you are: some evening take a step

out of your house, which you know so well.

Enormous space is near.

—*Rainer Maria Rilke*

CONTENTS

SUMMER 1970

TO GO

I WAS PAINTING the family house when my best friend snuck up beneath me and shook the ladder. Hard.

"The hell, Tony! I could have crashed down on top of you!"

"So you coming or not?" Tony demanded.

"I still haven't decided," I said.

"Maybe this will convince you," he said.

He was right: I looked down the driveway and saw a primitive four-wheel drive on its last legs, like a run-down jeep from a World War II film, stripped of all amenities.

"See, no doors, like we wanted," he said.

"Sweet," I said, climbing down to inspect close-up.

"And no roll bar."

"Impressive," I said. "Stunning."

Like me, Tony was twenty years old and thus considered the third-hand clunker he'd just picked up for $400 to be glory itself. No blinkers. No brake lights. The more deficiencies he listed, the more we liked it. Not only did it have no doors, but it also rather glamorously lacked jumper cables, a battery charger, a spare tire, a speedometer, and a safety manual with first-aid instructions—just in case. It did happen to have a couple of mangy seat belts, he confessed sheepishly, but even so, a cross-country joyride in a car this broken down, this lacking in rudimentary safety features, was our chance to face all the danger we could hope for, proving to ourselves and everyone else that we weren't just a couple of coddled college kids with too much Van Morrison in our heads. Best of all, there was no universal joint, whose function I vaguely understood was to keep the chassis from collapsing on itself. The plan was to pick up a U-joint at some junkyard along the way, but somehow, starting the journey while lacking that crucial item added the final irresistible element of peril we needed to get moving. Not that any of those niceties mattered. In the end, the point wasn't the vehicle, and it certainly wasn't the destination, however inevitable that might or might not turn out to be. The point was just *to go*.

Summer 1970. Without quite knowing how or why, we were feeling a whiff of the Vietnam War from eight thousand miles away. Everything was coming to a boil. Plane hijackings. The Beatles' breakup. Four students shot dead by National Guardsmen at Kent State. Over five hundred colleges shut down in protest, liberating a generation of wispy-bearded, mad-dog students to perceive something the rest of the country couldn't. A dog whistle of danger. The rest of the country—older, more cautious—may have heard a tickle in their ears, but it was the younger men and women of the sixties who turned up the volume, flashing *V*s to each other and generally scaring the bejesus out of what they scornfully called Middle America. Wanting in on the action, Tony and I hoped to become part of that rabble-rousing contingent. For the most part, our reasons were more personal than political. Tony suspected that his wife, Lisa, the mother of their year-old daughter, was cheating—he needed air. As for me, I had just split from my girlfriend of three years and it felt tragic—the end of love.

Tony and I both had student deferments that kept us safe from the war, a blessing we viewed with equal parts gratitude and guilt. We were safe, and somehow that made us crave danger. We wanted to at least touch, at least smell, something of the hell that was swallowing so many of our less-lucky cohorts. We needed a perilous rite of passage that would reveal all sorts of things about ourselves we couldn't possibly name.

I was half-packed anyway. It didn't take me long to throw the rest of my stuff into a duffel next to his.

Itchy as we were to get moving, we had one stop to make before we left: an impromptu afternoon cocktail party thrown together by our parents at the art gallery they co-owned. Tony and I were appreciative of their efforts, but it smacked of the ridiculous: a suburban gathering under the pink dogwood trees to launch their scruffy children into a world of adventure. The entire group assembled on the grass to wave goodbye: the well-intentioned Connecticut moms in their skinny Lilly Pulitzer dresses, serving us one last helping of wobbly Jell-O salad; the stately dads in their sad pointy party hats, offering final words of advice. Tony and I stood there, looking pleased with ourselves. No matter how long we lived, we knew we would never be grown-ups the way they were. The partygoers shook their heads helplessly, knowing we were destined for trouble and there was nothing they could do about it.

We grinned at each other as Tony gunned the car, spitting gravel. Within seconds, the party became comically tiny in our rearview. We heard the last words my father called out before he disappeared entirely.

"Keep your seat belts buckled!"

We hit the highway, gas at thirty-three cents a gallon, no goal but the open road west. Soon we were hurtling across the continent under our own steam, changing our landscape and even our climate as we went. What command we had. With one foot on the pedal we could conjure up rainstorms, make cornfields appear and disappear, all because we were on the move. All because we were young.

Next day in Ohio we paid our respects to the Kent State murder site. Like so many places considered remarkable, it was distinguished chiefly by its unremarkableness. Sober gray academic buildings seemed destined to stay in the background for eternity. A slope of sun-baked lawn had its grass cut too short, like the crew cuts of the National Guardsmen who had so recently opened fire on the students there. The place felt strangely empty, anticlimactic. We hadn't yet learned that death could be so arbitrary; how quickly it could snatch your life away.

We headed farther west, plunging deeper into the heartland of some kind of enemy territory. A truck driver in Indiana hurled a bar of soap at us, putting a crack in the windshield. "Dirty hippies!" An old-lady school bus driver—probably forty—tried to run us off the road in Missouri. *Easy Rider* with Dennis Hopper and Peter Fonda was up for two Oscars that year, and we were freewheeling the same way, braving the middle fingers aimed at us by any number of patriotic Americans. "Commie agitators!"

Lovely varieties of menace loomed everywhere. Tornadoes developed in Kansas, looking exactly like the dark omens they were supposed to look like. As they funneled gray matter up into themselves, the wind picked up speed from the flatness on all sides, whipping through the open cabin of our Cruiser and punching the canvas roof so hard we could barely hear each other singing. Tony's hair looked like an exotic variety of guinea pig, its fur whorled into rosettes. The wheat fields on both sides of the road looked disheveled, too, twirled and ridged by the wind. Suddenly, from deep inside the wheat, a bevy of disoriented pheasants flew out two feet from us, flailing through the heavy air as they sought shelter before the approaching blow. We needed shelter, too, and found it beneath the wood porch of an old farmhouse. No time to ask permission. The farmer and his wife descended into their back-yard shelter, and we rolled under their porch, where we slapped five and hunkered down till the twister roared past.

Next day in Oklahoma, we encountered a lightning storm. As the dry thunder boomed, we pulled over beside a cliff where a bunch of half-naked daredevils our age were defying the lightning gods by swinging out on a rope and dropping between spiky white bolts into the swimming hole below. An entire generation seemed to be on a suicide mission that summer. Stripping to our underpants, Tony and I joined them, screaming to the sky. "Come and get us!" The air sizzled like eggs in a bubbling black skillet.

It got even better before the Great Plains came to an end in New Mexico, and the rural flatness allowed us to track the solitary lights of a car approaching from the left on a collision course with us, six or seven miles away. We approached it eagerly. The other car was on a separate road perpendicular to ours, and both our vehicles must have been going the same speed, because the closer Tony and I got to the projected inter-section point, the closer the other car did, like a sideways game of chicken. It was exhilarating as we sped toward our rendezvous in the dark. They beat us there by five seconds as they whipped through the junction ahead of us, never slowing down. What we had no way of knowing, nor did they, apparently, was that their road ended there, with a drop of sixty feet. Their car went airborne and after a breathless few seconds landed upright at the base, popping off all four tires but otherwise remaining intact. Tony and I jumped out and raced down the embankment to find four passengers inside, laughing uncontrollably as they tried to stash their weed. When they finally opened the stuck door, gushes of smoke filled the air. Turned out they were two very handsome and very stoned Hispanic couples whose college had closed in Texas, apparently looking for some sort of road danger themselves. With one glance to each other, Tony and I acknowledged we'd gotten what we'd come for. This must have been the danger we were supposed to experience, or close enough. We'd been spared. Time to come to our senses, quit taking asinine risks, and get on with the business of finding the U-joint.

Hours later, we spied a cluster of lights in the distance blinking softly from a peaceful desert valley below. It was late—no junkyards would be open at this time of night—so we parked on a sand dune beside the road and tucked into our sleeping bags for the night. Falling asleep near my best friend under stars that seemed to fizzle with energy . . . I don't know what it was like for Tony, but I felt sorry for everyone who lacked the good sense to be us.

Bright and early next morning we entered a town that looked critically down on its luck: dirt-poor, dead broke. Where was everyone? No cars, no dogs. A few one-story buildings had chintz curtains thumbtacked into rattling window frames, proof of life. The place was on its way to becoming a ghost town like so many others littering the Southwest in those days: a tableau of the forlorn and forgotten.

I asked Tony to pull over so I could splash water on my face. He turned in to the parking lot of an empty diner where an iron spigot was dripping water out of an adobe wall. I hopped out and drank a palmful. The sky was beaming blue, our radio warbling a country song as I bent backward to stretch, then straightened to take in the sight of junkyards up ahead, a cornucopia of U-joints. Bounding back into the passenger seat as we drove toward them, I decided for one of the only times the whole trip not to buckle. Why would I, when any minute we were going to stop and pick up that damned—

"Tony," I screamed, "she's not stopping!" Commotion on my right: a flash of blond hair, a blur of giant truck. Instantly, a sense of wrongness swallowed the morning as the truck barreled into us with the force of an iron bull right where I was sitting. *Bang!* I was out, sailing through the desert air, hoping to make the wrongness right. It was working: I was escaping the bang as the country song grew fainter with my distance . . .

Go down, go down, you Hard Knocks Girl . . .

So this is what it felt like to fly—being pulled rather than pushed, not so much shot from a cannon as drawn toward a safety net up ahead. It was exhilarating. I could fly! There was something radically farcical about dog-paddling to stay airborne. The warm air was lofting me away so that even the sky was welcoming, its blueness assuring me I was safe, so invincible I could keep soaring for days.

But no. As quickly as I went up, I was coming down. The wrongness returned with a vengeance as I dropped, heading toward the pavement before I'd had a chance to do whatever I was supposed to do on earth. And then I was gone, face smashing the tar, entering the silent world in a heartbeat. In the instant of blacking out there was an image—a clock on the wall of Tony's and my old sixth-grade classroom, its hands racing double-time around the dial. It must have been the morning after daylight saving and the clock was being reset remotely from the principal's office. Spellbound, I stared at its unnatural speed and felt I was privy to a secret no one had ever been able to put into words before. Could I possibly do it—capture the secret in five or ten words? I clutched the words tight, trying to smuggle them back up with me through the layers of consciousness without losing any along the way. *Something*, we are all *something, something* . . .

But I was already losing them as I surfaced—only three words left: *we are all* . . . The others were sifting off into the sunlight as I opened my eyes. I was on my back in the clamor of the conscious world, in the middle of the street with my head cradled in the lap of a beautiful blond woman who must have been driving the truck. I gazed up into her sorrowful blue eyes and loved her like an angel. She looked to be a few years older than me, maybe twenty-seven, with a nimbus of sun glare framing her golden hair like a halo. Her words of comfort penetrated to my bones as she cupped my head with inconceivable gentleness. "Shhh, rest now, you're OK . . ."

Back in the Cruiser, Tony was weeping blood from his skull as he rocked back and forth amid a thousand glittering nuggets of wind-shield glass. He was making sounds I'd never heard him make before. Trembling with shock, I tongued a gap in my mouth that felt like five broken teeth but may only have been part of one. My instinct was to rise on all fours and scramble backward to safety, but the woman pinned me with her strong legs so I couldn't move. Two stony-faced cops called for an ambulance. A crowd of rubberneckers had materialized out of nowhere to take in the show. One of them, a tall, stooped man with vacant eyes, was speaking to the Raggedy Ann doll he clenched in his arms. "You seen that, Ann? He flewed through the air, you bet. If he'd stayed put he woulda pissed hisself to death."

"Where are we?" I asked, the only question I could formulate.

The woman said something I couldn't make out. I tried again. "Where in holy hell are we?"

I was swooning anew. Wooziness enwrapped me as I locked her face into memory, a pause on the cusp of consciousness. Then a phrase, wondrous strange as I blacked out again.

"Truth or Consequences."

PART I

WINTER 2010

FORTY YEARS LATER

CHAPTER 1

AWAKENING

I'M DROWSING IN the sunporch when the phone rings. It isn't a sunporch exactly, not the screened-in room with wicker furniture and potted ivy the words usually call to mind. It's more of an underheated home office than anything else. My desk is down there, the books I've published. Framed drawings of spaceships colored a few years ago by a pair of happy sons. Pressed wedding flowers worn by a loving bride back in those days when nothing could go wrong. And a humpy couch that's been my bed the last seven nights, since my wife asked me to sleep downstairs. It's my sixtieth birthday today. No one's home.

"Wake up, Danny boy!" sings the jolly voice on the answering machine. "Nap time's over. It's your most immature friend, offering the adventure of a lifetime."

Yes, it's Tony. *That* Tony. From *that* crash, forty years ago.

"Adventure of a lifetime," Tony repeats. "Better than pulling off that triple play when we were nine. Better than creating that junior detective agency when we were twelve. Almost as good as surviving our legendary you-know-what in New Mexico when we were twenty. C'mon, third base, pick up the phone."

Tony and I share the markings of a friendship forged in the school-yard. It's a multifaceted relationship full of the juvenile jealousies and mock sexual overtones that have managed to transfix us both since the jungle gym. We're pretty tight, in other words, even if our relationship sometimes seems stuck in those days when Tony would march around with arms outstretched like a stiff-limbed Frankenstein—his response to acquiring forty-eight stitches in his forehead during our fateful New Mexico mash-up. (Six plastic surgeries eventually fixed him good as new.) He's a great guy, in other words, if a bit pushy. A bit bossy. A bit ladder-shaking.

I adore him anyway.

But no, I think to myself. Just no to his invitation, whatever it entails. I'm hurt. Sad. It's all coming apart: this life, my eleven- and fifteen-year-old boys, my beautiful wife, the home we've built together. I've managed to screw it up. Now I have to unscrew it up. Not as easy as it sounds.

The family dog, Barker-the-Barker, looks at me plaintively as I pick up a washcloth to degoop his eyes. He's a rescue dog, mournful from some early trauma before we adopted him, with gunky tear ducts that give him a doleful air. I'm about to address Tony—"Come in, first base—" before he beats me to it.

"You sound awful," he says. "Did I really catch you napping in the middle of the morning? Or crying? Smart money's on crying."

"Bad connection," I lie. "I'm out in the sunporch where the signal's weak."

"Sounds fucked up to me."

"Loose wiring is all. The family's off shopping while I'm out with the dog, who's got this congenital—"

But Tony barely pauses before he's already talking again, asking the worst possible question:

"So how is she anyway, the lovely and magnetic Polly Reade?"

Wonderful from the get-go, that's how my wife is and has always been—literally from our first kiss. She had just hosted one of her legendary mandolin parties in Boston, and each of the guests had headed out into the night. I was the last one left, lingering beside her on the sofa. When finally I gathered myself to stand, she said, "Oh, don't go," and that was that. I kissed her, and she was beaming so broadly, all I got was her pearly whites. Snow was thickening outside the windows as we glided down the hall into bed, so warm and snug I felt something I'd never felt before: a glow of goodliness. I was with the right person. Afterward, my body felt flushed with optimism, and even better, with just the right touch of silliness. I ran outside and pranced naked in the dark yard, pelting snowballs at the window behind which Polly stood

"She's good," I tell Tony. "More than good—goodly. That's why we're going to fix it like new."

"Things are that bad?"

It takes a few juddering heartbeats to answer. These are words I'm nauseously fearful to hear myself say aloud, like a guy lost in the woods who doesn't panic until he hears his own voice crying for help. Nothing sticks. Nothing holds. Minus my family, I'm in a rowboat going over Niagara Falls with no oars.

"*Trial separation*, they call it."

Tony whistles, because he's the sort of guy who does that when hearing bad news. "She kicking you out?"

"Not exactly. We're staying under the same roof for the time being: easier on the boys. That's why I'm sure it's going to work out."

"Damn, Dan, that sucks! And I'm assuming it came out of the blue like it usually does, right? No clue?"

"Basically blindsided, yeah."

"Perfect. So let me ask you something else. Was there another time in your life when some perfect stranger did something like this to you? Kicked you to the curb, sent you flying, and I do mean literally?"

I don't have to think long. "Obviously, the car crash we survived by the skin of our teeth—the worst crash of our lives."

"Not the worst, Dan: the best. That's why we always called it our miracle crash. So, it's simple. We're going back. Name of the town, please?"

"You know perfectly well."

"It'll be healthy to hear you say it."

"It's too on the nose. Embarrassing."

"Say it."

I hem. I haw. Finally, I croak it out. "Truth or Consequences."

Yeow! My tooth hasn't bothered me in decades, and suddenly it aches with no warning, a dead nerve bursting to life. I'm too old for this crap. I want to slow things down, make sense of whatever Tony's proposing, but he keeps saying these words that are either the stupidest I've ever heard or . . . yeah, the stupidest.

"So that's the plan, Dan, a visit to Truth or Consequences, the land of spirits, filled with truth visions, screwball coincidences, all that supernatural stuff I never can decide whether to believe in or not, way out in the Mojave Desert where they tested the first atom bombs. You got connected to some spooky shit out there last time, Dan. We need to get you more of that mojo so you can crash-land safely again."

I shake my head. "Too deep for me."

"Fuck *deep*. Dan, after all we've been through, you can't deny me this."

My tooth stings again, a reminder of how much worse the crash could have been. How much worse everything could always be.

"You're insane," I tell Tony. "That was forty years ago—"

"OK, so forget the spooky shit," Tony cuts in. "Come because Dodge is bad for you right now. I don't know the whole story, but whatever you and Polly have gotten into, you could both probably use a breather. We'll come back when Dodge is safe again. All right, ready? Watch closely as I prepare to seal the deal," he says. "The main thing I've been saving up my sleeve. Ready? Blue eyes. Yellow hair swept back like Farrah Fawcett. You said she looked like a cheerleader, or prom queen—what'd you call her, the babe with the halo thing? Who crashed into us and you couldn't stop mewling about her for years?"

"The Guardian Angel," I say, quietly remembering. "Telling me I was OK . . ."

I've never forgotten her. Maybe she could answer some of the questions that have baffled me all these years since the crash, like how I managed to escape when her truck filled my open doorway. Did I deliberately jump or was I catapulted, when there wasn't time or space for either? Most of all, was there a reason, in all those miles of empty desert between us, why she happened to connect with us in the first place? I've never been one of those "everything happens for a reason" kind of people. But maybe, every once in a while . . .

"Sold!" Tony says. "So what time you want me to pick you up out here?"

"What? You mean you're—already there?"

"Flew in yesterday. Figured you'd cave, so I wanted to prepare a desert castle even you couldn't say no to. Your very own plane ticket too. Happy birthday. I'm emailing it over now."

Ping! My phone displays a ticket to a place that's warm.

"Tony, you know what? Your presumption is endearing. But this is one adventure you'll have to have without me. I'm staying home to fix what's got to be just a bump in a sixteen-year marriage. Group hugs. Family rituals. The boys got Mounds bars from me under their pillows just a few nights ago—"

"Mounds—?"

"The point is, we're solid. We'll do anything to avoid—"

Barker-the-Barker lifts his chin and starts barking everywhere at once.

"Gotta go, Tony, someone's here."

I click off to investigate why a man is skulking over the frozen grass. Blue uniform. Shiny badge. Oh, he must be hawking tickets for the policemen's benevolent society.

Nope.

CHAPTER 2

NUMBER-ONE DAD

WARMTH. THE AIR outside is cold up here, but the plane is stuffy. I press my forehead into the cool of the plastic window on my way to meet Tony in Albuquerque. Divorce papers are tucked inside the pocket of my carry-on; I can't see them, but I know they're there.

How do you say goodbye to your family?

Dear monkeys,
Had to clear up some old business from afar.
Take care of Mom and I'll be back as soon as I'm able.
Love always, Dad.

Before leaving, I'd placed the note on their night table and hoped they wouldn't notice my shaky penmanship. Then I touched the sacred relics: the stuffed turtle, the edge of their pillows.

Now, in the plane, I dig my keys out of my pocket and look at the key chain they made me a few Father's Days ago: #1 Dad!—with a crayon drawing of two Huck Finns fishing on a riverbank with their old man. It's a classic corny image of early Americana—stick poles and straw hats—and it scalds me now as something I always meant to do with them but didn't. My intention: not to leave for good but to come back an improved man. Can I say this? A better man.

Because Tony's right: rather than grieving for a wife who doesn't want me, why not take a step back? Try to be that better person I always hoped I could be. That better person Polly fell in love with. Why not take myself within spitting distance of one of the globe's most bizarre travel targets, the atomic test site that carved out a whole new perspective on modern life. Better to focus on a part of my life that was fortunate by anyone's count, a part of my life when a couple of college kids could throw a duffel in a car trunk and off they'd go, lickety-split, don't look back.

And why not try to find that anonymous blond woman while I'm at it? I know it sounds desperate, distracting myself from my real wife with some apparition from forty years ago. But she seemed so wholesome, that apparition, so tender and trustworthy. Even if her halo was a hallucination, as of course it must have been—one of the components of a near-death, Shirley MacLaine–type experience—I still can't shake the sense that she holds the key to something without which my existence will be incomplete.

I know it sounds self-important. I know it sounds like I'm clutching at straws. But I've never forgotten her over the years, never quite gotten her out of my mind. Despite the violence of the collision and the fact that she was the one who clearly caused it, I've never felt angry with her. Mystified is more like it. Enthralled. Bewitched. Maybe it was the backlight of the sun encircling her face or the shock of the impact, but I idolized her as a golden-haired beauty who comforted me in my proverbial darkest hour. Makes sense, I guess: she was the one who let me know I wasn't dead or maimed. It was her face that hovered in the blue above me, her voice assuring me I was OK. Might it be possible that this guardian-angel person could recollect what I've had no luck recollecting all these years since—the cryptic blackout words I'd mumbled aloud in the moment of coming back to life in her lap?

Of course it was possible. Anything was possible in a town with the name this one had.

We are all . . . what? What was the rest of it? Did she hear? Could she possibly remember? Maybe the words didn't capture some eternal staggering truth, but even if they turn out to have been worthless, they were the words of a twenty-year-old who thought he was about to die, and I need to know what they were.

I'm terrified to leave. I admit it. And I don't even know what I'm terrified of, exactly. All I know is that I'm more terrified to spend another night shivering on one side of the wall while my family is snuggled up watching *America's Got Talent* on the other. No matter what strange and frightening place I'm going to, it can't be stranger and more frightening than that.

CHAPTER 3

INJURY

SHE WAS SO happy. That's what I loved first about Polly. From our earliest dates I couldn't help but see that she defaulted to happiness. I credit her father, who made up bedtime stories for her when she was little, adventure stories about a girl named Patricia who faced all sorts of goblins but always vanquished them in the end—or at least escaped their clutches. Polly believed in happy endings and I wanted desperately to share her belief. Like everyone, I'd had bad breakups in the past and I was determined not to make the same mistakes again. But how could we ever be unhappy when those teeth of hers kept showing up so gleaming white when she smiled? And she was always smiling.

We were only a few dates in when I found myself rubbing the place where a wedding band should go. Not a nervous itch, just a way for my body to tell my brain that something belonged there, on the base of my ring finger. Eventually I took the hint from myself and asked her to marry me. When it came time to move her into my New England farmhouse, I was corny enough to carry her over the threshold. We were nuts in love when the boys arrived. Nuts enough to track Spencer's name in the snow, fifty feet wide, so it could be read from an airplane. Nuts enough to conduct family hugs at the drop of a hat. "Oh, look, Jeremy finished his green beans! Time for a family hug!"

I was always singing to them at bedtime: "Dark Eyes" to Spencer, "Green Fields" to Jeremy. I invented a Yiddish Alfred E. Neuman routine for their benefit: "Vot, me vorry?" We traded houses for a week with a young family in Paris and did nothing but walk for seven days—Jeremy on my shoulders the whole time, while whiz-kid Spencer memorized the entire Metro map. Flying home, Polly pronounced ourselves "functional"—a word almost never used because of its ubiquitous evil twin, "dysfunctional." I wrote a children's book for them and perched them on my lap at the kitchen table to read *Little Charlie Tucker and His Very Noisy Nose*. I woke them in the middle of the night for Mounds that we'd eat on the stairs, in the dark.

We were OK. Our family was OK.

So what happened?

It wasn't any of the major things people think of. I didn't cheat. She didn't cheat. We had enough money—not a ton, but enough. We hadn't forgotten how to kiss, how to hold each other's gaze. But I have an attention problem—a problem paying attention to people who aren't me. Most of the time I'm unable to get out of myself enough to really hear and feel the people in my life. It's a drag for everyone concerned— me included—like having a camera stuck in selfie mode: every time I try to snap a sunset, there's my face beaming back at me, shit-eating grin front and center like an idiot. *Me me me!*

But it was worse for Polly. I heard her but I didn't. I felt her but I didn't. If either of the boys suffered so much as a bee sting, I was all over him with kisses and big-boy cuddles. Not so much with Polly. She was a grown-up; I figured she didn't hurt the same way. How withholding was that? Now that it may be too late, I finally realize that every time I took off to some weekend conference without kissing her a proper goodbye, I hurt her. Every time I came back and it was the boys I hugged first, I hurt her. It wasn't that I loved the boys more, exactly; it's just that they were easier to love. No undercurrent of misunderstandings, miscalculations, endless explanations. I loved my wife lots. But it wasn't the same.

Still there was hope. She believed I was better than I seemed to be. Where was that really good guy she only caught glimpses of? The one who braved a sleet storm to fetch her chicken soup when she was sick, who surprised her by cleaning up after an eight-person dinner party so she could sleep? Why didn't he show up more often, that man she could rely on to come out of himself whenever she needed him to? She would try to summon what she named my inner mensch, playfully unbuttoning the top of my shirt and calling to the space between my ribs: "Come out, wherever you are." Her warm breath on my chest never failed to stir me. She bought a small ceramic gargoyle, and when I had an irritable spell, she would place it next to me on the kitchen table. To remind me. I needed reminding more and more. Yet still I didn't see it coming. Not really.

The final strains. Overcrowded school and work schedules. Televisions that lacked the mute function. Leaks in the garage roof we could never find the source for, dripping, dripping. Worrying, worrying, another kind of drip, about things we needn't have bothered about. Plus, a rescue dog who couldn't rescue us, constantly barking at chairs in case they might move of their own accord. And finally, toward the end, a minor but, in a sense, fatal accident.

No excuse. Driving Jeremy home from school a few months earlier, I had taken a shortcut through a mall parking lot—anything to shave a few seconds off an errand—and didn't notice a projectile careening toward us from the side until it struck with surprising force, shattering the window next to Jeremy. Ironic, with my dreadful driving record, that it turned out to be merely a runaway shopping cart. It could have been a lot worse, I told myself, but then, everything always could. What if his car seat had failed and he'd been banged around when I braked? What if he'd been slashed by the broken glass? What if, what if? He was fine, but I vowed then and there to swear off all but essential driving for the foreseeable future.

An ambulance arrived, standard safety procedure. I sat in the back with Jeremy, squeezing his little-boy fingers as the siren moaned on and on, sounding like all the recriminations I could ever hurl against myself: that I was careless, irresponsible, too much into myself to pay attention to the outside world, another privileged jerk who assumed the road was his own personal property to take liberties with, even at the cost of endangering his son.

I remember a conversation on the sunporch at night, the window reflecting us against the darkness. I remember telling her it wasn't too late to call it off; we didn't have to cause this injury. She drew her shoulders back.

"You're one to talk about injury," she said.

CHAPTER 4

ONE-ARMED HUG

ALBUQUERQUE INTERNATIONAL SUNPORT is bright and shiny, like most American airports. Except that ABQ offers itself up as a gateway to magical happenings, even to the point of calling New Mexico the Land of Enchantment. Bring it, I say.

"Danny Rose."

"Tony Wilson."

He looks me over appraisingly, taking a contemplative sip of the Yoo-hoo chocolate drink he's toting. "Your eyes are red. Crying on the flight?"

"Napping."

"Uh-huh."

"Jesus, Tony, enough! This may come as a jolt, but I haven't had a good cry in years."

Thus, our sentimental blowout in the airport. Warily, we do our one-armed hug—the second arm used as spacer to ensure a little distance. It's how American males of a certain disposition do it. At the same time, a subtle half yawn stretches Tony's face, one of an arsenal of yawns he perfected long ago that still serve to express a range of functions, only a few of which express boredom. More often his yawns signal how *not* bored he is—he's paying such attention that he needs to take a catch-up breath. He's moved by seeing his childhood chum for the first time in two or three years.

"Well, anyway, your cell phone is cooler than mine," I say.

"Possibly. But your backpack is cooler."

He's just being polite. Because Tony is effortlessly cool. Both our cell phones are black, but his is savvier black, somehow. Blacker black. I've got an ordinary laptop-and-cell-phone backpack, while his is more like a European satchel. I'm carrying a club soda, but he's sipping that chocolate drink anyone else would have the good sense to keep out of sight. On anyone else, a streak of excess sunscreen on the side of his nose at this hour would look dorky, but on Tony, it's perfect. All part of his Tonyness.

As for what he's wearing? I'm hard-pressed to summarize. Over the long haul he's become a walking palimpsest to me, his life's changes layered over the baseline of elementary school. At the moment he's sporting Ralph Lauren moccasins, but I also visualize his baseball cleats from Little League days. Up top he's wearing a preppy pinstripe shirt, but I also see the buckskin jacket from our hippie years, with a few dear, dried daisies still wound through the buttonholes. God knows I don't want to be mawkish about our buckskin jackets, but I miss those daisies. They had such a short shelf life.

"Hiya, handsome," calls a grandma cowgirl from across the waxy corridor. Tony blows her a kiss and doesn't seem to mind when it turns out to be the janitor behind us she's calling to. What does Tony care? If the grandma's not yet a fan, she soon could be.

Outside, the balmy night air is a whisper of joy on my skin. The stars sparkle as though buffed with a jeweler's cloth. I sense Tony cranking himself up for an apology as we walk toward the parking lot.

"Now, my choice of rental needs explaining," he says. "See, how I figure, we grew up having a thing for snazzy car crashes: the James Dean effect, leave a pretty corpse, all that. So my thought was to get us the ugliest rental we could find as a safety measure, given how humiliating it would be to die in a compact Pinto."

He clicks the key fob—*bleep-bleep*—lighting up a gleaming-blue Mercedes. "But just couldn't do it." He shrugs. "Sorry."

The Mercedes sits there, sleek with menace. I toss my backpack into the trunk atop his golf bag, and we resume our time-honored positions: he drives and I ride shotgun. Why mess with a good thing?

"By the way, speaking of nothing, it wasn't a Mack truck that mauled us back in 1970, like you always say," Tony says. "It was your average two-ton pickup."

"Pretty sure it was a Mack truck."

"We'll find out soon enough."

"That we will," Tony sings, pinching my cheek with affection that hurts. Otherwise it wouldn't be affection, right? He steers the car skillfully through the maze of airport roads and turns south onto Route 25. "Two hours straight down. T or C, here we come!"

"Tears?"

"T or C, for Truth or—"

"Got it. Just misheard."

All that's visible in the darkness are the hulking shadows of distant mountains on both sides, vaguely oppressive hippo shapes as Tony turns to me expectantly and settles in with a new Yoo-hoo from the console. "So start at the top," he prompts. "You were crying the first time you called me in sixth grade."

"Seriously," I grouse, "that's the best origin story you can come up with, the source of all our meshuggaas?" But it's true: I was crying. My mother was standing over me in the kitchen, haranguing me to make the call. She'd gotten it into her head that I didn't have enough playmates and needed prodding. She was right—I was a dreamy kid who didn't notice how many friends I did or didn't have. I guess she worried that I was too entrenched in my own world but didn't realize she was sparking a friendship that would not only last long after both our mothers had died, but would stay locked in sixth-grade mode for the duration. Because when Tony was sent off to boarding school the next year, he held on to these reference points as home base and remained defiantly adolescent despite the usual pressures to grow up. To a considerable degree Tony has managed to stay loyal to our early selves in this manner ever since, a manner I admire despite the fact that he's fixated on the crying phone call, which is his favorite way of annoying the hell out of me.

Meanwhile, Tony and I continued our adventures during school vacations—falling through the ice of a nearby river on three separate occasions, capsizing Tony's Blue Jay sailboat during a sudden summer squall. Our exploits accelerated once Tony got his driver's license and we discovered the thrill of close calls, nearly crashing in brightly lit parking lots, nearly crashing on dark dirt roads. To the outside world we must have looked foolhardy, but to ourselves we were hot-rod outlaws, so indestructible that we assumed the occasional vehicles we bounced against were indestructible too—bumper cars on the interstate.

Coming back to myself I look over to see what Tony's thinking. Who am I kidding? He's a brick wall. Maybe if I try probing a bit?

"So, how're you doing, meanwhile?" I ask with forced nonchalance. "How's your marriage?"

"Hunky-dory. Marriage made in heaven."

"Why are you so hot to take this trip? What's in it for you?"

"Not a thing, Danny boy. It's all about you, just the way you like it."

"Why do I not believe that for a—?"

"Well, since you asked so nicely, I did receive a fairly momentous phone call a few days ago . . . but in due time, sugar plum, all in due time."

"Meaning you're never going to tell me, right?"

Tony merges into the middle lane, keeping the speedometer on seventy-five, the posted limit. "Oh, thanks for reminding me," he says. "The one and only rule for this trip, if you don't mind: we're not spilling our guts about anything personal."

Of course—same stupid rule as forty years ago, when we were too lost in our male fog to even begin discussing our issues. I knit my fingers and press outward in silence, remembering what I wished I knew then and find myself wishing I knew now.

Tony uses his blinker to change lanes, purely good breeding since there are no other cars at this hour, nothing but wide-open spaces as far as we can see. "So, without getting gooey," he says, "what was the tipping point for you and Polly?"

An honest question deserves an honest answer. I breathe into the empty ache at my core, accessing the info, and tell him about the tussle I had with the shopping cart in the parking lot, how Polly considered it yet another example of how oblivious I am to what goes on around me. She never put it this way, but what a spoiled ass I could be, half expecting traffic to bend to my will. Tony responds as expected, some wisecracks, a couple of bad puns. "Attaboy," he says with a proud smile. "Showing the road who's boss. How many accidents does that make altogether? Eight? Ten?"

I sidestep the question, ashamed to tell him. "Yeah, but this one was different," I say. "It was the only time I ever had one of the kids with me."

Tony stops smiling. I can feel the weight of his judgment pressing on me. The night outside seems a little darker than it did a minute ago.

"No one was hurt," I rush to say. "Still, what kind of father puts his kids in jeopardy for a fucking shortcut? I think that's what got her wondering about me, deep down. It makes me wonder, too, I have to say."

"Ouch," he says soberly. I'm relieved he doesn't say something like, "Empty shopping cart? How the mighty have fallen." Instead he blows out two cheeks full of air, a gesture of concern. "How're the boys, anyway?" he asks.

Never mind the answer—I can't even bear the question. "Tony, do you mind if I draw a veil across that part? I tried calling them from the plane, but they didn't pick up. They're beautiful. It's a beautiful home. That's all I want to say."

This statement is too sad for Tony. He tightens his grip on the steering wheel, keeping his eyes straight ahead. Outside, the distant mountains are like brooding hippos, their sodden breath heavy on us as our vehicle whips through the dark, the air in the car so thick it almost has a smell to it, like burning wire. I'm filled with a sense of urgency, like there's a pinch of desert sand lodged in my throat, like I'll choke if I can't capture whatever I can of the past before it dissolves forever. The shadowy hippos have lumbered away, leaving nothing but empty desert acreage washing out for miles in every direction. Faraway porch lights seem lost at sea, signaling to our own lost lights. Static electricity forks the horizon.

God, I love this hour. It reminds me of when I was seventeen and had a summer job working the night shift at the Arnold bakery. My task was to stack boxes of bread into the eighteen-wheelers before they drove off to fill grocery-store shelves across the country. The boxes were warm from the oven-fresh loaves inside, and my coworkers always punched open a carton for us to snack on through the night. Most nights when I'd finish at 2:00 a.m. I'd grab a few loaves and drive around my silent town, stuffing them into mailboxes—a nice surprise for my friends to discover later, after the sun rose. I felt happy spreading the wealth, but also lonely with no one to share the darkness. One time I myself got a nice surprise when I approached Tony's mailbox, and there he was, sitting on the stone wall, awaiting my delivery at two in the morning, with a half smile on his face. Just wanted to say hi, he said.

I fight an urge to hug the man now and not be one bit embarrassed. "I'm never going to get rid of you, am I?" I ask instead.

Tony decides the best response to this is to stick his tongue out at me, then to adjust his rearview mirror, though there's nothing back there to see.

"By the way," Tony says. "I never got around to asking you. Did you ever figure out what a universal joint is?"

I feel a stupid joke coming on. "A universal joint is what our generation was in search of that summer."

Tony doesn't bother to groan, choosing instead to fix his gaze on me with one eyebrow raised: the infamous "hairy eyeball," circa 1963. Then he says, "You're a bucket of laughs, Danny. No wonder it's taken your wife so long to dump you."

Tony shoots me a worried glance to measure if he's gone too far this time. "Oops, sorry if that was over the line," he says. "But you're OK with a little roughhousing, right, Dan? It can only be good for you to laugh."

There's a hint of vomit in the back of my throat. My pulse is around ninety. I've been feeling a slow crush in my chest the last two hours—the vise grip of missing my boys. I squeeze my ribs and cough out a laugh.

"Sure, Tony," I say. "It can only be good to laugh."

The night continues by itself, without any help from us. The radio picks up a stray signal carrying a jubilant Mexican tune from south of the border somewhere, complete with what sounds like a walrus tooting along merrily in time with a bass drum. After a minute the signal sails off into the night again, plunging us back into the dark hush.

"Hey, I just saw a speed sign that wasn't full of bullet holes," I say, changing the subject.

"So?"

"Just thought it worth mentioning. Have you been noticing the caution signs? Dust Storms May Exist. Zero Visibility Possible. You can't say we haven't been warned."

Indeed, we have. Almost as well warned as when I spied a sign in a third-world country years ago warning of hairpin turns ahead. Scareful of Accidents, the sign warned—the words *scare* and *careful* sharing space together on the same sign—a good optic to keep in mind. I visualize a split screen: Tony and Dan driving down the desolate road as twenty-year-olds, Tony and Dan driving down the same desolate road as sixty-year-olds, each together and alone, lost and found, both careful and scared at the same time.

"Meanwhile, notice all the handcrafted memorials beside the breakdown lanes?" Tony asks. Now that he mentions it, they're nearly as numerous as mile markers. Plain wooden crosses. Ornate metal ones with beaded flowers or deflated balloons or tattered ribbons. Sometimes they're solitary. Others come in family clusters: mommy, daddy, and a scattering of baby ones.

"This *is* the crash capital of the country, after all," Tony points out. "This state, this road. Despite having one of the lowest population densities around, something like three people to a mile where we're headed, they keep finding novel ways to clobber each other. Bunch of reasons; I did a little Googling. A, it's the main corridor for drugs coming up from Mexico. B, the local population is partial to various forms of grain alcohol, so that a high percentage of the six thousand drivers who use this road every day are plastered. Plus, there's very little police presence, C, which makes sense 'cause if you were the law making ten bucks an hour down here, would you give a shit?"

The odometer needle flutters to ninety before Tony takes it down again, purely cautionary since we're the only car in sight. "This here's the big league of reckless driving. From here down," Tony says, "we've basically entered the kill zone."

I've been fingering the #1 Dad! keys in my pocket. "So it's deadly as well as depressing."

"Doubly so for us, since we already have a history here. Speaking of double, look at that cross smashed in half! As if one crash in the same spot wasn't enough." Comfortably, he rolls his head against the leather cushion behind his neck. "Remember last time we were this deep inside New Mex?" he asks. "We swapped ghost stories to stay awake, like the one Mrs. Seiffert used to tell when we had to stay in for recess, about the woman who always wore a yellow scarf around her neck? And finally on her wedding night her hubby unwound it and her head fell off—"

"Stop, that one still spooks me out."

"But the spookiest thing back then was the real-life New Mexico military men with their regulation crew cuts. We could feel them out there on their secret bases, even if we couldn't see them—the epicenter of enemy territory to a couple of pinko peaceniks. At last we decided that we'd pushed our luck long enough and that at the next town we'd stop and find that universal joint. But by that time, it was too late for any junkyards to be open, so we decided to pull over and crash on some sand bluffs beside the road—"

"Don't use that word here, please—"

"Sorry, we decided to *retire* on some sand bluffs."

But the word *crash* seems to have beckoned something new from the darkness. Or maybe it's a mirage. But there's something peculiar about a pair of approaching headlights. They're traveling way too fast, for one thing, getting brighter by the second—

Zzzzzzzhhhyp!

An old-style family station wagon rockets past us going the wrong way in our lane, its lights streaking. Tony barely has time to yank the car sideways.

"Holy shit, do you realize how close that was?"

"She must have been doing 100!"

We burble a minute, our hearts pogo-sticking as the station wagon disappears behind us. "Thank God we were driving defensively," I croak.

"No, that's what we were doing wrong. Being defensive made us sitting ducks. What we gotta do is fight fire with fire like the old days!"

With that, he stamps the pedal to burst like a horse from the gate. The needle jumps to one hundred, prompting two aging Connecticut boys to whoop like they're twenty again.

"See what happens when we try to be good?"

Tony scopes out another radio station until it rewards us with an oldie: "96 Tears," by Question Mark and the Mysterians, one of a million songs that used to flick the switch for craziness back in the day. Adrenaline pounds to the tips of our ears as Tony cranks the speed to

110, 120! He's crushing the horn—"Too many teardrops for one heart to be crying"—scaring us both shitless as he turns off the headlights to plunge us into blackness for five seconds, ten . . . can we make it a half minute? "Whoa, that dip I didn't see coming!" Tony roars. This used to be our favorite cheap thrill, not actually as lethal as it sounds, when we had the road to ourselves like we do now. But no we don't, because suddenly we're nearly climbing up the rear of a multicolored VW bug coughing along at sixty. Tony slams the brakes and we have time only to glimpse the bearded freak of a driver giving us the finger before we spin out, round and round, coming to rest in the breakdown lane, slanting backward. A cloud of road dust settles on our skin, light sand with flecks of green plant needles mixed in. The VW has puttered out of sight. Tony and I look at each other, chastened, then bust out laughing. It's the first real laugh we've shared since laying eyes on each other at the airport.

"Oh my God, that station wagon—it was like her foot was glued to the gas pedal!" I say. "The kill zone is right!"

"Did you see the yellow scarf flapping out her window?"

"Liar, you're completely making that up," I tell him, but nevertheless it gives me goose bumps.

"Anyway," Tony says, gesturing out the window to the sand dunes running alongside the breakdown lane, "recognize these?"

Maybe I do. Faintly at first, a memory tugs itself free from a nest of clinging cobwebs in my brain. "Wow," I say. "The bluffs where we spent the night before entering town."

We clamber to the top of the soft wall of sand, twelve feet high. From here we get our first good view of the twinkling lights of T or C nestled in the valley below. Assuming the Guardian Angel is still around, which I feel in my bones she is, is it all that crazy to think she could be one of those lights down there, reading Virginia Woolf or doing her needlepoint? Or am I going overboard? I've been idealizing her so long I can't stop now. Don't want to stop now.

"That mountain to our left is supposed to resemble an elephant," Tony says. "Called Elephant Butte, though I call it Elephant Butt because I like to bore myself with childish humor. But this one right in front of you, that's T or C's very own Turtleback Mountain."

It's just a jumble of rocks to my eyes, but I take in the windless desert air, worlds warmer than the sunporch I left a lifetime ago.

"Didn't I tell you this was a good idea?" Tony says. "Just wait till you see the desert castle I rented for you. You're gonna say, *Oh, thank you, thank you, best friend, for finding this incredible sanctuary for me to lick my wounds.*"

I do feel strangely moved. Transported, even, as though the brief interval of our lives between 1970 and now was just a fleeting fantasy, a month at most since we were last standing on these very grains of sand. Our lives in a twinkling, complete with goose bumps. The height of the bluff we're standing on, the steep angle to the road below—both are so familiar it's as if I could reach down and pick up something I dropped here last time. A ballpoint pen, maybe, that might still write.

CHAPTER 5

CAPITAL *C*, CAPITAL *S*

LEAVING THE HIGHWAY ramp, we merge onto the main drag through the outskirts of town—a dark, empty straightaway of ghostly lots behind crushed guardrails. Is that a fence made of beer cans cemented together? Are those two pawnshops next to each other both out of business?

"Yeah, the place was poor then too," Tony reminds me. "Median income's less than half the country as a whole, so not exactly top ten. Of course, it was a sunny morning the last time we were here, not midnight and scary-looking like this, but do you remember your first impression?"

"Same one I have now. That it was a good place to look for a junk-yard because the whole town's a junkyard."

It's not a put-down so much as stating the obvious, no offense intended. Now as then, lot after lot is strewn with truck grilles, bed frames, refrigerators on their sides. A row of ragtag motels all proclaim Vacancy; one of them is in such a permanent state of vacancy that the word is painted on the cinderblocks with no room for *No*. Though there are enough *No*s elsewhere to make up for it. No spitting. No guns. Even a burned-out dumpster with an all-purpose *No No No* spray-painted on its lid.

As if to make up for that, the word *Bud* is also everywhere. Budweiser signs on windows, Budweiser signs on walls. A string of plastic pennants announcing Bud Bud Bud Bud, the lifeblood that keeps the town afloat, apparently.

The street is wider than such a small town would seem to warrant, two lanes in each direction with a tar median in between, and seeming even wider because of the lack of human activity at this hour: not a person anywhere. After a few blocks we fall silent, overcome by the sheer misery of the place.

At last a sign of life. In one window the shades are up, and the interior of a bedroom is lit in flickers of reds and blues. We drive past slowly enough to make out a Betty Boop cartoon on the TV screen inside. A few blocks farther we encounter the dubious comfort of a printed welcome: a banner draped listlessly between two dead streetlights. "We've been waiting for you!"

"That's not too creepy," I say.

Tony is busy looking at a pair of drunk-driving billboards looming over a couple of brown cinderblock hovels. "Driving drunk? Or just driving tired?" asks one. "You have a defender with King Counsel!" states the other, beneath a jumbo-sized likeness of a movie-star lawyer in a crisp business suit, his cowboy hat poked into a crown with jewel points that flash neon green in the dark.

"Glad to see the ambulance chasers are thriving, anyway," Tony says, just before we shudder over a craterlike pothole—a jolt that jostles loose a growing grievance in my brain.

"Tell me again why I'm not having my midlife crisis in Tuscany?" I gripe.

Tony ignores me, clearing his throat as a reminder for me to go easy on the self-pity. "So, as we continued toward downtown, do you remember anything special?"

"We stopped so I could splash water on my face. There was an outdoor standpipe of some kind."

Tony turns the car into an empty parking lot beside a collapsed diner. "This one."

"Really?" I step out to inspect an iron spigot dripping water from an adobe wall.

"It's rusted out," I report. "The knob doesn't even turn."

"Forty years, Danny. Hate to see what *our* plumbing looks like."

Once I'm back in the car, Tony proceeds slowly in the direction of downtown. "Now at this point an odd thing happened last time. Jumping back into the car, you decided not to rebuckle."

"Truly odd, right?" I say. "It was one of the only times the whole drive

I decided not to bother. Not a conscious decision; I just figured we'd find a junkyard any minute."

"Notice another odd thing, Danny? You're not buckled now either."

Which is equally odd. "What happened to the warning beeper?"

"Yanked it. Hate those things," Tony says. "Anyway, we've now gone one mile from the spigot, we're going up this slow rise, and—"

It must show on my face, the slow dawning of a recollection, because Tony nods. "Yup, I had the same reaction when I got here yesterday. Like it happened just a few weeks ago, right?"

We continue another minute, entranced by memory. "It's the two-mile mark now," he tells me. "Notice anything familiar?"

Eerily familiar. There's a curve ahead into the main part of town, a classic fantasy curve that I must have dreamed about a hundred times over the years. But first there's a side street to our right—

"*Bang!*" Tony says, lurching to a halt in the middle of the street. "This is it. She came out the side street right there."

There's no traffic in the middle of the night, so we get out and walk around.

"This I've been saving," he says with something un-Tony-like in his voice, almost like reverence. "Seeing it without you would have felt like cheating."

"Thank you."

"Are you kidding? We got whacked here together."

Our voices are low, the words hanging in the street between us. But why is my heart beating so fast? It's not only the energy of identifying with a twenty-year-old's vigor. It's something more. Defiance. My life force saying no! I didn't give it up then, and I'm not giving it up now!

I wonder if Tony's heart is racing too. But that's exactly the sort of intimacy we'd never dream of sharing with each other.

"So here we are at the Crash Site, capital *C*, capital *S*. Like our own personal grassy knoll."

"Of course it is. Who else is gonna aggrandize it for us?"

I get a warm chill off the midnight air—admiration for the sheer strength of his ego. The moon has risen, casting a pale glow over the scene. It's the same moon that must be hovering over my boys right now at home as they sleep, I can't help thinking.

"There must have been a gas station on the corner," Tony points out. "See the oil stains? The bolts on this nub where a sign must have been? Other than that, I bet this place hasn't changed a bit." He circles back to where I'm standing, mesmerized.

"Two timeless questions present themselves immediately," he continues. "One: How didn't she notice us when, as you can see, she had clear visibility half a mile in all directions? And two, the old mystery: How did you escape when the front of her pickup must have blocked your exit?"

"All I remember is shouting, *Tony, she's not stopping!* Then lying in the street, looking up at this blond . . . fantasy."

There's the faint trace of cartoon music stitched into the air, like in some memory bank from long ago. "Knoxville Girl"? The words *not stopping!* echo in the silence, along with the sickening sound of steel biting steel.

"OK, time to review what we do know," Tony says. "*Bang!* You flew. Soon there was a crowd shouting for an ambulance and cops who didn't look fondly on a couple of sniveling college kids."

"We thought we'd fallen into enemy hands, for sure. The hospital must have been on a steep hill because the ambulance felt like it was going straight up. And it must have been a Catholic hospital because the nurses were wearing nuns' habits." My tooth suddenly acts up again, a reminder to go easy with the memories. "I remember insisting to everyone in the ER that I wasn't a gutless draft dodger or crazed druggie. I was Daniel, a nice Jewish boy from Connecticut. Funny how quick I was to affirm the respectable self I'd been so eager to ditch just a few days earlier."

In response to my prattle, all the doctor did was chortle, "Gee, I hate to carve up that hippie beard of yours," as he put a couple of minor league stitches in my forehead. The nurses giggled at that. Even in my terrified state I could see there was some serious flirtation going on between the staff.

"They patched me up well enough for me to decline the hospital bed they offered," I remind Tony. "I preferred to sleep outside that night under some yew bushes."

"I had no choice where to sleep," Tony says. "Not with forty-eight stitches in my forehead."

"You weren't even conscious till that afternoon. I stuck around until the following day when you told me to get out of your hair. You didn't want me to keep seeing you in such a gory state. Finally, you just about threw your crutches to get me to leave."

"When they released me," Tony says, "I hitched to the police station where they'd towed the car to get my documents from the glove compartment, which I had to pry open with a crowbar." Incongruously, he starts smiling. "I mean, talk about grotesque. If you'd been belted in—"

"I know, Tony. Believe me, I know."

"It was sheer metal, no padding."

"I realize."

Tony starts making chopping gestures with his hand. "Oh, gnarly, Dan. I don't know why I'm laughing—"

I wait for him to collect himself: pure sixth-grade nervous mirth, I suppose, plus the joy of a good horror show. In time he settles down, wiping his eyes.

"Sorry, Dan. I swear I'm not laughing at you. At us! What a couple of overprivileged twerps."

He slaps himself in the face to knock himself out of it.

"Because, Danny, I mean if we had been paying the slightest attention to what our parents were yelling at us . . .

"Me, couldn't read for six months, had to drop out of college, looked like Monster Mash for a year until I started getting my surgeries." He lurches into his vintage Frankenstein routine for a minute, with stiff limbs outstretched. "But the point is you, Danny: bulletproof! Blasted within an inch of your life, yet you fly free? That's the invincibility you need to get back now, from this very spot where you were most invincible ever."

From the invisible interstate two miles away, an eighteen-wheeler rumbles by, followed by the annoyed blast of another truck's air horn. Closer to hand, a broken glass sign from the 1930s advertises a hot-spring "spa." Oh, right—I distantly recall hearing that the town was famous for "medicinal waters" long ago.

"Tell me true," Tony says. "Is this not better than staying home cleaning the dog's eye gunk?"

For the past few minutes we've been standing side by side, facing the hallowed ground of the Crash Site. Now the site has exhausted itself for me. It's time to turn and face my companion squarely.

"Tony, what are we doing here?"

"What do you mean?"

"I mean, I get it about me. I'm here for all the reasons we did or didn't talk about last night. But what are you doing here? Something to do with the 'momentous phone call' you got a few days ago?"

Tony scuffs the tip of his moccasin along the ground, a gesture I remember from Little League, when he'd be thinking something private from his position at first base. It usually meant he was about to make a decision of some sort. And here it comes.

"OK, I'm really sorry to do this, Danny, but I have to break our rule now."

"About not spilling our guts?"

Without fanfare he takes out his wallet and hands me an old photo, frayed to fuzz at the edges. "You remember who this is?" he asks me.

"Are you kidding? I had the same picture in my wallet for years."

We stare at the photo: the one-year-old with a baby biscuit between her lips next to her father, a twenty-year-old with a baby biscuit between *his* lips.

The baby's name was Caroline. She'd been only a few months old when Tony and I hit the road in 1970. When we got back, Caroline was gone—her mother, Lisa, had absconded with the infant in our absence. Tony had spent the rest of his twenties trying to track them down, supplementing his budding construction career by driving a cab to fund the search for his daughter. He'd even hired a private detective. Two, actually. Cost him a fortune, in every way. Of course I remember. I'd carried her picture in solidarity, until I'd had my own kids and their photos had replaced hers.

"Horrible," I say, shaking my head.

"Back before the Internet, people could just vanish into thin air," Tony says. "It took me forever to accept the fact that I'd never see her again. Finally I forced myself to put it behind me and build a new family. Whenever it flashed in my mind I sealed it out. So . . . ready, Dan? Here's the new headline. She just contacted me."

"Your baby?"

Tony nods. "Only she's not a baby anymore. She's forty-one. All those years I spent searching, it never really sunk in that someday she might grow up and come looking for me. But that's what happened."

"Called you out of the blue?"

"Which is why I called you out of the blue. I had just gotten this call from Caroline that she wants to see me, except her name's not Caroline any more, it's Hannah. She's an Orthodox rabbi now, Danny, can you believe it? Her stepfather apparently was some sort of raving Zionist."

I blink, trying to put it together. "So that made you want to revisit here why, exactly?"

"Had crash, lost daughter. Or lost daughter, had crash. I don't know which order. They happened back-to-back. The two events are fused in the center of my being."

"I'm still missing something."

"What don't you get?" Tony says impatiently. He stamps his foot to mark the territory. "This here Crash Site is ground zero, where everything changed for me. Until this spot, I had a daughter. After this spot, no daughter. So before I go reunite with her, I had this urge to check in here, restore my life to its factory settings."

I sort of get it, but still don't see why Tony needed me here with him.

"Put it this way," Tony says. "Practically every major event in my life, you've been at my side. Capsizing in that summer squall—you were there. Smoking dope the first time—you were there. Seeing our first naked lady through a peephole into that burlesque club—you were there." We do our ritual bow to the immortal stripper Hotcha Hinton. "Now this reunion with my daughter is about to take place, maybe the last major event in my life, and I'm a little nervous."

Nervous? Tony? This *is* a big deal.

"I mean, I could have come out here without you, if you'd have thought this whole idea was too far-fetched, like any half-sane person would have. But I had a feeling you'd be just idiot enough to buy it, and with you next to me I could get myself warmed up, psychologically amped . . ." He clears his throat to summarize the issue. "I lost my daughter right after I was here with you, so being back here with you sort of undoes it, or gets it ready to be undone. Make sense?"

"Sense enough, I guess."

"This is what I needed to do," he says, with a tremble of conviction in his voice. "And it's working, Dan. Just standing here with you at this minute, I'm pressing the reset button."

His eyes are closed. Passionately. In all these years, have I ever seen this person with his eyes closed passionately? It's almost scary to see him without his cover of coolness to protect him. It makes me rethink the belief I sometimes have, that we wouldn't be friends if we met for the first time today, that the only reason we've never murdered each other is because we're both grandfathered in for the duration. But this look on Tony's face right now makes me think we might have both made the cut after all.

Suddenly he opens his eyes, chipper again. "OK, time to experience the castle," he says, jamming his wallet back in his pocket. "What're you waiting for?"

I'm waiting because I just had a vision. Or something. Christ, this place is strange. Did a gangly man really materialize from around the corner, clasping a Raggedy Ann doll to his chest? I swear he seems half-familiar, like I've seen him years ago.

"Hi, I'm Summer," the man says, shambling up to us with a diffuse gaze that doesn't quite take us in. "Spring's coming but I'm Summer all year round, 'cause that's my name, Summer. Right, Ann? If summer comes, can spring be far behind?"

Tony and I look at each other. "I think that's our signal to call it a day," Tony says. "Good night, Summer."

••

Four blocks from the Crash Site, we're standing before a structure. My friend throws his arm around my shoulders. "Welcome to the castle, Danny boy: our very own no-tell motel."

"I can hardly find the words."

"Just feel the love, baby. Soak it in," he says, giving me a particularly well-aimed noogie on my arm.

The rest of the block looks even worse. Motor homes in every state of disrepair. At the one next door, a stubby cactus twines itself through a nest of car radiators. On its porch sits an exploded microwave.

"Not only is it not a desert castle, but it also happens to be a single-wide trailer! How do I even know it's called that? Since when did I become an expert on trailers? You've turned me into trailer trash!"

"Shhh, Dan, you'll wake the neighborhood dogs, who're insanely aggressive."

I breathe, but only because I have no choice. "What's that stink in the air?"

"I doubt it's the dead coyote," Tony says, pointing out a stiff carcass against the curb, flattened so it's like coyote cardboard, not an ounce of juice left to cause an odor.

It's been a long day. I want nothing more than to sink into bed, but there's this Bates Motel thing happening in front me, along with a Walmart bag stuck on the three-inch thorns of a dead mesquite tree that frames the driveway. I reach to yank it free, only to have it shred on the thorns. Now instead of one piece waving in the stale breeze there are four. In disgust, I rip them off, tossing them to the dust. Ordinarily I'd never dream of littering anywhere, but this is one place I'll make an exception, turning my attention to an eyesore in the middle of the yard, a jumbo metal basin the size of a first-generation satellite dish.

"Ahhh, that," Tony says, proudly following my gaze, "is our own private tank for soaking in the hot springs. A far cry from the chichi tourist hot tubs in Santa Fe. This is southern New Mexico, featuring 385-gallon steel stock tanks for swilling hogs. That's the difference, in a nutshell. Up north they have tubs; down here we got tanks."

"It's a can, Tony. A giant tuna can in the dirt. You won't catch me soaking in that thing."

Tony bats his lashes coquettishly. "You don't think it'll be romantic? You 'n' me under the stars?"

When even this fails to lift my mood, he resorts to the tried-and-true method of getting me in a headlock.

"Off me, fool," I yelp, but it takes a full minute of grunting before either of us is able to wrestle free.

Two sixty-year-olds winded on a desert street, Hopper and Fonda panting with hands on knees as they struggle to catch their breath.

CHAPTER 6

QUAINT IT AIN'T

I WAKE UP to the *blaaang* of a ukulele chord, woefully out of tune. It's Tony, sitting cross-legged on my bed, tuning a toy ukulele he must have found in some cobwebby shed outside. Looking around the bedroom, I find I'm not as mortified as I expected to be. The single-wide is clean and bright, not funky. The floor is gleaming-new white birch, not beer-stiffened wall-to-wall. I'm grateful.

"So the new regime begins now," Tony announces. "No more sleeping during the day, for starters. I assume you've been doing that double nap thing, taking naps on top of naps just to get yourself out of the way, little trial deaths like dress rehearsals for the real thing. That's stopping now."

I pull the sheet back over my head, ashamed. "How do you know about double naps?"

"You forget how I spent my twenties," Tony says. "Think that's fun, feeling this bad but knowing you still have fifty years to get through? You're lucky—you'll be in the ground soon no matter how bad it gets. Shall I proceed?"

"Yes. No. I don't know. Maybe if you could stop farting on my pillow I could make some headway—"

"Breakfast in five!" Tony sings, sailing out.

Before long I'm ready to emerge from under the sheet, like a turtle cautiously venturing his head out. I stroll into the kitchen to see Tony browning a slice of Wonder Bread with a steam iron.

"No toaster?"

"Or pots or plates or silverware," he says, cheerfully handing me a metal ice tray he's used to fry an egg. "Things are pretty minimal around here, though alternative health care appears to be in full flower."

He refers to an advertising flyer he must have found in the dirt, judging by the ants scampering over it. "Not only your typical sex-astrology tarot readings, there's also 'Zen livestock care' and something called 'Dale Evans belly dance instruction—available over the phone.'"

"You're exaggerating."

"Bet your ass I'm exaggerating. Every chance I get!" Tony says, Frisbee-ing a disc of burned yolk across the room into the kitchen sink. "This is like the world's wildest exaggeration spot: no one would believe a word of it anyway, so why pretend any of it's true? Hippie culture meets Wild West. Marriage of New Age and stagecoach days. Look, here's an ad for a black-widow-venom weight loss clinic. And an RV park offering colonics. Which reminds me: check out the painting over the couch."

It's a sight. A scary portrait of a woman sporting a kind of dirty aura the same shade of amber as the beer bottle she's gripping. She stares at the viewer with booze-blitzed eyes, complete with mocking curse-smile. Within the Miller High Life bottle caps around the perimeter of the painting, her sinewy arms are folded across her chest in defiance.

"Creepy enough for you, Danny?"

"I wonder who hung it here."

"A frequenter of junkyards, I'd say. Speaking of which, care to take in the view?"

Outside is a blighted landscape. Beyond a few blocks of trailers, the alpine desert stretches out brown and bare, one mile high. Drought has stunted even the cactus. Scrub sand runs all the way to the soot-colored mountains in the distance, punctuated here and there by colorful clusters of auto graveyards. Everything within view cries, *Parched, parched!* My lips are instantly dry in the desert air.

But it's the blue of the sky that really disheartens me—the proverbial blue out of which unexpected danger springs. From horizon to horizon, it's a blemish-free hue, a seemingly harmless shade that hides every kind of peril no one's ever prepared for. A false blue, in other words— the deceptive blue of a baby blanket made of flammable material, or the seductive blue eyes of a serial killer, charming as death. I distrust it on principle.

"Make out the turtle now?" Tony says, nodding to the nearest mountain. "See, that granite outcropping on top is the hump, and out front's the paw—"

"Fuck the turtle," I say.

He looks at me curiously. "Comin' back to himself, that's the Danny Rose we know and love," he says, then hops off the porch and makes his way to the yard sale next door. "Howdy, neighbor," he says to a lizardy old man sunning himself in a plastic lawn chair, camouflaged so well into the jetsam of his yard that I hadn't noticed him until now. "How much you want for this lampshade?" Tony asks, picking up one that's dented on two sides.

The man doesn't bother putting down the *Betty and Veronica* comic he's reading. "Ain't for sale," he says, reaching into a box of frozen fish sticks on his lap. Tony inspects other items. A suitcase with cans of pineapple pulp inside. A plastic fan with two broken blades. "How much for this?" he asks, holding up something that might once have been a George Foreman grill.

"Not that, neither."

Tony picks through a few more items, getting the same answer before it dawns on us both at the same time. Holy shit, it's not a yard sale. It's just a yard.

Of course. Without cellars or attics, it looks like many hardworking trailer folk understandably store their extra stuff outdoors. It so rarely rains that nothing rusts and, honestly, rust wouldn't be the worst thing that could happen to it anyway.

The street in front is extra broad, like the others in the neighborhood: double-wide streets for single-wide trailers. Back when the town planners were laying it out, they must have figured they had the whole frontier to expand to, so why not broaden the streets to accommodate the growth that was sure to follow? Except there was no growth. Not one car has come down the street since we stepped outside.

A shovel clangs somewhere, harsh and sad.

"Time to motor," says Tony, stepping over the coyote cardboard and making for the Mercedes. "Dare I say destiny awaits?"

• •

"I guess the logical place to begin would be the police station, go through their accident records," I say as we turn the corner. "Tried that yesterday, before you got here," Tony says. "They destroy all records after five years."

We're driving past the police barracks as we speak, open nine to five. The cop cars in the lot have expressionistic paint jobs: scurvy patches peeling from the hoods.

"Then I guess the hospital."

"All background info protected by privacy laws. They'd kick us out the door."

"What, then—town hall?"

"And ask for what—the Department of Daniel Asa Rose? I hate to break this to you, but not everyone in America was tracking our historic passage across the continent forty years ago."

"Then I guess we just keep driving around and see what turns up."

"My sentiments exactly," Tony says, looking pleased that after all these years we're both of us still ready to rely on dumb luck. It's reassuring that on some fundamental level character traits don't change much over a lifetime. "But why're you lugging that thing with us?" Tony asks, referring to the backpack I've patted into place beside me.

"Can't leave it unguarded. My whole identity's in here: laptop, cell phone, contacts, calendar . . ."

We navigate a couple more blocks to the "historic district" of downtown T or C, two one-way boulevards named Broadway and Main that circumscribe what passes for the business center in opposite directions. It's not exactly a ghost town. A few thrift shops are open; a vacuum cleaner rental shop seems to be doing OK. But what does it say about your financial situation if you need to rent a vacuum cleaner? Main Street especially is a stage set out of a cowboy show, the unpainted wooden buildings fronting a main drag redolent of shootouts. But Broadway boasts an organic eatery—no, two!—and a few art galleries heroically trying to sustain a bohemian underclass. We park on Broadway, also grandly wide, as if once upon a time the town threw open its arms and proclaimed, "Someday we're gonna be a star!"

"So here she is, the town we never got to see," Tony says. "Notice, please, the tumbleweed bouncing down the middle of the street, symbolizing the romantic rootlessness of the Wild West, right?"

"I guess."

"Wrong," he says. "Welcome to the Fake Wild West. Tumbleweed is actually a thistle plant that slipped in from Russia in the late 1800s. Quickly drove out so many farmers, they were thinking about fencing in the entire state of North Dakota. Such a hardy little sucker that after the first atom bomb, nicknamed "Gadget," was detonated on the barren plains an hour north of here, tumbleweed was the first plant to regrow at the site.

He sees my admiration for his research and huffs on his knuckles, then pretends to shine a badge on his chest, sixth-grade style.

"What I admire about this particular specimen is the crushed beer can inside, so it jangles as it scampers down the street. Did I not tell you we'd see some zany shit?"

Yeah, he told me. Now can I take my nap? I rub my upper arm where last night's noogie is blossoming into a bruise. The whole place looks like it hasn't changed since 1970, or 1930, for that matter—a time warp from the Dust Bowl, except with extra es in "shoppes" and "grilles," which, along with the forced cheer of random walls painted orange and red, are a desperate attempt to be cute. *Calling all tourists—hello?* Sandbags slouch dejectedly in each doorway—protection against the periodic ravages of the mighty Rio Grande—but the river doesn't live up to its billing. Instead of a gushing green, it's a thin soup of sluggish brown, shrunken from the banks with sticky algae on both sides.

Empty. Empty. I've barely formulated the thought, *Where is everybody?* when I'm nearly run over by a motorized wheelchair with red, white, and blue streamers driven by a large man whose white beard is braided into pigtails. "Out of the way, dick cheese!" he growls as he races down the street. Some of the colored bulbs on the back of his chair are duds, but most of them blink well enough to depict an American flag with dead spots.

As for real American flags, they're everywhere—outside the moribund bank, outside the moribund post office—and everywhere ragged. And why does almost every store have a handmade warning taped to its front door: "Beware of winds . . . hold door tightly during winds." So it gets a little breezy? They've got nothing better to bother us about? As for the exchanges between the few people going about their business—"Still got your marbles?" "Stayin' outa jail?"—their conversation barely seems worth the breath.

I hate picking on the locals. It's cheap. They're doing the best they can—surely better than I would in their shoes. Hell, *better* than in my own shoes. I try a positive spin by focusing on the wonderful tang in the air, a gun-smoky perfume like an airborne intoxicant, pungent as onions sizzling in bacon grease. It may be the stink from last night, come to think of it, except today for some reason it's delectable.

"Maybe T or C's like Sedona or Bisbee before they got noticed," I suggest, hopefully. "Like Taos before it got twitched up."

"Yeah, good luck with that. We're in a different universe down here, Dan. Quaint it ain't. Have you checked out the DWV building with its Driving While Intoxicated program?"

It's an incongruously spiffy building with bold lettering. Drunk driving is not something the town sweeps under the rug, apparently; it may be as close to big business as the place comes. There's even an official blue sign stating that the DWI program has adopted this section of the road to keep clean.

ADOPT-A-HIGHWAY
LITTER CONTROL
DWI

Yet the three initials at the bottom are undersized, as though the DWI is ashamed of itself. The painted stripes in the DWI parking lot carry the same whiff of apology—they're only about two-thirds regulation width, so there's no way a car could fit between them. Maybe they were drinking when they painted them?

"Drive-through liquor store, check," says Tony, driving again. "Dog alarm systems, by which I mean chain-link fences with snarling dogs behind them—check. Y'know, if we were inclined to be respectful, which we emphatically are, we could see the poverty as a clever self-defense mechanism."

"How's that?"

"Those cartels a couple of hours south of here? T or C's too poor for them to bother with."

Trucks! Truck! Trucks! We got 'em!

—comes an advertising jingle on the radio.

Cars! Cars! Cars! We got 'em! S-U-Vs! We got 'em!

Things are getting livelier. We pass the parking lot of a deserted motel where two junior-high-school girls with eagle feathers in their ears are making out and flicking us the bird for noticing. We pass something that looks like a soup kitchen for worn-out cowboys, rowdy enough to wave their hats and hoot at us as we drive by. Around the corner is a rough and scratchy bar called Candy's. Then another of those banners we saw last night, slung loosely between two slanting telephone poles. "We've been waiting for you!" How does it manage to sound plaintive and threatening at the same time?

I notice two things: that I'm fiddling with the #1 Dad! keys in my pocket, worrying them like rosary beads for their calming effect. Also, that I keep girding myself for impact on my right, like a truck might come charging for me at any moment. Can't Sleep? You Could Be Disabled! says a billboard above a legal office. Call the King for Cash You Can Count On! The ubiquitous chain-link dog alarm system depicts a fang-baring canine with the words Try It and I'll Tear You a New One, while three real-life rottweilers on a metal restraint gnash the air, giving proof to the warning. Out front, a bright orange Hummer sits idling, its license plate gleaming with the letters *KNG*. The tinted window is cracked open so we can see the top of a cowboy hat poked into the crown with jewels, a natty dresser shined up sharp as a movie star. Inside, weighing down his side of the Hummer, the King sits dispensing legal wisdom into his phone so forcefully, we feel the rumble like the bass notes of a grizzly bear. "He has no case! What about *no* does he not understand?"

"Yeah," Tony says, "gossip is that the King swings the biggest dick in town. And how's this for postcard pretty?" Tony points to the local jail directly across from the King's office. A handful of inmates in jumpsuits the same orange as the King's car pace back and forth within their individual chain-link fences, like an outdoor kennel run, getting their exercise in full view of the passing traffic. What's next—stocks in the public square?

Oof! We hit another pothole. Tony slaps off the radio and turns in to a bargain gas station. While he's away, I try again to call my sons. More radio silence. I turn my attention to the old heap of a car at a nearby pump in which sit two pretty lady goths with skin white as cream, dressed in black with matching black ponytails. One is hunched over her palm, fastidiously counting coins. The other seems in physical distress of some sort, breathing hard in the passenger seat with the door open, unable to haul herself out.

At the other pump, two teenaged punks are horsing around in their high-rider, its suspension bars three feet high. Tony emerges from the bathroom in time to hear the ugly names they're tossing between themselves that are meant to be overheard by the women. Kneeling to check our tire pressure, Tony calls to me in a voice equally meant to be overheard. "Remember when people actually used words like that? Can you believe what cretins they were?"

"*Cretin*'s the word."

Their gas tanks filled, the punks glare at us as they climb back into their ridiculous ride. *Rev, rev!*—the acknowledgment that they heard us is there in the noise as they drive off, loud but not as loud as it could be. How do you like that? Message received. After the punks buzz off, the goths prepare to leave too. The one in distress shoots me a broken smile that cuts through me; something hurts her so bad that she moves like a turtle half-crushed in its shell, hauling its carapace along behind. But suddenly their car starts roaring in neutral, its accelerator stuck. They're so flummoxed that I go to help and find the floor mat jammed around the pedal with all kinds of junk mixed in: cheap toys in crinkly cellophane like you'd get from a carnival or vending machine. I free the mat and the revving stops, giving me time to see the mortified look on the women's faces—extra attention from guys like that is the last thing they need—before the car jolts into gear and off they jounce, too flustered to shout thanks.

The meter on their pump reads $7.68—exactly two gallons' worth. People are watching their pennies in this town.

"Huh," Tony says, climbing back in. "Car they were driving was a Plymouth cop-mobile from the late sixties, if I'm not mistaken. Probably the same kind the local fuzz was driving last time we were here."

There's no time to reflect on this intriguing dynamic—or to wonder when I last heard the police referred to as *the fuzz*—because the gas station is now being invaded by a cluster of gray-haired bikers, like a swarm of hornets darkening the air. They look more dangerous for being middle-aged, as though time has tanned their hides even tougher. In a violent scrum of metal and exhaust, they come to rest twenty feet from us, all eight or nine of them. *ZAAAAAR yah-yah-yah-yah-yah*. Even in neutral the decibel level is such that Tony instinctively sinks to the level of his steering wheel. It's the proper response. A smell emanates from them—black leather and fried clams—and it's a scary smell.

For some reason the act of aiding the goths has given me a shot of something I've lacked for a long time: spunk. Out the car I go, sauntering toward the bikers like I'm on a school picnic. The glare they train on me is pure truculence, designed to stop an eighteen-wheeler from even dreaming of entering their lane. With a belligerent thrust of his wrist, one of the bikers cranks his engine even louder as if to say, *Does this pork chop honestly want to be our dinner tonight?*

But like all noise, the revving eventually has to die down. When it does, I've almost finished my leisurely stroll toward them.

"Good-looking bikers!" I say, reflexively adopting a Southwestern twang without even meaning to. "Damn, I envy you. Never had the balls to ride a hog myself."

It might not work every day, but today it does. Despite the lip rings and full-sleeve tattoos, they turn out to be about as threatening as a group of podiatrists.

"So I'm wondering if any of you remember Farrah Fawcett, pinup girl of the seventies?" I ask.

General snickering follows. "Ain't no one likely to forget that red bathing suit" is the general consensus. There's the sound of beer bottles knocking in agreement, the sight of throats opening to receive massive quantities of suds.

"And my follow-up," I say as Tony half yawns nervously from his seat. "Anyone remember a woman around these parts who looked like her?"

But the bikers aren't from round here, it turns out. They're down from the hills, in town for their weekly horseshoe tournament.

"OK, related question," I say. "Me and my cohort here were in a little scrape way back when. Splattered from hell to breakfast by a Farrah Fawcett beauty queen but lived to tell the tale. As royalty of the road, you have any idea why impossible escapes like these happen with such regularity?"

Did I push the twang too hard this time? It's hard to get the right balance. But it may have won me a few points, due to the kinship of crash vets. There's much chin rubbing as they pass around a bag of sunflower seeds.

"You with the muscles," I prompt. "Mr. Manhood! I'll bet you have an opinion."

It sounds like I'm messing with them, but they know I'm not really, so they answer me straight.

"Destiny, dude," the man replies. "Everything happens within the universal flow. I've come out of five crashes spitting glass each time. Lesson learned? Don't ride faster than your patron saint can fly."

"Wasn't your time to go, plain and simple," volunteers the guy next · to him, who looks like Robin Hood's chief lieutenant, Little John. "I believe when your number's up, it's up. But you can crowd it a bit, this way or that."

I turn to address the group as a whole. "So what do you think, fellas, and be honest now because this is important. Think I could whup Little John's ass?"

They laugh. The guy is easily six feet four and 240 pounds.

"Hell, anyone could whup me now," Little John says, lowering his eyes bashfully. He takes a swig from a buckskin purse that could be rum but could just as well be Juicy Juice.

"So we've all been there. Anyone else?" I ask, directing my attention to a bulky woman who looks like the momma of the bunch, wearing a prison-grade padlock around her neck, her name welded on top in cursive. "What about you, Dayna? What's your take?"

Dayna commands silence. Dayna commands respect. Dayna commands so much everything that I expect her to crush a Bud can in each hand before she speaks. But she doesn't need to. Her words carry power enough on their own.

"Likely you have unfinished business here," she says.

The sunlight blinks as a plane flies by, unseen.

"What that might be, I don't have a clue," she continues. "All's I know is, T or C's a peculiar place. If something was meant to happen anywhere, it'd happen here. I'd be on guard, I was you. Might just catch up with you this time."

Tony clambers upright in his driver's seat, alarmed. "Are you saying we're pushing our luck, like we dodged a bullet last time and it was crazy to come back?"

Dayna hoists herself back on her machine and kicks it into gear. "I don't know what to tell you except stay on your toes. Serious explosives you're playing with."

There's the sound of zipping up as several of the bikers finish relieving themselves in the sagebrush. Little John performs the traditional dipping motion with his knees to rid the last drop. "As for your Farrah double," he says, "you might try the town museum where my cousin used to work. Supposed to have photos of every high school senior going back to the Apaches, practically."

Then the sound of hornets reswarming as they turn a wide circle, waving on their way back to the highway. "Happy trails, amigos!"

Feeling good, I take a wad of gum I hardly knew I'd been chewing and fasten it squarely to Tony's forehead. "To the museum, Jeeves!"

CHAPTER 7

THE STORY OF AMERICA,
WRIT SMALL BUT WRIT SPICY!

"GETTIN' YOUR JUJU back, that's how we're gonna track down the Angel!" Tony congratulates me, removing the gum from his brow after the bikers roar off. "You do have your moments, turtle dove, I'll grant you that. Even picking up the lingo. 'Splattered from hell to breakfast?' Where'd that one come from?"

But I've never known whether my proclivity for adopting local dialects was a talent I should take pride in or a weakness I ought to hide—a knack for adapting to changing circumstances or an inability to stay true to who I am. Nevertheless, I can tell that Tony's admiration, if that's what it is, is more ambivalent than it sounds. With me in ascension, he's in decline. As often happens with friends who forged their friendship in the schoolyard, it's a seesaw: somebody up means somebody down.

The museum's not far, and we drive past a few ramshackle spas into a more upscale residential area, past double-wides, which coming from a single-wide we regard as unspeakably ostentatious; past two-story stucco houses so gussied up as to have screens in their windows; past two well-dressed old ladies strolling arm in arm, each attached by a plastic tube to her own little portable oxygen canister wheeling along behind them like toy poodles.

Suddenly Tony slams on the brakes. Then, yeah, I see it too. The multicolored VW bug from last night. The one we almost hit on the highway sits parked in front of an honest-to-goodness head shop, like they used to have in the heyday of dope culture. It's an artifact from the seventies, complete with a suitably cryptic sign out front: It's Harry in Here.

Inside, whoa. It's like someone's set the clocks back forty years. I'd completely forgotten how black light whitens shoelaces, the teeth on Bob Marley posters, the price tags on R. Crumb comix. I'm high, instantly, a contact high from smelling the patchouli incense. Tie-dyed rules: dizzying racks of tie-dyed T-shirts, crowded displays of tie-dyed sneakers, baseball caps, and baby diapers. Overhead some sixty or seventy license plates are loosely tacked to the ceiling: Texas, Montana, Ohio. In the middle of it all is the bearded freak from the highway last night, looking like he stepped out of a time capsule complete with body paint and love beads. Time travel has been rough on him. His round face has wrinkled, his body thickened. Years of purple haze have shellacked his fingernails yellow. But his sensors still work fine: he lifts his nose and sniffs the air, left and right. "Fresh meat!" he declares, locking his attention onto Tony and me. "Welcome, newbies, to the Bermuda Triangle of the Southwest desert. I'm Head Shop Harry, stoned since '71!"

He takes off a tie-dyed top hat to bow low. Tony puts out his hand. "Tony and Daniel, how're you doing?"

"I'm dandy, it's the rest of the world I'm worried about." He squints, putting two fingers to his lips to signal a developing insight. "Wai-wai-wait," he says, "ain't you the two honeymooners who climbed up my heinie on the highway last night?"

He grabs a rifle and aims it at our faces. There's a moment when time stands still . . . until out pops a tie-dyed flag with the word "Peas" on it.

"Nah, only kidding. The way you were driving, you're crazy enough to fit right into this town. Case you hadn't noticed, we got the wildest mix of people in the state, a veritable love fest between scalawags and castaways."

He looks at me, shaking his head yes, no, yes, no. "Don't even think it," he says.

"Think what?"

"That there are lots of places that boast their own alternate reality. Not to sound competitive, but there's only one T or C, and we have the highest concentration of mischief-makers anywhere: medicine men of various stripes, blackballed college presidents, a genuine Tibetan lama who moved here 'cause he said the secret of life is summarized in the town's name—"

I'm enjoying the show enough that I don't mind playing straight man. "What about bona fide medical people, like with degrees?" I ask.

"Let's just say it's not a town you want to get sick in. The hospital, Saint Ann's—"

"We've already had the pleasure," Tony says. "Forty years ago."

Harry's mouth falls open. "Oh, Mommy. You're lucky you made it out alive!"

"Well, that's where the ambulance took us."

"You took the meat wagon? The driver back then was famous for dragging patients by the belt, then forgetting to latch the back door, so they'd roll out the back going up Hospital Hill." Harry shrugs and goes back to his list of local luminaries: "Varmints, drifters, dopers, quality cranks hiding out from the law. Take this renegade here." He squeezes the cheek of a customer who looks like an investment banker except he's wearing tie-dyed PJs. "Escapee from one of the more prominent financial families in America, ain't ya, Rocky." Rocky pays no mind, picking through a rack of tie-dyed jockstraps as though selecting bowties at Brooks Brothers. "Not to mention the celebs out in the hills, the Sandra Bullock–type dudes, the Val Kilmer–type dudes who may or may not be partial to a hemp pancake mix I blend for them personally."

"I don't get why you say *type dudes*," I say. "Is it Van Kilmer or isn't it?"

"I like to insert a little vagueness between me and the world," Harry says. "Half the people here aren't who they say they are anyway. Wiser to say you're a Tony-type dude, you're a Daniel-type dude, 'cause how do I know you're not a couple of movie stars impersonating Tony and Daniel?"

Unusually quiet, Tony is observing Harry with unease. I know what he's thinking: the guy sounds more than a little like him. Same rat-a-tat delivery, same lotta things. A doppelganger situation—not so much their energy as their knavery.

Harry closes the door with exaggerated care, as though putting the lid back on a jewelry box.

"Have you made the acquaintance of our noble savage yet, our homegrown genius savant, Summer? Some say Summer was a brilliant meteorologist who had a nervous breakdown. Others say he was some sort of child star pianist with autism whose parents dropped him off here before proceeding to kill each other in a domestic dispute. If you're asking me what I think keeps him going . . ."

He prompts us with an impatient "c'mon, c'mon" gesture. "The local water, people! Summer ingests its magical qualities in the form of one daily coffee per day, accompanied by a single scoop of vanilla ice cream, which he procures at the Sunset Grille. Never pays, just gets up and walks out with his doll. Someone gives the Grille twenty dollars a week to cover him."

"Who?"

Harry raises his arms heavenward. "Now you're asking one of the town's great mysteries. All we know is his routine never varies. Wakes midafternoon and patrols the town all night, our very own roving sentry."

He regards us a moment, calculating. "Summer's one of a kind, but here's what I'll do: you buy a psychedelic pillowcase, and I'll tell ya why we got so many other nut jobs running around. Aw hell, I'll tell you anyway." He gives us the finger as though we've bested him. "They're only partly the result of the A-bomb they lit back in the fifties. No one evacuated 'cause the government said it was just an ammunition dump that had blown up. In addition to the lunacy *that* caused, hospitals near and far used to make a practice of shipping their ding-a-lings to any remote place that had hot springs to soothe 'em down. Cheaper than asylums. They settled here, and then guess what? They procreated with the locals to create a new race of aliens. Kaboom, you got a town built without right angles."

With these words, he appears to fall asleep—long snore—then wakes himself with a start. "So you bimbos gonna entertain me or not? Shoot me some questions, dammit!"

"Actually, I was wondering," I say. "You've barely mentioned Native Americans. Aren't they part of the population too?"

Harry points at me like I've asked the million-dollar question.

"I'm gonna treat you to a history lesson! Want it in black light or regular?" he asks, flicking off the fluorescents so the black light kicks back in.

"Regular would be fine," I say.

On go the fluorescents again. I attempt to smile at Tony, but he's still looking out of commission.

"In the beginning," Harry says, adjusting his belly to get all parts of it comfy, "this was a swamp where mastodons roamed. Something about the aforementioned magic water gurgling up through the mud-flats attracted 'em. When Homo sapiens came along, they said, 'Ho, this water rocks!' Even Geronimo, they say—it was the only place he'd ever lay down his arms, chilled out by righteous ingredients into some state of mud . . . sanctity!"

Tony takes a breath. I need to take one too.

"So it remained, a spiritual oasis until a hundred years ago, when the Great American Fathers in their wisdom decided to dam the Rio Grande, thus making a resort in the desert called Elephant Butte. Since the worker-bees weren't allowed to drink within X miles of the dam, they paddled downstream and built a town here to accommodate their earthly needs. Meaning booze. Meaning women. Meaning lawlessness in general and specific. Ka-pow, you got yourself a town with wall-to-wall cathouses—you can still see their remains around today, along with empty cavalry bullet shells worth a penny apiece. Welcome to Hot Springs, New Mexico, a shoot-'em-up filled with gamblers, gunslingers, and every variety of reprobate who could get the thrills he wanted for the cash he had on hand. It was about as wild as the Wild West ever got, and no longer a sacred space where man and beast could come to purify themselves—unless maybe it still was, way down deep in some secret mystical way. Cue the spooky music . . ."

Harry interrupts his chronicle to toss a package of Zig-Zag rolling papers to a grizzled customer who looks like a silver prospector from the 1890s—chunks of turquoise on a leather shoelace around his neck under a broken black cowboy hat. "Get outa here, girlfriend," Harry says, declining the dollar bill offered in return. "I still owe you from when you fixed the crapper, remember?

"OK," Harry says, turning his attention back to us, "so the dam is built, the Native American workers are rounded up and freighted down to Florida, where they start dropping dead from the humidity, and what does the town promptly do? It dies again. From nothing to nothing, or maybe to something we can't measure, wink-wink. Now it's Depression era. People blowing away like dust in the dirty thirties. But this place has an amazing ability to rise from its own ashes. So just before it's about to give up the ghost, it decides to capitalize on its water, which turned out to have a mineral content eight times that of other hot springs. Including lithium. Yeah, *that* lithium. No wonder Geronimo used to get all kumbaya with his frenemies. They've done studies in places where there's lithium in the drinking water, and guess what? Waaaaaaay more grooviness. Your organs soak it up, apparently. Soon doctors all over the country were writing prescriptions for our junky little burg. All the rage: patients limp in on crutches, skip out to tell their friends. The Healing Town, they called it—the Town of Health."

The words "health" and "healing" break open a bubble of hope in my chest. "So the water works?" I ask.

"Put it this way. I pooh-poohed it till one time I fell in a bathtub and suddenly thought, 'Did I just take a drug I like very much?' But buyer beware, it's not for everyone. Some people are repelled enough to get out of town as fast as they can; others are magnetized to stay like they can't get away. Or at least they keep coming back. The vortex grabbing hold!"

Tony and I share a look. Keep coming back. Is that us?

"Hate it or love it—one or the other. Like they used to say about Santa Fe: if it wants you, you can't leave. If it doesn't, you can't stay. You'll know pretty quick."

"And the ones who stay?"

"Half sink into the potholes, never to be heard from again. Though there's a nasty rumor the potholes will be paved in time for this year's Fiasco, by which I mean Fiesta, the annual spring parade featuring a dozen mini-Geronimo stand-ins."

Harry notices the incense stick has ashed itself out—the shop reverting to its baseline odor of a week-old roach—and lights a clump of sage to wave in the air.

"OK, back to health and healing. So the town is farting merrily along, building resort hotels around the hot springs, but it ain't long before something bad happens again, and this takes the form of Big Pharma, just beginning to put natural cures like hot springs out of business. Because who wants to soak in dirty wet mud oozing up from the netherworld when you can take a nice clean pill? Just like that, the town is ready to curl up and die again."

The prospector blows a kiss on his way out the door. "Strawberry rolling papers due next week!" Harry hollers before the door clangs shut.

"OK, new chapter. It's late forties, right? What's happening in the world of entertainment?"

My hand is waving in the air like I'm a contestant on some television quiz show. "Early days of TV."

"Correctamundo," Harry says, as if addressing a live studio audience. Then, with a surprising amount of knowledge, he tells us how some of the most popular radio shows turned into daytime TV shows to target stay-at-home housewives. Most failed in various ways, including scandals of all sorts. Some were discovered to be rigged, and ratings plummeted. Yet one managed to rule the airwaves for nine years: *Truth or Consequences*, hosted by a showman named Ralph Edwards, whose on-air greeting each week was, "Welcome back. We've been waiting for you!"

"Ha!" I wallop Tony in the shoulder. "Ha!" On second thought, I wallop him again.

"It became the granddaddy of all radio audience-participation shows," Harry resumes, "requiring contestants who fail to answer trivia questions to perform quote/unquote 'crazy' stunts for various rewards. Get the beauty of that? The contestants who fail get the prizes! The fuckups triumph!"

A breeze flutters through the shop, making the license plates on the ceiling rattle cheerfully.

"So in 1950," Harry continues, "to celebrate the radio show's becoming such a hit on TV, Ralph comes up with the best publicity stunt ever. He announces that he himself, mighty king of broadcasting, will telecast live for one day from the first American municipality willing to take on the name of his show. Being the great reinventor of itself that it was, a certain desert community leaps at the chance, and on April Fool's Day—you can't make this shit up—votes forevermore to officially change its name from Hot Springs to Truth or Consequences, New Mexico."

"Great, 1950, right when we were born," Tony says. "We've been living our whole lives in parallel to a game show."

"The day comes for the telecast, and the town goes batshit," Harry resumes. "Police sirens. Flat champagne on ice. Ralphie flies out with a plane full of grade B Hollywood stars and becomes what can only be called a god in this burg. You have to realize there were only three TV channels back then, so catching a glimpse of any kind of star was seeing royalty. And in some ways it was a windfall. Give the devil his due. Cash exchanges hands. Ralph promises to come back every year to head the Fiesta-Fiasco parade. True to his word, he does it every year for the rest of his life."

"So, a happy ending?" I ask.

"Dude!" Harry scolds me. "What have I been saying? This town is cursed as much as blessed. It keeps rebirthing itself only to find new ways to die."

"Got it, sorry," I say.

"No sooner has the razzmatazz died down, but the town realizes it sold its soul to the devil. Twenty-five grand is barely enough to cover the expense of the name change and a little park—the Ralph Edwards Park, naturally—in a town that already has more vacant lots than it knows what to do with."

He opens the cash register drawer, making a toy alarm go off. *Help, armed robbery! Help, armed robbery!* Snatches a couple of twenties and slams the register shut.

"So we became a joke, the town that named itself after a game show that rewards failures. No one remembers that the town's original name told the truth—that we really do have amazing hot springs. With a little luck we could have become a major health destination on the map of the world—"

"So the town got screwed," I say.

"No!" Harry says. "The town screwed itself. Like it always did. Ralph was just doing what Ralph did—promoting himself. No one forced the town to sell its birthright. We can't blame anyone but our sweet little selves for being left holding the bag, by which I mean respiratory diseases of all kinds. Emphysema, asthma, bronchitis, you name it—that's why everyone has an oxygen tube up their nose, in case you were wondering."

The Story of America, Writ Small but Writ Spicy! • 51

"I don't get it. What's the connection?"

Harry stares at me like I have the mental capacity of a yam.

"Who do you think were some of Ralph's biggest advertisers? Big tobacco! You can still see it on YouTube. 'Pall Mall proudly presents.' 'Chesterfield happily brings you.' The town swapped its health for a shot at Tinseltown glamour and got stuck with nothin' but smoke, literally. That's the legacy—the sight of all these old-timers sitting on their porches sucking their fags down to the nub."

Harry does something uncharacteristic: gives us time to absorb that image before resuming.

"So now in the present day, when the town's lost 10 percent of its population and looks like it's finally gonna become a ghost town like so many others in this godforsaken desert . . . guess what it's come up with this time. A spaceport!"

Harry squeezes the bulb of his nose, clown-like. *Hwank-hwank!*

"A spaceport! Meant to be the first port for commercial space travel on the planet, being built twenty miles from where we're standing. If that ain't the ultimate parting shot, shooting for the stars! Sound familiar? And given our success rate, what do you think our chances are? Let's hold our breath for this one, shall we?"

It doesn't take more than ten or twelve seconds for Harry in a kind of rapture to start turning purple. Tony and I watch in morbid fascination as the color deepens, the veins engorge. Is he going to do it all the way? Is he that aggrieved or maddened or sad? Finally he lets it out in a great outpouring of blubbery air, a kind of reverse sigh, free of judgment, full of rue.

"So in summation," he concludes wearily, "quite a town. It's had a wild ride, and it gives its citizens a wild ride. It'll break your heart or heal your soul, sometimes neither and sometimes both at the same time. The story of America, writ small but writ spicy."

After such a delivery, what next? A tuckered-out Harry has the answer. He becomes businesslike. "So tell me what exactly I can do for you fellers today?" he asks.

"Oh," says Tony, grateful to grab hold of the conversation again. "We're trying to find a woman for my friend here."

Harry considers this as soberly as though we'd asked where to get a good enchilada. "Well, let's see. There's Dee from the car wash, but she got run over recently by an ATV—"

"No, we're looking for a woman who nearly ran *us* over, forty years ago," Tony says. "There doesn't seem to be any record of her anywhere."

Still businesslike and only slightly insane, Harry grips our necks and pulls us into a huddle close to his perspiring beard. "Well, did you check the local newspaper?" he asks in a fruity stage whisper. "Come in, Earth! The ravishing editor Judi Simpson has a record of every car crash for the past sixty years!"

He releases us, to our astonishment. A newspaper, what a great idea! Have we been just too taken by our own self-importance to think of the obvious?

"*Shalom aleichem*, y'all," he says, straightening up and kissing cheeks all around. "One last word of advice. Your karma ripens faster in the desert kingdom. Whatever's supposed to happen to you happens fast, so pay attention."

CHAPTER 8

ANOTHER CRACK AT DEATH

FORGET THE MUSEUM. Forget the police station, the library, the funeral parlor. The newspaper, that's the place to go. Still safekeeping my backpack, we drive to a building on a rise just outside of town. A patriotic theme: the doorway is bulwarked by sandbags painted red, white, and blue. Inside, old color photos of Ronald Reagan festoon a counter that bisects a cluttered but empty newsroom.

Up strides Judi, all five feet of her, with the energy of a spitfire and more than a trace of the beauty she must have had in her youth. Tiny and fierce, she's a brook-no-nonsense newspaper editor like Lois Lane in command—smarter and more hard-boiled than Perry White ever was. "Spit out your business, or get out of the way."

Tony snaps to, loving her moxie: "We're looking into a forty-year-old car crash," he tells her. "Who the person was who hit us, how we made it out alive, if the whole thing had any meaning we can benefit from today. How does that strike you, just off the top?"

Judi scoops up a monster-sized Persian cat who hates us on principle. "Just off the top," she says, "it strikes me as one of the stupider questions I've heard this week. 'Had any meaning?' Accidents happen. That's why they call 'em accidents." She raises her eyebrows to certify that she's once again put us in our place in no time flat.

"No doubt you're here to see if we covered it," Judi continues. "And I'll bet you dollars to donuts you were too hopped up back then to have a date for when it happened."

"We don't. Just bright and early one summer morning, 1970."

She shakes her head with a *tsk.* "And you don't even know the month," she says. "What're you fixin' to do about that?"

"We're fixin' to look through all the papers for that summer, June through August, until we come across it. Assuming you have copies."

"Oh, we have copies. The post office requires that we do. But what makes you think Bite-Size here's going to let a couple out-of-town sharpies plow through my property?"

Bite-Size snarls for emphasis, less cat than fat brown bat.

"I was hoping for professional courtesy," I tell her. "I'm an old newspaper person myself. First job out of college. Ink in my veins."

"You and about four thousand other outa-work wretches," she says.

Beneath the chilly façade, Judi has a soft heart. Eventually she transports the cat through the newsroom and locks her inside an office—the cat glaring feline hatred the whole way—and comes back lugging an armload of flaking newspaper bundles, each tied with white string. She drops them on a composing table behind the counter and invites us to dig in.

"Any trick to removing the string?" I ask.

She slides a pair of scissors down the table.

Snip! Revealed to us is the entire summer of 1970. Which is mostly about car crashes—clearly the paper's bread and butter. The "rollover" section, they call it: issue after issue, page after page, a grim display of the wrecks that took place in and around town. How could one locality sustain so many crashes? Yet there they are, photo after photo: trucks on their backside like overturned dinosaurs, convertibles flattened like wads of cardboard. Headline after headline. "Car Burns after Flip-Over." "Hunters Injured When Vehicle Blows Up on Impact." "Car Plunges into Lake with Two Small Children." Week after week, wreck after wreck. High-speed wrecks on highways and low-speed wrecks in parking lots. We've hit the mother lode of wrecks, but where's ours?

Judi stands there, observing us with smoke curling out of her nostrils like she has all the time in the world to watch us make fools of ourselves. She finally leaves to take care of a subscriber at the front counter. Tony and I take turns reading aloud to each other. "'Bicyclist Killed When Struck by Truck. A ninety-one-year-old man was struck and killed while riding his bicycle early Wednesday morning on a rural roadway. The driver told police that the rising sun was shining in his eyes and he didn't see what (continued on page 3).'"

My turn. "'Three Injured When Pickup Hits Washout. Three young men were treated for injuries Sunday evening when their vehicle dropped into a washout in the road. The driver stated that they were driving along when all of a sudden he noticed that the road was no longer (continued on page 5).'"

"Maybe here's a clue as to why so many," Tony says, putting on a pair of tortoiseshell reading glasses I never saw him wear before. "'The driver fled before officials arrived, but inside the vehicle was a thirty-pack of Budweiser, still cold, according to Lt. Hamilton.'"

"And look at this one," I say. "'Officer says he witnessed suspect exit his car door, then fall against his vehicle while urinating on himself. Officer approached suspect and asked if he could recite the alphabet but when he got to 'e' he commenced urination of the officer and was placed under arrest.'"

"And did you see the last line?" Tony says. "'Suspect is employed by the county sheriff's department.'"

Page after page. Chips of old newspaper break off and fall to the floor, making me feel that urgency again: get the info before it turns to dust. After an hour of searching, we're through June and still not finding ours. What we are finding, becoming almost as plentiful as crashes with each passing issue, are more and more drug busts. This was the summer of '70 when drugs were worming their way into the heartland from both coasts. To judge by these articles, hippies were the evil unknown to Middle America, indistinguishable from drug dealers and draft dodgers and free-lovin' stoners. In almost every issue there's some kind of warning issued by the police department on how hippie drugs are ruining the country and corrupting a whole generation of Americans. "Hate cops?" one says. "Next time you need help, call a hippie." I had forgotten how bitter the sarcasm was.

One cop in particular appears to be leading the local charge: a barrel-chested man, big and buff like the Babe Ruth of anti-hippies, glaring out with a pugnaciousness beyond the call of duty. In one shot he kneels heavily on the back of a skinny longhair in his custody. In another he poses by a cop car with two decals on its rear window: Law and Order and War on Crime. From the distance of forty years it's plain to see how the hostility was heating up. Plain to see that kids like Tony and me were the enemy.

"Oh shit, this is bad," Tony says suddenly. He looks up at the ceiling and takes a deep breath. "Mary," he says, "that's the name that just came back to me. Out of the blue. For the Guardian Angel. I must have heard someone say it at the time."

"Any last name?"

"Just Mary. I don't know if it's right or not, but this isn't good at all."

"Why not?"

"Too woo-woo," Tony says, averting his face like a sailor who doesn't want anyone to know he's seasick.

Back to work. Another hour passes. Where's our wreck? Finally toward five o'clock we reach the end of August and haven't scored so much as a single mention. The discouragement shows.

Bite-Size is back, head cocked in Judi's arms. "You bad boys learning something about your place in the universe?" Judi asks. "Thought you were kinda special, and didn't even merit a footnote. You sure it wasn't something you smoked up?"

Stating the obvious like that, the very thing we're starting to wonder, suddenly makes Judi feel sorry for us. She eases up. "The only other thing I can think to help you is the crash box," she offers.

"The what?"

By way of reply, she elbows past us and leads the way into an adjoining garage stuffed with crates and cabinets. She directs us to push some file cupboards out of the way, exposing dozens of cardboard boxes, one of which bears the date 1970. "These are the photos that didn't make the cut," she says.

Inside are negatives depicting the gorier images unsuitable for a family paper. Stretcher after stretcher covered with dark blankets. Carnage in black and white. Bystanders are stunned. Some guy in the background is pushing his cowboy hat up so you can almost hear the long, slow whistle he lets out. It's like a daguerreotype of spectators after a Civil War battle.

One figure keeps showing up more than the others: that anti-hippie cop we saw before, massive arms folded across his chest, the very picture of the opposition. This implacable force was what the college generation was up against. Meantime, his companion, a skinny, squirrely cop, flits in and out of the images, taking measurements with an old-fashioned yardstick.

Half an hour later the negatives have exhausted us. Judi's getting crankier too. "Know what I think, the real reason you're back?"

"We already told you why."

"Nuh-uh. Most people would have sense to leave well enough alone. Not you two. You gotta come back to the very place that nearly got you killed. Pretty dumb, if you ask me. The crash dummies! Here's my theory, from watching you bust up most of my afternoon." Judi gets a canny look on her face, regarding us as she strokes the bat-cat's fur behind the ears. "You've come back to take another crack at death."

We don't like hearing this, and our reaction shows.

"It's to finish the job you started last time. My money? I'll be running a picture of you two on my front page before long. 'Crash Dummies Cost the County Again'—this time for needing two crosses put up. Like we don't have enough expenditure in that department already."

"Well, Danny boy, I think we've gone as far as we can here," Tony says, pulling me by the arm. "Out to the parking lot with us."

"Thank you," I say to Judi.

"Your funeral," she says with a shrug.

Out in the parking lot, I'm rattled by many things. I'm rattled that we found nothing about our crash. I'm rattled by Judi's theory—especially since we came so close to being killed last night by that pickup speeding the wrong way up the highway. Mostly I'm rattled that Tony looks both ways before crossing the parking lot. Uncharacteristic caution.

Suddenly he grabs my arm again. "Danny, look!"

What we're looking at is a Toyota Land Cruiser driving into the parking lot where we're standing. Same vintage as ours. No doors. Nearly the same shade of green. It comes to a stop ten feet away.

Tony and I've got a full-blown case of the willies. We stare at each other to make sure we're not seeing things.

"It's not the same green," I assure him.

"And it's a year or two off," he assures me back.

Yet it's the same model. Way too eerie for us to handle just now. All we can do is stand there and nervously say, "Ahhhhhhh!" to each other and wait for the next thing to happen.

Which is this: a man steps out of the Land Cruiser, wearing a T-shirt with these words: You Can't Fight It!

Turns out Mitchell is a chiropractor with an office on Broadway. He's here this particular moment because he has a classified ad to put in next week's paper. We tell Mitchell our circumstances as neutrally as we can—our history with a car that was almost a dead ringer for the one he's driving. "Dead ringer, huh?" He's appropriately skeptical, but eventually he gets rattled too.

Mitchell invites us to sit in his Land Cruiser for a minute. I'd forgotten how high up the seat was, what an overview it gave. The old sensation comes back, like we're in the wheelhouse of a lobster boat; the seas may be rough, but we're rougher. Only this time, at age sixty, we feel like the slightest wave could capsize us. Both of us bolt from our seats.

"Let me ask you this," Mitchell asks Tony when we're back on steady ground. "In the years since your crash, how many classic green Land Cruisers with no doors have you seen?"

"Two? Maybe three?" Tony says, sounding like he's swallowed a mouthful of chalk dust. "How many for you?"

"Now that I'm thinking," Mitchell says, "I saw one when I first got here a bunch of years ago. Looked like it had been there a long time."

"Where?"

"In a junkyard a few miles east of town, called 'Farwell' after the owner. I have no idea if it's still there or not."

"C'mon!" Half fearfully, half eagerly, Tony and I push each other into our car and head outside of town. Driving gives Tony the authority he needs to get hold of himself again, or at least conceal his feelings. Could the Land Cruiser Mitchell saw actually be ours? If so, could it provide any clue to the woman who hit us? The sun's starting to head down, lighting the line of mountains in front of us a ghoulish orange. In a few minutes, we're weaving through a narrow, treacherous pass—hairpin turns with more than one wooden cross where a car went over the edge. The final curve takes us into a straightaway that opens up on all sides, and we see the horizon in every direction as the mountains fall back behind us. I can't deny a sense of awe as we emerge—a sense of *we have come through!*—as hanks of sunlight pour down through rips in the cottony clouds.

On our right stands a series of old signs propped up in the sand like long-forgotten tombstones. Most are blank with any painted message long ago sandblasted off by the elements. But one retains the outline of a few letters: *F RWE L*. We park and step out into a strong wind. An old man is leaned up against the backside of the sign, whittling.

"You Farwell?"

"Last time I checked."

"How you doing?"

"Still above ground," he says. His voice is a cross between a whisper and a growl, a nicotine baritone as if he's been pounding cigarettes for breakfast since he was ten. Roused by our approach, two ancient Weimaraners rise on long, unsteady legs. They quiver forward to sniff our crotches.

"Hounds won't bite you none," Farwell informs us. "Mighta used to, but no more." He laughs soundlessly to himself as chips from the wood he whittles are carried off in the wind.

"We were told you had a junkyard out here," Tony says.

"You just missed it."

"What do you mean?"

"Mighta found it if you'd come six months ago, but everything's gone now. Wife and me had the yard all those years, but she went and got cancer. I wasn't inclined to keep it on my own and six months ago had some trucks crush 'em for scrap and haul every last bit to Cruces. You see what's left."

Indeed we do. Nothing. Not a speck. The sand is smug, like it's swallowed everything it had a mind to. We're on the downside of a dune overlooking desert of a different dimension—the edge of a void like none we've encountered so far. It stretches out like a death sentence, flat and empty toward the horizon.

"You wouldn't remember a Land Cruiser by any chance, would you? Green?"

"Used to be I could tell you the fender on every model. Nowadays my memory's like Swiss cheese."

The dogs move in a tight circle to rebalance themselves, shivering on their lanky legs. Tony chucks Farwell a Yoo-hoo from his six-pack.

"Obliged. Yeah, I come out here sometimes to see where it used to be," Farwell continues, cracking open the can and gazing out over his lost fiefdom. "Not a stitch left. I feel like my whole past has come to nuthin'. No sign I even lived."

He stretches now, and I can make out the round outline of a chewing-tobacco tin inside his shirt pocket.

"Still got my hounds," Farwell croaks. "Gray ghosts, they call 'em, on accounta the color of their coat."

The dogs look up anxiously. "See that tar road out back the side of that rise?" Farwell asks. "No, you don't, 'cause the sand ate it down. Like it eats everything down, by and by. Back in my grandpa's day them roads used to go to the mines that were everywhere in these hills, closed down after the price of silver dropped in 1893. Most of 'em caved in since then, the roads returning to sand. Long before that, this whole vista used to be pine trees, most of the Southwest a forest smelling of vanilla, with bark that fit together like jigsaw pieces." The thought brings a smile of comfort to his lips for a second.

Tony does an unlikely thing. Right there in the middle of the conversation he hauls out his golf bag from the trunk of the car and starts smacking balls into the distance. It may be tactless, if there's such a thing as desert etiquette, but I take it as a sign of health. The old man is bringing him down, and he's taking steps to keep his spirits up.

As for me, I can't get my mind around any of it. Time. Sand. Cave-ins. The DNA of the desert is a mystery I can't begin to decode. I wonder if this expanse we're overlooking has a name.

"Jornada del Muerto, Journey of Death," Farwell answers. "Deadliest part of the old trade route from Mexico up to Santa Fe. This here death stretch is ninety miles of hell. No water, no shade. They used to say if the thirst don't get you, the Apaches would. Or the quicksand. Or the rattlers." He lifts his pant cuff to reveal a brick strapped to the underside of his shoe, and now I see his left leg is several inches shorter than his right. "One of 'em shriveled me up pretty good a few years back."

This isn't tall-tale telling; it feels like he's telling us straight.

"You wanna talk dark, though?" Farwell says. "It's the flip side to all that airy-fairy talk you might hear back in town."

Behind him, the thick clouds are tumbling over one another in the dwindling light. Tony smacks out another ball, but it doesn't go far against the wind that seems to have reinvented itself now that the sun's almost sunk.

"See them little piles of rocks out there? There and there?" He points. "The unmarked graves of those who died building the dam, and plenty more uncounted for. Shoot-outs and such. The rocks are to keep coyotes away, but come spring the buzzards gather on the trees. I've counted more'n a hundred waiting to feast on the remains from the body parts they still find litterin' about, thanks to a serial sex murderer back in the nineties with his storage bin right up the road where he did his torturing. Over fifty victims and still counting."

Tony is trying not to listen as he tees off again.

"Darkness aplenty," the old man continues. "There are places you drive around here, you'll have four Black Hawks on your tail, guaranteed."

"Black Hawks . . . Native Americans?" I ask.

"Helicopters!" he snorts. "The military has bases out here that don't exist! They're doing blacked-out things all the time: secret missiles, who knows what. Those UFO sightings people are always seein' as far as Roswell? Maybe they're aliens, but then again, could be the dark makin' itself known."

"Speaking of rattlers—holy shit!" Tony says, focusing his camera phone on one a few feet in front of him.

"I'd keep your distance I were you," Farwell warns.

"But he's such a cute little fella, all coiled up."

"The little ones got the freshest venom. And they coil before they strike."

"Don't worry," Tony says, circling around the rattler to get better angles, "I just want one shot . . ."

Quick as a bullet, Farwell sidearms a stone directly into the snake, which slithers off with a companion hiding two feet away. "They come in pairs," Farwell explains as his dogs shake on jittery knees. Tony looks very exposed on the hillside with his bare ankles in suburban moccasins. Literally rattled now. It's obvious he's suffered a blow to his dignity. Teeing off again, he kind of glares at me and kind of doesn't, a subtle expression he would never admit to having.

"You don't look too good," I tell him.

"Tired is all." His cell phone rings. "You'll excuse me," he says, walking off—but carefully this time.

Nearby, a tall cactus with spindly arms looks as if it's dancing in the wind, a thorny scarecrow against the fading sky.

"Not a stitch to prove I was even born," Farwell resumes, surveying the dunes. "Seem to recall being a bony runt at one time, though."

"I've still got my belt somewhere from last time I was here," I say. "Looks like a dog collar."

Farwell snorts appreciatively, more of a machine-gun wheeze. "Maybe if we sat out here with a bourbon and Coke it'd all come clear."

We share the wind a minute in companionable silence, peering over the denuded sand falling away in sweep after sweep like a desert ocean, flowing out to the horizon.

"Sands of time," he says. "Even the rocks are in a state of motion. Dissolving. Enlarging. We're just seeing 'em at this stage of their journey, but their span is over millions of years, through the bright and the dark."

"Hard to imagine anything dark right now, under a sky lit like this," I say.

"It's more of what's inside you," Farwell says. "This here's one of those places will bring out whatever you've got goin' on inside. If it's for good, it'll bring that out, and the opposite too."

"You always alone up here?"

"Sometimes a wild goat or two will stray over. I feed 'em like kittens." He kicks his bad leg out to access his pocket, then pops a palmful of pills down in one dry gulp.

"How old are you, if you don't mind my asking?"

"Seventy-two used to sound old to me. Now it's 'bout the same as sixty."

"I guess a lifetime's not that long a time," I say. "I mean, it was only a few lifetimes ago that we had the Civil War. Only a couple of lifetimes before that when George Washington was walking around. It's like, I wouldn't be all that amazed if he were to step right out from behind that cactus there now."

"Well, yes you would!" Farwell laughs. The stick he's whittling shakes as he chortles soundlessly at his own humor.

His phone call finished, Tony makes his way back toward us, revived.

"Sorry to break up the party, gents," he says. "But something's come up. I gotta go home."

Even Farwell registers the shock. "The hell? And leave your partner here?"

"He's comin' too," Tony assures him. To me he says, "Sorry, it's just that Patty's got a fashion show to get ready for and I completely forgot to get the gutters cleaned."

Fashion show? Gutters cleaned? What's next—a garden party with Jell-O salad?

Tony sees my expression and tries to make amends.

"Look, Dan, I'm sorry if that's a flimsy excuse, but I've got a marriage that's running on bald tires. Could blow any day. I have to keep the peace as long as I can."

"I thought your marriage was A.1. steak sauce."

"It's a *marriage*, for God's sake." Tony looks at me with pity. "Dan, I'm sure you like to think you're the world's worst husband because it gives you some jolt of distinction, but in actual fact it's me who thinks he's the center of the universe."

"Sorry," I say. "Maybe I've been contagious."

"Yeah, that's a good Danny boy. Even my self-centeredness is about you."

Tony watches as Farwell limps a few feet away on his brick to settle the dogs' unease. "So the point is, it's an emergency. No time to waste."

"But what about getting my mojo back?"

"Didn't pan out. And the new regime I wanted to put you on was always a long shot. But hopefully the desert heat helped you a little."

"What about the Guardian Angel?"

"Figment of our imagination, Dan! Or may as well have been. Maybe it was a double hallucination, from the good folks who brought us double rainbows. Who knows? There's not a shred of proof she ever existed. Maybe Judi was right. We smoked up the whole thing. In which case, who gives a shit! We need to get on with our lives!"

By way of convincing me, he tosses a pebble at my sandal, hitting me in the toe. "We're not gonna find anything, Danny. The whole town's a giant junkyard, except the one we want has fallen off the face of the earth." Another pebble hits me with more urgency, bouncing off my chest. "I mean, no offense to this nice man here, but show me one piece of evidence there was ever a junkyard here. We're disappearing even as we speak, like every minute here we lose more of who we were! Which is not the sort of issue I want to be dealing with. Let's go back to something real."

I have to admit, this new plan is agreeing with Tony. He's looking more vigorous than he has in hours.

"Tell you the truth, I'm glad Patty called when she did," Tony admits. "I don't like things getting this freaky. That banner everywhere—"We've been waiting for you!"—and then my coming up with Mary's name, even if it's wrong, not to mention that chiropractor's Land Cruiser. I, for one, know when I'm out of my depth."

The wind has whipped up another notch. "Blow's coming in," Farwell growls, soothing the dogs who are moaning and skittering about. "See on the horizon how the sky's getting blurry? You'll want to find shelter before the dust storm hits."

Which is nonsense, in my opinion. The sky's just smoky at the far edge, where there must be a wildfire. The old man's eyes are as shot as his memory. I'm losing patience with everything.

"I didn't want to tell you this," Tony is saying now, "but I've had a creepy feeling ever since I invited you here. Like right after I hung up from calling you, I opened the window and heard a huge car crash a few blocks away. Then I started getting spam offering electric wheelchairs. I mean, these things take their toll, Danny. C'mon, tell the truth, aren't you a little relieved to be leaving too?" Tony asks.

I don't answer, which Tony takes as a yes.

"So, pardner, let's saddle up and head home!" he says, hoisting his golf bag over his shoulder. "We can drive to Albuquerque and catch a redeye by midnight. How'd that cowboy song go? 'Move 'em, move 'em, move 'em . . . keep those dawgies movin' . . . head 'em up, ride 'em in, cut 'em out, rawhiiiiiiide!'"

Quite a performance. There is that moment when the first stars hang in the evening sky, not quite sure whether they'll stick around for the festivities or maybe just kick back and rest in the unseen infinities.

"I'm staying," I say.

Tony drops his golf bag to the sand. "You're what?"

"I've got no home to head back to," I say simply.

Now it's his jaw that he drops.

"Just till I get back on my legs," I say, "my feet, whatever the expressions is."

Tony raises his voice. "Have you forgotten you almost lost your legs in this town? Don't push your luck! Plus you have to take the boys ice fishing back home, remember? How could that slip your mind? February's like the best month!"

Tony's the picture of innocence as he picks a grain of sand off his tongue.

"OK, no biggie," Tony concedes, calming down. "I'll be with you in spirit. Won't take me long to straighten this out with Patty. You sit tight, play a little solitaire. I'll be back in a jiffy to finish finding Mary or whatever the hell she calls herself. So you won't mind if I take the car, right? I'll drop it at the airport since you've sworn off driving anyway."

The gray ghosts are beginning to howl now, their butts banging together in the wind. Farwell and I shake hands goodbye. His thumb is missing, but he's got a strong shake.

Tony and I leave him whittling in the wind and head back for the mountain pass. In seconds the hound howls are replaced with windblown radio static. Tony is looking vastly relieved since his decision, cheerful enough to give bad advice. "Ask Judi to whip you up a home-cooked meal. It'll all turn out great, so long as you don't, you know—ouch."

A gust slams the car sideways as we round the first turn into the pass.

"I don't mean shoot yourself, necessarily," he continues. "I mean fall under a bus, for instance. Or *shoot* yourself under a bus! Even better. Accidentally on purpose. I wouldn't be mentioning it except you're not wearing your seat belt again. For like the fourth time today."

He's right. I buckle in. We finish the pass in blackness and drive through town, which is equally unlit, the stores shut tight against the evening like the stage set of an abandoned cowboy town. In a minute we're pulling up the driveway of the desert castle. My heart stops when I reach into my pocket to find it empty.

"I've lost my keys," I say quietly.

"Oh."

Less quietly: "Tony, I've lost my keys!"

"Well, it's not like you're going to need them here. I'll lend you the trailer key and—"

"No, the keys to my home! To my life! I'm lost without them!"

#1 Dad! key chain!

Tony looks at me as though he figures I'm a lost cause, anyway, and there's nothing more he can do about it. Leaving the car running, he scoots into the trailer and rummages around without turning on a light, coming back hyperventilated a minute later. "Stop worrying, they'll turn up when you're least expecting them," he says, back in the driver's seat. "You'll find your way. You always do."

I'm dizzy but able to fake enough courage to climb out of the car and stand straight.

"Wait: possible change of heart," Tony says, putting the car in reverse but keeping his foot on the brake so most of the block is lit up emergency-room red. "Maybe I shouldn't leave you alone in your state. 'Cause if you do something rash, I swear—"

"I'll be OK. Go."

"You sure?"

"So long as I have my trusty backpack," I say, slapping it with more bravado than I feel and placing it on the driveway.

Tony keeps his foot on the brake. "Yeah, it's better this way," he decides. "All those biblical dudes who ventured into the desert—you think they were buddy movies? No, it's gotta be just you drilling deep into your soul with no distractions. To say nothing of Mary. If I stayed, what if she developed a crush on me instead of you? That would throw some kind of wrench into the works, huh?"

"Enough, I get it."

"Sayonara, kemosabe," Tony says, taking his foot off the brake and—

The sound of my laptop crunching is accompanied by the helpless peeps my cell phone gives off, like a bird whose head is being squelched.

The block is hospital red again. Tony has reapplied the brakes.

"Did something very bad just happen?" he asks.

I'm on my knees, cradling the remains.

"Oh my God," Tony says. "Did something very bad just happen?"

Not bad. Devastating. From inside my backpack there is an ugly whirring noise, like a grinder doing its best against coffee beans made of steel. I can't bear to look but fit my hand inside to feel warmth where warmth is not supposed to be. As if it was an exertion for my priceless technology to be run over by such weight. I open the backpack to behold the ruin that is the shattered screen of my laptop. My contacts, calendars, correspondence—everything I need to stay in touch with the world and with myself has been flattened. Who I am and what I do. My precious identity.

"Ho, no! I can't believe you made me do that!" Tony stammers, hiccupping with guilt. "You planted it practically under the wheels! Sorry I'm laughing. I do that when I'm upset sometimes."

It's a poetry ambush, an impish benediction in some sort of clandestine code as I stand here speechless, watching him try to swallow a series of nervous microburps.

"Tell you what," he says between trembling intakes of air. "You stay put. I'll fly home and come back with a practically brand-new laptop for you to play with. You like that? Huh? Am I the best friend you ever had? Not just the best but the *best-y* best? C'mon, gimme a smile . . ."

It's gibberish, a kind of infantile gobbledygook meant to camouflage the fact that I am standing here immobilized while Tony is very clearly inching the car forward, away from me.

"I don't blame you for not seeing the poetic justice of this right now, Dan, but I swear you'll thank me someday. To be completely cut off like you were forty years ago, with a chance to really get down and dirty with your innermost self, out beyond all your reference points without even a car to escape in . . ."

Tony's desperate blather fades down the street like so much useless stammering to cover up the fact that he's actually leaving, for God's sake, leaving as *in going, gone*, as in *I'm being left alone by myself*.

Stepping on a mesquite thorn that punctures my instep, I limp into the castle and lock the double deadbolt behind me.

"Help!"

PART II

TWO MINUTES LATER

CHAPTER 9

SHIT SNEAKS UP ON YOU

SILENCE IN THE single-wide. Not a cough. Not a sneeze. It's the silence of a cave after a cave-in, once the earth has settled. Silence that makes you aware of the limitations of your breathing. Don't like it. Not one bit.

I retire to the bedroom, seal the windows, close the curtains. The strain of the past couple of days is hitting me hard: the divorce papers, the distance from my children, Tony's surprise departure. Whatever puny courage I possessed has left me. I'm cowering worse than I did at home, where at least I had the dog to divert me. So many questions. Are the boys brushing their teeth? Are they asking their mom where I've gone? I want to squeeze their shoulders and assure them that everything is OK. If only I believed that.

Eventually the brute force of the wind arrives, down from the mountain pass. Farwell was right. It is a blow, and it comes from every direction at once, bringing with it sounds both unfamiliar and unnerving. The insidious squeak coming from the bathroom reveals itself to be a roll of toilet paper unspooling by itself in the draft. The persistent clatter coming from outside is the license plate banging on the door. It's against these and other noises that I recoil from the world, barely daring to move.

My aim is to shut myself down, get as near comatose as I can for as long as I can. I lie down and close my eyes extra tight, the way my monkeys do when they're pretending to be asleep. Soon I'm only vaguely aware that dust is beating like hail against the shingles, almost a lateral tornado. Down I dig deeper into my cave-in, that place where nightmares thrive. I dream that the four grand old maple trees in front of my New England home have no roots. They're toppling, replaced by four roadside crash memorials, one for each member of my family. I dream that Barker-the-Barker has frozen to death, flat and stiff as coyote cardboard. *How will I tell the boys?*

And dreams even darker come as the hours spin by. Cars skidding into our family house, smashing into the boys' bedroom windows. My wife gathering Spencer and Jeremy around the kitchen table to tell them about the family separation—no, that dream was real. The storm continues, lifting and slamming the metal sheet that serves as porch roof, whipping the mesquite branches to slice the outside walls. I burrow down further to a place akin to my postcrash blackout state, from which I try to access the secret words: *we are all* . . . What comes instead is an image of my sons being gently rocked in the arms of the lovely goth women from the gas station, of all people, accompanied by the faint strains of a country song I seem to recall from decades ago:

> I met a little girl in Hard Knocks Ville
> A town we all know well
> And every Sunday evening
> Out in her home I'd dwell

Daylight comes at intervals, but I avoid it. The storm dies off, yet the cave-in continues, along with a need to pee. I'm upright long enough to limp to the bathroom, but the sole of my foot throbs from the thorn puncture, so I go back to my default: the horizontal position that asks nothing of me. I'm vaguely aware of internal gears shifting, prompting me on an almost granular level to get up, lie down, get up. I'm not sure what's propelling me, but eventually I open the front door—a kind of sleepwalking that leads me down the porch steps.

I'm remembering being outside the boys' darkened bedroom door, listening to Polly strum her beloved college mandolin as they were dozing off. I can picture the dim nightlight and the sound of cars hissing by outside. I can see the baseball trophies lined up on the bookcase. For the first time, I'm feeling left out of my family and don't know what to do.

Turns out I'm just looking for a new place to resume being horizontal, and I find it on a sidewalk bench a few blocks away, amid a band of passersby whose commonplace gumption astounds me. Where do they muster the moxie to stand up straight and take what comes? Conversations are animated, like between those two old friends joshing each other, pretending to take offense at something one of them says, stealing something from his pocket, then snatching it back with a *gotcha!* How do they know when to smile, when to frown? How do they forgive each other the everyday misdemeanors that erode a friendship, much less a marriage? I'd try to join a conversation except I'm trapped inside myself, stuck in a cycle of *me me me.* Slow panic rises as the words of that unknown song turn sinister.

> I took her by her golden curls
> And I drug her 'round and 'round
> Throwing her into the river
> That flows through Hard Knocks Ville

Running out of sleep at last, I'm rescued by a shadow falling over me. I picture the Angel telling me to rest easy, but when I open my eyes it's an old man clasping a Raggedy Ann doll, his face framed by a crystal blue sky that's been airbrushed by the storm, more falsely benign than ever.

"Are you one of the crazies?" he asks, peering down at me.

Good question. I'm lying on a sidewalk bench, near the Crash Site. Apparently, I've come to consciousness a stone's throw from where I came back to myself as a young man forty years earlier. I rise to a seated position, rub my grizzled chin. How long have I been under? The storm must have been a doozy. Looking around, I see flowerpots shattered, mounds of sand churned up against windowsills, porch chairs crumpled.

"I'm not one of the crazies either. I'm Summer—that's a good name for me, you bet. You're Dan-Rose-wife-kicked-him-out."

He sees my surprise. "Word travels fast when you're having a good time," he explains. "I'm having a good time. Are you having a good time? Oh, don't ask so many questions, Summer. That's rude to ask so many questions!"

These last lines are delivered in falsetto. I run my tongue over my front teeth, gritty from the storm. "I'm confused," I say. "Is that the voice of Raggedy Ann?"

"You bet. She was real good to me a long time ago in the hospital, so I use her voice to settle down. I can do other voices too. Guess who this is. Boop-boop-de-doop-oop!"

"Betty Boop!" I say, with more enthusiasm than I intended.

It's not a bad imitation. I recall the Betty Boop cartoons I saw through a bedroom window that first night with Tony. "Do you live on the route coming in from the highway?" I ask.

"You bet, uh-huh. Word is you was in a car crash on that road once. We got a lot of crashes there. Thirty-nine to be exact." His mouth moves as he mentally counts a series of numbers to himself. "Thirty-nine, that's right. You know why? 'Cause it's empty, that's why. OK, I got a good one for you, ready? Why do cars traveling on an empty road hit each other?"

"I give up. Why?"

"'Cause there's nothing else for them *to* hit!"

It's like a Zen koan. But Summer isn't looking at me to gauge my reaction; he's staring off diffusely to my left at nothing at all.

"Good one, huh? Did Summer make a good one?"

"Summer made a good one."

"A good one, you bet. Are you a man or a woman?"

"Man."

"See, I could have told you so. Seventy-three percent of all people killed in car wrecks are men. Sixteen percent of men drive as fast as they can into the bottom of the dam. Oh, now you said a swear word, Summer. Don't talk dirty!"

"Damn's not actually a swear word."

"Yes it is too," he snarls. Chewing on his tongue, he builds himself into the start of a rage. A powerfully built man, despite being stooped, he calms himself by adopting a professional radio broadcaster's voice. "Weather and traffic on the ones. Sunshine now with moderate delays and a chance of hail later on—"

"Wait, are they really predicting hail for today?"

"That's not today. That's March 2, 1970, the day Mother brought me here," Summer says mildly, still clasping his doll, so threadbare the gray cotton is slipping out in spots.

Nineteen seventy, did he say?

"First-class memory, that's what I've got, you bet. Give me a calendar date since I got here, and I'll give you the traffic report."

"That's OK, I believe you."

"Give me a date!" he snarls.

For lack of anything better I pick my wedding date.

"Traffic and weather for September 5, 1994. Sunny and hot with winds out of the east. Relative humidity stands at 13 percent, barometer holding steady—"

Who cares if his stats are real or just useless numbers he's accumulated from decades of being glued to a radio. It's mesmerizing to watch as he winds it down. "That's very good, Summer," I say. "You must be very—"

But Summer interrupts me, nodding toward a group of men milling in front of an adobe office building—the rowdy cowboys who hooted at Tony and me our first morning in town. "See those guys over there? They're not crazy either. They're trying to beat the bottle. C'mon, let's go make friends."

· ·

I let myself be led to the porch where a group of men stand around wearing every sort of hat: camouflage boonies, greasy tractor caps pushed back on the heads, Stetsons bent across the front, their brims creased down in a manner signaling defeat at life's hands. But defeat that didn't come without a fight, the glint of rebelliousness not quite guttered out.

"This is Dan-Rose-wife-kicked-him-out," Summer announces before wandering back down the street. I stand there feeling I've just been handed off, like a toddler being dropped at day care.

I'm remembering how on a crowded Rhode Island beach the boys were all of a sudden drifting dangerously close to an invisible undercurrent. Polly was beside me. Panicked, she took off down the beach running so fast her feet barely touched the sand. Without knowing what was happening, I started running toward the water too. She braved the waves that her husband failed to see, and together we yanked them from the swirling water. As Polly sprinted up toward the pavilion with Jeremy in her arms, our fellow swimmers erupted into a standing ovation. Polly always seemed to attract more than her share of those.

"Quit yer braggin'!" someone growls from behind the railing of a beaten-down porch. Turns out to be a man with extralong white pigtails in a motorized wheelchair.

"Excuse me?" I say.

"I've had a hundred women kick me out! And that includes my mother, my sister, all my aunts, and the girl next door I ended up marrying twice, so don't think you're something special, Brother Fancy-Pants!"

"Colonel, colonel, this ain't a sweepstake to see how many women despise you," says a laid-back man I recognize from Harry's head shop—Clay, his name turns out to be—the prospector with turquoise necklace and broken black cowboy hat.

"Bullshit-kicked-him-out!" pursues the man. "I been tossed on my ass by women in most all thirty-eight states—you don't see me boastin' about it!"

That said, he pops a wooden clothespin in his mouth and chews on it avidly.

Turns out that this is a splinter group of Alcoholics Anonymous. And as in AA groups the world over, the oral fixation is pronounced—that clothespin, as well as cough drops, Tootsie Rolls, garlic cloves. I gather that this particular group deviates in significant ways from the standard AA franchise. My source on this is Clay, the grizzled prospector whose lack of teeth doesn't stop him from enjoying a toothpick, rolling it from one side of his horsey gums to the other.

"Call ourselves Assholes Anonymous," he says with satisfaction. "Not very original but for the fact we been kicked out of every other AA group in town. We're more an outlaw AA, a maximum-security AA that makes its own rules, the lowest of the low, USDA-certified rock bottom."

"Why were you all kicked out?" I ask.

"Being psychopaths, basically. Getting sore and playing pick-up sticks with the furniture. That sort of thing. Bringing guns to meetings."

"Loaded?"

"Why wear a gun that ain't gonna put 'er down?"

Clay is relishing the bona fides of his compatriots, continuing with a roll call we've all heard before, a kind of humble brag that declares *we're the most fucked of all!*—but right now I'm alarmed by my reflection on the lenses of Clay's paint-spattered granny sunglasses. Holy shit, it looks like I've aged three years in the last few days. I've become a member of the ghost army of the walking wounded, complete with listless gait and glassy stare. When the porch door opens, I can't think of a single reason not to shuffle inside with the rest of them.

The room features a long redwood table covered by a bright yellow plastic tablecloth, as though for a picnic. Pictures of red hummingbirds and orange butterflies flit among its coffee stains. The walls are dinge-yellow, with black finger smudges around the light switches. The single window is propped open with a broken stick. Spaced at intervals along the inside wall are empty cans of tomato paste. But the room smells amazing. Strong coffee is being brewed on a card table in front.

"Let's get to it," Clay says. "Who's got the spike?"

"I do." A railroad spike is produced.

"Who's got the story of the spike?"

"I do," says someone shaped like a tree stump in OshKosh overalls, crew cut on top. "It's a reminder that anytime you're outa luck, you can always pick yourself up a railroad spike, walk into a store, and tell the man you'll clean out the cracks in his sidewalk. You can carry that sucker from Minneapolis to Miami if you have to, cleaning sidewalks the whole way. Plus, it's good self-defense for loners, which we generally tend to be."

With that apparently ritual story, the meeting comes to order. "Who wants to start the intros, short 'n' sweet?" says Clay.

"Hell, I may as well," says a guy with colorful clocks tattooed across his knobby bald skull. "I'm Real Dick: wino, dope fiend, would-be best-selling cookbook author, and pissant malcontent."

"Welcome, Real Dick."

"As most of you know, I call myself Real Dick to distinguish myself from Phony Dick, who's cooling his heels back behind bars again. Where I joined him this weekend, sad to report."

"Taking your swigs a little too openly?" Clay asks sympathetically.

"Don't ask me, ask him!" Real Dick replies, pointing at himself. Left unclear is whether the other, incarcerated Dick is an actual person or some psychological stunt double. A car drives by outside, trailing a chorus of Mexican tubas that turns flat in the distance.

"My turn," says a man holding a flyswatter with the slogan "Do other banks bother you?" "I'm Bird Brain, and I'm a gutter-crawling asshole of the hopeless variety."

"Hey, Bird Brain, what's the scoop?" they say, even though they give every sign of having heard it many times before.

"As most of you blowhards know, I chose to live in T or C just because there's only one stoplight. Can't say why the notion of one stoplight appealed to me: it just did. Anyway, I'm here to tell you that shit sneaks up on you, that it do."

This tickles Clay's funny bone for some reason. "That it do," he laughs, as Bird Brain whacks at a fly on the tablecloth before him, missing by a mile. "That's a good one, Bird Brain. Who's next?"

Next to take possession of the spike is a gray-faced man with an eye patch covering who knows what kind of injury. "Yeah, well, I'm Hap Hazard, and I am the end-all and be-all of bad. Watch out now 'cause here comes the haphazard man!"

"Howdy, Hap . . . Howdy, Haz . . ."

"I mean, I am a public-health hazard, but at least I only been drunk once in my whole life."

They know the drill. "How's that?"

From out of the corner of his mouth he fires a stream of tobacco juice expertly into one of the tomato-paste cans, an act of self-congratulation. "Lasted thirty-two years!"

With appreciative guffaws, the spike is passed to the tree stump in overalls. "You're up, Moon Dog."

"As you all know, they call me Moon Dog 'cause I used to have a penchant for Mogen David, MD, six bucks a gallon. But I'd appreciate if you'd use my real name, everyone. I've earned it, ain't I, with eighteen years' sobriety? My sobriety's old enough to vote, for cripes' sake! Anyway, it's nice not to be on a wanted poster anymore, though it is kinda lonesome not being wanted." The spike is paused halfway en route to the next person. "Oh, and for anyone out of the loop, I just wanna say this here spike comes from yours truly. I was the one used it to Miami that time."

"And we appreciate it, Raydeen," Clay says. "Thank ya as always, sugar."

Raydeen! Sugar! Of course the ghost army contains female transsexuals as well as male. How small-minded of me to assume otherwise.

Next up is a soft-spoken man wearing blue eyeliner. "I'll pass," he says, handing the spike down the line.

"Let the record show Doctor Tom passes," Clay declares, turning his attention to the man in the wheelchair. "Colonel, the floor's all yours."

The energy being galvanized by this next speaker can only be called electric. He's like a human thunderhead gathering all the airborne ions in the room before detonating his delivery. "I," he says, "am Colonel Roy Joy: three hundred pounds of pure stinkin' boy toy and high-performance masturbator to boot! Hee-haw! Massive self-manipulator and jack-off of all trades!"

"Rip-roarin' Roy!" everyone cheers.

"Roy Joy is all boy!"

"All boy!" sing the others. It's a little like call-and-response in a gospel church, cowpoke version.

"Since French Kiss bought the farm last year," Roy Joy resumes telling the room, his rasp like a bullhorn, "I'm the oldest of the group, asshole emeritus you might say, thus the code name *Colonel*." He stops to pinch his nose dry with callused fingertips. "No news to report since this morning's meetin', so in conclusion let me just say I would dearly love to find me a woman I could check up and down for ticks, backwards and forwards too."

"All right, that's enough outa you, lover boy," Clay says, not unfondly. "Who else we ain't heard from this mornin'? Old son, wanna give it a go?"

Courtesy dictates that no one look at me as I decide. I really don't want to speak. But shit sneaks up on you, that it do. I take a deep inhale of the great coffee smell and manufacture an ounce of cheerfulness I hope won't sound as phony as it feels.

"Hi, I'm Dan, and you're probably wondering what I'm doing here."

"Something about crashing into a beautiful blond, word has it," says Clay, taking a sip of coffee under the broken brim of his cowboy hat.

Before I have a chance to clarify, there's an outburst to my left.

"Chairman! Your Honor!" shouts Roy Joy, nervously tugging on his fly. "I object on the grounds that how do we know she's beautiful?"

"Settle down, Roy Joy," Clay warns him, and signals me to go again.

"See, I'm recently separated—" I begin again, and again am interrupted by the same interrupter.

"Separated? I think not!" shouts Roy Joy. "Fucktard looks like he's in one piece to me!"

I thought there was no "cross talk" in AA. Like isn't that one of the cardinal rules? I make the mistake of saying as much out loud.

"Well, fuck you too then, Miss Prissy Hoops," Roy Joy shouts. "No cross talk? I say let's see you try and stop us! We're sons of bitches and fathers of whores—now who's gonna tell us right from wrong!"

"Colonel," Clay warns again.

"But this fart ripple is fucking things up and bringing me down!" Roy Joy says. "Someone shoot this day-tripper. He sure as hell's not Christ so get him off the cross. We need the wood!"

Snickers roll through the group.

"Now that you bring it up," says Hap Hazard, "I'm kinda wondering myself what makes him think his crash is better'n anyone else's."

"*What's he got against our crashes?* is another way to put it," says Bird Brain, banging the tablecloth with his swatter again with no better luck.

"Girls, girls, Dan's not here to out-crash you," Clay warns.

"Then he's wastin' our time!" Roy Joy shouts, raising a huzzah. By way of encouragement, Real Dick claps him on the shoulder, raising a cloud of sawdust from the unidentifiable fabric.

"Let me elaborate the animus I got against Richie Rich here," Roy Joy goes on. "I seen him and his sidekick nosin' around town 'while back, lookin' down their nose from the cockpit of their Rolls Royce. Coupla haters, that's what they were, who'd need to put a quarter in the jukebox just to know what they was feelin'—"

I realize I don't have to sit here and take this, yet I can't escape the idea that this is a place I'm supposed to be, that these are words I'm supposed to hear.

"What's he back for?" says Bird Brain. "More to the point, what's in it for us?"

I try to raise a word in self-defense but am cut off by Roy Joy. "I'll tell you what he's back for," Roy Joy says. "He's finding our shithole interesting! And us losers colorful! Even with all the teeth he has, he still can't chew through his own horseshit."

My adversary has worked himself into such a state that he swivels his wheelchair to address me straight-on, so in-my-face I can't help staring at a perfect circle of blackheads on the bulb of his nose. "I ain't gonna sugarcoat it for you, Dandy Dan. Your head's been up your ass so long, you think the view is the Grand Canyon! Look around, cock splat. You think you're the only one got trouble? Well, boo-hoo to you. You wouldn't last two weeks here with trouble of the real variety."

"Roy . . . Joy! Roy . . . Joy!" comes the chant, like a chorus out of *Jerry Springer*.

"Matter fact, I give it one week before you collect your marbles and skate back to your gold-gated community. But before you go, I got a parting gift." Adroitly, he writhes himself up to a standing position and pulls down his pants, offering a stupendous display of his fat white ass, luscious as a honeydew.

"Take a hit a that, Chicken Little. You want to taste trouble, take a hit a that—"

He freezes midmoon, silencing the hoots, and puts a hand to his ear as though hearing the strains of a French horn in the distance, summoning hounds to the hunt.

"Wait, listen: your boyfriend's callin' you to come out and play cowboy some more. Go on, don't wanna keep him waitin'. Git!"

It's a jeer they can clap to. "Git! Git! Git! Git! Git! Git!"

Clay, one of the few not joining in the chant, raises his eyebrows to me on my way out the door.

"Sorry, old son."

CHAPTER 10

DOOR NUMBER TWO

SERIOUSLY, DID THAT JUST happen? Did I just get my ass handed to me by some of the orneriest customers I've ever met? Appears that I did. So I have a choice. I can either shut myself down again, go directly back to the horizontal position for who knows how long—or I can stay upright, face what comes. Hard choice, but most folks seem to manage it.

What the hell: I'll take what's behind door number two.

I walk down Charles Street, a little energized by the drubbing I just got in there. Partly it's the thrill of being called on my shit. Regardless of whether there was any truth to it, it's kind of heartening to think they got my number. Maybe I am just a half-assed tourist looking for distraction. But hey, at least I'm not limping. The cave-in must have lasted long enough for my puncture to heal itself. And hey, another thrill: no one knows where I am. Tony may know the general vicinity, but does he know I'm taking a right on Broadway at this moment, free to go any direction I want with no one to tell me *boo*? Fuck Tony's abandonment. I could reinvent myself like everyone else in this woebegone town.

Besides, as I was exiting past him back at the meeting, didn't Clay send me a farewell cheer to counteract the jeers? "Head up, tail down, and plead not guilty!" Or do I just wish he had?

Anyway, it's worth walking unhurriedly to take in things I overlooked before. The year 1935 is stamped in the corner of many still-durable slabs of sidewalk, proving that the asphalt mixed by Roosevelt's WPA has held up better than the tar they've used to patch the potholes all these years since. The buildings, too, with their flat-faced cowboy fronts: they may be from the 1930s, but they'll outlast us all unless the vibrations from the eighteen-wheelers en route to the spaceport destabilize their supporting beams. It's yet another gamble of the sort this town seems to specialize in: cement trucks weakening the foundations of the past on their way to redreaming the future. Yet another throw of the dice, and brave, I suppose, in its way.

It feels un-American to be without a car. I'm disenfranchised, like a teenager who's been grounded. On the other hand, the slower pace is kind of nice, allowing me to see how wrong I was on my first take of this town. Those cop cars with the scurvy-looking paint jobs? They're retired cars, stashed out back; in front are brand-new cop cars with tastefully muted colors and an elegant town logo on the driver's door. The side streets in one unfortunate neighborhood may be named after all the local mines that didn't pan out—Tin Street, Platinum, Nickel, Copper, Lead—but the street signs sport little yellow rocket ships to remind everyone of the spaceport that's conjuring itself from the desert floor twenty miles away. Though most residents I pass seem to prefer more earthly things to talk about.

"Seen *Gunsmoke* last night?"

"Good one, all right. That Miss Kitty—"

"In our dreams, Willie, in our dreams . . ."

Ignorantly wrong, was what I was. That's communication—not superficial at all but meaningful code signifying that people are present and accounted for, at least for the time being, and meanwhile shoring each other up.

"Old enough to know better." "It's nasty but I'm gettin' there." Most of it is shorthand for "still in the game." And sometimes they're even able to bring a little neighborhood news to the exchange:

"How's it goin'?"

"All right 'cept for that wind last night."

"Did kinda rip up the flags again."

So that's why the flags in this town are ragged! You arrogant fucktard, Rose . . .

There's a sense to the place—more method than madness. The chain-link fencing may be monotonous, but here's one golden-ager down on his knees mending his links with green fishing line while his wife whiles away with her dirt whacker. The reek of cigarette smoke may predominate—most every passerby exudes a scorched cloudbank of Kools, most every car radiates the fumes of week-old Camels—but it's overlaid by that delicious T or C aroma, sharp and tangy as the burn from a barbecue. The dogs may bare their fangs, but their hearts aren't in it. When I stop to look them in the eye they scamper away, whimpering. Then what a howl they put up, at their safe remove: the humiliation of having had their bluff called. Could the whole town be like that? More bark than bite?

Giving Candy's bar a wide berth, I turn the corner and encounter a large "We've been waiting for you!" banner draped outside of what turns out to be the town museum, which I've totally forgotten about. I pounce on the black entrance mat, expecting the door to open automatically; I guess I'm still acclimating. Inside, a tall woman whose nameplate says *Dotty* waves me in with a bright smile while continuing to speak on her phone. "They found a body behind the school playground last night—"

I've got the place to myself, wandering room to room as Dotty's voice fades away. Here is the mastodon head Harry mentioned, then a life-size model of Geronimo at the height Spencer was before he got his growth spurt. Like rattlers, I guess—sometimes it's the small ones that pack the most punch. In another room, history fast-forwards to the modern world, where in an open bin are scores of what the bikers told me about—posters of the local high school's grads going back decades, pasted on cardboard and sheathed in plastic. It doesn't take long to determine that the Guardian Angel's photo is not among them, at least not the way I remember her. I'm neither surprised nor discouraged. I'm used to her proving elusive by now but still hoping she'll turn up when the time's right, whatever that means. Meantime, my attention is drawn to the front page of a 1950 newspaper framed behind glass.

CITY OF HOT SPRINGS CHANGES NAME
TO HONOR RALPH EDWARDS

Voters of Hot Springs, New Mexico decided March 31 to change its name to Truth or Consequences in honor of Ralph Edwards and his radio show. . . . It was a great day for the citizens of this health resort to become associated with such a great humanitarian as Ralph Edwards, since

he has the facilities to tell the world of the great health
benefits here.

It was the most unprecedented action ever taken
by a city anywhere. . . .

It is now the plan for both the town and the
radio program to work hand in hand for the betterment
of humanity over all the United States. With the great
resources of this town, and the advertising facilities of the
radio program, there is no reason to doubt that the town
will become the greatest health resort in the entire nation.

Wow, they really did buy it hook, line, and sinker. The vote, according to
the article, was a landside of 1,294 to 295. I shake my head at the sheer
grandiosity. Forget Athens. This was the most unprecedented action
ever taken by a city anywhere. I guess that's the self-regard it took to
keep one step ahead of the bulldozers all these years.

And what's the date of the newspaper? April Fools' Day. Harry wasn't
kidding—joke's on us. A genuine old-timey laugh track sounds down the
hall. I follow the guffaws and find a wing devoted to the *T or C* game
show: photos of sugary Shirley Temple and Nazi sympathizer Charles
Lindberg and everyone else who ever marched in the annual parade,
along with over-the-hill celebrities who went on the TV show. Few of
them even bothered to inscribe their photos. And then, just in case I'm
not sure who enlisted such blinding star power, a voice bellows out the
windup to the great wizard himself on a black-and-white loop playing
on a mini plastic TV in a room of its own:

"Hello there, we've been waiting for you! It's time to play *Truth or
Consequences*! And here he is, America's prime prankster, your *Truth
or Consequences* man, Ralph Edwards!"

Out pops a thin figure, nimble and glib. "Howdy, friends!" Quick
with a smile, oozing charm, there's something magnetic about Ralph's
unabashed hucksterism. I'm instantly drawn to the snake-oil energy,
just like audiences of the 1950s must have been, and take a seat on a
wooden church pew to watch the reel roll.

Cue the housewife. "Ralph, Ralph, they've got my husband decked
out in washerwoman clothes!"

"What's that you say, Bev? Your husband, Lew, in washerwoman clothes? What the dickens?"

"Is he OK, Ralph?" cries Bev, fretting as she watches her husband in a glassed-in laundry room, flailing as soap bubbles from an out-of-control washing machine rise to his chest. "Is he gonna be all right?"

Pretending his collar's too tight, Ralph yanks it loose with two fingers and sticks his face sideways with a faux panicked expression. "Gee whillikers, Bev, I'm not sure what kinda trouble's heating up in there! Looks to me like Lew's in some hot water!"

He's a likable phony, an ingratiating charlatan born in the can that canned laughter comes from. Harry was right: Ralph was such a good con man that people didn't mind being taken to the cleaner's—quite literally in this case. Perhaps because they didn't mind, I surprise myself by minding for them—feeling protective of these townsfolk who didn't realize they were being made fun of. Each time a local bank teller consented to put on a pair of donkey ears, or a janitor to wear his wife's bra, it was Ralph winking to the national audience and saying, *Look at the rubes we rounded up for you this time: too dumb to know we're mocking 'em!* All these years later, I'm insulted on their behalf.

"Lew is all right, Bev," laughs Ralph at last, hugging Bev, who shelters in his arms. "It's just a stunt man, don't you see? Bless your heart, doggone ya: your husband's in on the whole prank, that dirty rat!"

Exultant organ chords accompany the wife sobbing with relief as she clings to Ralph Edwards, who made everything better in the nick of time.

"Oh, Bev, he had us both going, but don't feel bad, you won the jackpot: a trip to sunny Acapulco!"

Applause and laugh track. Hee-haws out of a shit-grinning past.

Outside again the sky is selling a similar bill of goods, pretending everything's ducky down here—a disingenuous, clear-conscience blue that covers a multitude of sins like a finish coat of whitewash. But it was under this peaceful sky that settlers eradicated the Native Americans and massacred the buffalo. Ralph's unctuous buffoonery is like an earworm I can't get out of my head.

"Sorry we won't have time for more *Truth or Consequences*, folks. This is your host, Ralph Edwards, saying goodbye, hoping all your consequences are happy! Goodbye, everybody!"

..

A block away I'm climbing a hill to a water tower painted with a mural of Native Americans sitting proud on their noble steeds while buffalo cavort, happy as kittens. The hill is made of sand, dissolving under my feet like angel-food powder as I climb, getting close enough to see the graffiti spray-painted below the mural. "Go Tigers! S&T 4ever." From this height, I'm able to take in a bird's-eye view of the town below, T or C laid out in all its glory, sweet as a toy village under a Christmas tree. On the interstate, a baby Walmart truck looks like a Tonka toy as it slugs its way up the desert hills. Closer by, local traffic moves through the streets in every direction, flowing effortlessly through the Crash Site like the ordinary intersection it is. A multicolored VW put-puts out of the head shop's parking lot. An orange Hummer maneuvers through the city streets like a tank among rickshaws before it turns into the driveway of a stucco palace next to the golf course—the King going home for lunch, most likely: raw lion heart. I can make out the whoop of kids scrambling dirt bikes through the dead-end streets, the tink-tink of teenagers carefully hammering their car engines, the clack of cheap trailer doors slamming shut. Then this *craaaaaack!* from the general vicinity of Candy's bar. Was that another gunshot?

Elsewhere a Tibetan lama strolls peaceably by himself, radiating wisdom like a beacon of saffron serenity.

So Roy Joy's right. I am finding the town interesting, not least of all because somewhere down there lives the woman I'm determined to meet. The aroma of barbecue reaches me, stinging me with yearning for a home-cooked meal. I raise my nose, and suddenly there's the turtle more or less decipherable at last atop the peak. The paw, the hump. So it's not just a pile of rocks up there? Seen from this angle, can the mountain range even be said to lend the town a Podunk sort of majesty?

From out of nowhere, my phone starts bleating. I didn't even realize I was carrying it, but I guess being run over didn't completely kill it. My first crazy thought: it's the Angel having gotten wind I'm trying to find her. But it was just the phone reactivating itself somehow, picking up a stray signal at this altitude.

I dial home. Get a ring. Connecting: my wife's voice!

"You've reached the Rose household, home of the boys and Polly. Leave your message at the beep."

Her voice is like the first taste of food after fasting. But "Home of the boys and—"

"Oh hi, Dad," says my oldest, picking up. Oddly blasé.

"Hey Spencer, good to hear your voice!"

There's the sound of a keyboard being tapped. The dog barking in the background.

"Spence?"

"Yeah, you too." More tapping. "Dad, I'm kinda busy right now."

I try to match his nonchalance. "Wassup, son?"

"Nuthin' much. Chillaxing."

"Oh. Well, I'm calling from the desert."

"What? Oh, desert. Cool."

"Spence, can you give me 70 percent of your attention, please?"

"Oh, just missed! You distracted me, Dad!"

I hear the oven door opening in the background, its hinge squealing. That means his mother is there, preparing dinner. I can almost smell the cauliflower roasting in balsamic vinegar. A weather report in the background is predicting fourteen inches of snow.

"Spence?"

"Dad, uh, hold on . . ."

"I get it," I say. "You're angry about my leaving, you're hurt, but if we're able to talk—"

"Uh-huh. What? Sorry, I was distracted."

"Can you speak into the phone, please? I can barely make out what you're saying."

"Hold on."

"What're you doing now?"

"Talking to Kyle."

"You're supposed to be talking to me."

"I'm talking to both of you."

I try a lighter tack. "Well, you're getting to be a pretty nimble typist, anyway."

Tap-tap . . . tap-tap-tap-tap—

"I said, You're getting to be a pretty good typist."

"Yeah. Dad, can you call back another time? I love you, but right now I'm trying to get this really difficult power-up—"

"Forget the power-up! I want dialogue!"

"Sorry, Dad, I'm in the middle of things! Anyway, I hate talking on the phone!"

"Then let's email."

"I hate email too!"

Tap-tap-tap-tap—

"Spence? I get that this is hard for you."

"Just . . . when's it going to be over, Dad?"

"I can't say for sure, hon. I'm hoping to make it better than before."

"No, I mean this conversation. Because, not to hurt your feelings, I'm kinda doing four things right now. Sorry. And *24* is about to come on."

"OK, well, is your mother there?"

"She's setting the table right now."

"Then let me speak to your brother."

"He's busy too. Sorry, but now's like the worst time."

"Hey, while you're on your computer, you might want to research some fishing spots for us. And give your mom a message for me, please. Tell her—"

"OK, bye."

The connection is gone.

· ·

That's it? is my only thought. That's as high as "S&T 4ever" goes? Human beings are that small, able to stretch only eight feet to tag our names, maybe nine on tiptoes? We can send fireworks to explode against the sky, but how high are we sending them, really? Three hundred yards at most? If we look down from an airplane, it's obvious that even the most breathtaking fireworks are only the height of a few upended football fields. And the plane itself, only about one hundred football fields high, give or take. A rocket ship, even one that goes to the moon . . . such a puny thing, spindly and frail. And the moon itself is such a tiny distance away, just at the edge of where the void begins.

A Walmart bag slaps me in the face, bringing me back to earth. But instead of flinging it behind me, I'm moved to put it in my pocket. And then to notice where it comes from: a family of torn plastic bags nesting on cactus thorns, purring like coyote pups as the wind slides through them. I reach carefully inside the cactus and find another bag to put in my pocket. My fingers weave through the barbs, retrieving the red-and-white shards of an Arby's coffee cup. I pocket them too. A black-and-gold tobacco tin. The burnt umber of a candy wrapper. And another, this one dusty blue. Sometimes there's nothing to be done except the thing right in front of you, bit by careful bit. On it goes, until finally I know what I have to do next.

CHAPTER 11

SWAPPIN' LIES

THE ASSHOLES ANONYMOUS react to my return in different ways. Clay snaps up the brim of his broken cowboy hat, the equivalent of opening his eyes wide in astonishment. Raydeen grabs hold of her spike in case she needs to fight. Roy Joy yanks the clothespin out of his mouth like he might otherwise swallow it. "By god, he's back for a whuppin'!"

"If it's OK with you, I'm going to start over from the top," I say, standing defenseless before the others, who are about as friendly as a tribunal from the Spanish Inquisition. "Hi, I'm Dan, and I'm an asshole."

"Hey, asshole," a few of them mumble, grudgingly.

The words stick in my throat. "I'm a little nervous right now. Actually, I'm a lot nervous, so I'm just going to say it again, louder this time: Howdy, ladies and gents. I'm Dan, and I'm such an asshole I can't believe it!"

This warms them up a mite as they play with my name, trying out various iterations. "Welcome, Danny cowboy, Danny Crockett, born on the wild frontier."

"Doodoo Dee-Dee, I don't give a rat's crap," shouts Roy Joy, tugging on his fly. "Get on with it, dick hammer!"

I take sustenance from the scent of coffee in the air. And carry on.

"First off, I want to apologize," I say. "My attitude may have been . . . flippant or whatever. I get that way sometimes when I try to cover my nervousness. I've been overcompensating 'cause I'm a little lost right now. A little lonely."

"It's the high lonesome of the alpine desert. We all got summa that," Clay says, cocking his chair back on two legs and sending me an encouraging smile.

"Pretty depressed," I say.

"Ain't nothing 'pretty' about it," Clay says supportively, to a general susurrus of consent. "You're packin' some serious woe."

Roy Joy is having none of it. "How the stars do tremble," he says.

"Give him room, Colonel, he's speaking his piece," Raydeen says, giving a solid boot to the back of Roy Joy's wheelchair.

"No, Roy Joy's been right all along," I say. "Gave me my comeuppance fair and square. I have had my head up my ass, and I'm obliged to the man for calling me on it. Too much pity for myself and not enough for everyone else."

"Now you're tellin' it, keep it rollin'," comes a chorus of voices. Hap Hazard is moved to shoot a ray of tobacco juice into his can with dead-eye accuracy and hunkers down further to my words.

"Look, I don't mean to get slobbery," I say. "I'm just sad is all. Sadder than I want to own up to. I'll tell you what it is. Not having my two boys? That's like the Twin Towers of my life going down in a heap of rubble. I feel like I want to run into a tree and knock out my two front teeth. And here I am so far from home, I don't even know how I got here!"

"Oh, yes you do," Bird Brain assures me with a wink. "We all know exactly how we got here, though we pretend we don't."

That's when I realize most of the people in the room are as smart as I am, and then some. Everyone is brilliant in their own way, as old Mrs. Seiffert used to say. Someone hands me a cup of coffee, and it tastes as good as it smells.

"True enough," I admit. "But now I'm questioning . . . everything! Is anything real? The love with my wife didn't turn out to be real, or real enough, and now I can't get near enough to fix it. Every time I get close it's like—"

"—like she's developed an allergy to you," Raydeen cuts in. "Even the slightest contact makes her sneeze."

"That's exactly right," I say.

Roy Joy doesn't like the conversation getting so far away from him. "Someone pass the mustard so I can stick it in my eye."

"You'll have to excuse our temperamental friend here," Clay tells me.

"Roy was in a little wreck like yours once upon a time but didn't end up so lucky. Could be what his hostility's about."

"My animus!" Roy Joy puts in. Evidently it's a word he's proud of.

"Basically, from the fact you're up and about, you had what's called a soft landing on a hard road," Clay tells me. "Roy here had the opposite: hard landing on a soft road, plus a little guardrail action to keep things interesting. Landed in the sand with a broken neck, been in a wheelchair since '68. So he may be inclined to be a little more homicidal toward you than he might otherwise."

"Plus don't forget I lost my mother at the tender age of fourteen," Roy Joy tells me with eyes as sad as a basset hound's.

"You were only fourteen?"

"No, she was!"

Hee-haw! Roy Joy has regained top billing in the room. Hoots and hollers explode from almost every chair, complete with fist bumps and congratulatory winks. Nevertheless, I'm emboldened to hold the floor. I don't care if they make fun or not. I've got something to say, and I'm going to say it.

"And the most asshole-y part?" I resume as the room reluctantly quiets down. "The most pathetic part I'm almost too ashamed to share with you? I still harbor hope that she'll want me back. How's that for pitiful? I still believe that if I stay away long enough, she'll rediscover how much she loves me. I mean, talk about an asshole."

I listen for an objection, but Roy Joy just mutters into his beard. I have the feeling my words are being heard in a new way. No one is scoffing.

"I'm just not willing to let my family be done, is the thing," I say. "We have to keep playing badminton on spring evenings after dinner, all four of us. I don't care if that sounds like a fairy activity to you—it's what we like to do. Maybe we're overprivileged and you think I deserved whatever came to me in my L.L. Bean khakis, but those were our little joys. And hiking. We used to go hiking, and the boys would hide behind boulders, thinking we couldn't see them. Everyone's kids do that, right? They think they can't be seen. Which will happen soon enough, for real, of its own accord. So please don't let that day come too soon when we can't see each other anymore. Not yet—I'm not ready, not yet, not yet."

I gather myself together, but not really. "Tell you the truth, I'm not even sure what I'm saying. It's like I'm still in midair and haven't landed yet. All I can say is that I couldn't live up to my wife's goodliness. And by kicking me out, it's like she's taken all the goodliness out of my life."

The illustrious members of Assholes Anonymous scrape their shoes and look down at the tile floor. Even Roy Joy is embarrassed, or touched. Raydeen self-consciously scratches an itch in her crew cut with the point of her spike. The only sound is the coffee maker lisping in the corner, whispering tales of trouble without end. At last someone is stirred to speak.

"There're all kinds of pain," says the man wearing blue eyeliner, with quiet authority. "Right here in this building there once was pain we can't even fathom. Not many in town know this, but this building was the town hospital back in the forties, run by the Sisters of the Sorrowful Mother before they moved it up the hill and called it Saint Ann's. Heard many a yarn about amputations being done without anesthesia right here in the space we share today. Endless screaming. Matter fact, those bolted stairs in the hallway led to the crazy floor above us where they stuck the more rambunctious patients. Awful things that went on out of sight from the rest of the world." He draws in a long breath through his nostrils. "There are so many kinds of pain in the universe, but the pain of losing your family, that's one that'll shake the ground right under your feet."

He offers me his hand and I take it. "Tam, Tammy, better known in some circles as the late Doctor Tom, pleased to meet you," he says. "Princeton, Class of '65. I'm the emergency-room doc at the local hospital here."

Besides the blue eyeliner, he's wearing black clogs and two nametags on his hospital shirt. "Doctor Tom" says one, and "Tammy" says the other. An iconoclastic doc, T or C style, awaiting surgery to make him the woman he's meant to be. A wave of sympathy washes from him, warm as pancake syrup.

"Sure enough, ain't much fun to be drop-kicked out of your life," volunteers Bird Brain, sticking out his hand. "I know how it is: My family snuck out on me one night when I was dead to the world. When I come to, damned if I didn't find myself alone!" He shakes his head as though still shell-shocked by it all these years later.

We're listening so hard to each other we can almost hear the piti-ful cries of the long-ago patients upstairs, hoarse from not being paid attention to.

"I don't mind telling you I bawled for a week, when my clan decided they'd be better without me," says Real Dick, also putting out his hand. Hard hands, one after the other; strong hands, with lots of history to grab hold of. I'm honored to be shaking them. "Bawled like a baby dropped by his momma."

"Y'know, speakin' on the subject," says Clay, stretching back so the overhead fluorescence catches the speckles of paint on his sunglasses, "I've had more than a few jobs in my lifetime. Bridge painter in Alaska. Horse wrangler in Mexico. Firefighter in Oregon. Fairly awesome jobs, and I'll tell you what. Being married ranks up there with the worst of 'em for danger, 'cause you fail at that, it's worse than getting trampled by a runaway horse. It's your soul gets flattened."

"Or not," says Bird Brain. "Could be a chance for your soul to get bigger." He puts his finger in his ear and wriggles it violently for a minute. "Damned if I know what I just meant by that!" he says.

Clay has settled back, satisfied with the way the discussion is going. "That's why in a way I envy you, old son," he says. "Play it right, you might wake up and stop thinkin' you're so damn special, you lucky shit!"

I guess the astonishment shows on my face, because others are quick to amplify it for me.

"The indignities are heaped upon you, but indignities will help you see the light!"

"Your heart's cracked in half, but that means it's wide open . . ."

"Like a revelation: 'Ah, suffering! That's the look on everyone's face!'"

I shake my head. It all sounds like important information . . . but how to take it in?

"Could be a worthwhile time of your life," Clay summarizes for me as Real Dick steals out the back door for what I assume is a cigarette break.

"Just think back on what Roy Joy said when you first come in last time," Clay continues. "That just because your wife separated you from your family, you're still in one piece, a complete human being unto yourself."

I'm eager to hear more, but we're interrupted by a ringing from behind the building, iron on iron. "Time to circle 'round," Clay says, and the group wrestles themselves up from their chairs to put their arms around each other's shoulders, Roy Joy supported by compatriots on either side. "I'd like to thank you all for showing up this morning, with a shout-out to old son here who owned up to his asshole this very day. He didn't run and hide—he came back to find out the reason he's here, because each and every one of us has a purpose for being where we are, if we can just figure it out in time."

"Amen," says the group.

"So I want to invite him to join our patio powwow taking place directly after the meeting. And remember, till next time . . ." Here everyone joins in unison: "Keep your pecker up and your posse close, 'cause you never know what tomorrow brings!"

Out I shamble with my fellow soldiers. I study the back of Roy Joy's T-shirt, displaying a tie-dyed American flag with all the colors melding into each other. "These Colors Run When They Have To!" says the legend. Outside, in a white chef's hat, Real Dick has just finished ringing a triangular dinner bell of the chuckwagon variety, before tending to a barbecue pit from which the T or C aroma emanates. This is the source!

"Betcha had no idea Real Dick was a gourmet cook," Raydeen tells me with a glow of pride. "Executive chef of the Waldorf Astoria in Florida at one time."

The clocks on Real Dick's skull glisten with sweat as he stirs what looks like oxtail in a stew with beans, carrots, and potatoes. He inserts a few sticks of mesquite into the fire, crushes sage between skillful fingertips. Thick slabs of bacon sizzle on a side grill.

"C'mon, take a seat," Clay tells me, patting an overturned five-gallon paint pail beside him. "We'll just be sitting 'round swappin' lies."

The backyard is fenced in by knee-high cactus on three sides and ornamented in the center by a dead brown stub of a tree like an old roach. At the base of the tree is a porcelain sink filled with dirt and planted with a couple of zinnias for color. Kittens, more or less wild, roam the yard. "Good for catching rats and snakes," Hap tells me. "They can confuse a rattler to go bite hisself!"

Roy Joy sits in a shaft of sunlight with his eyes closed, soaking up the heat. Where it's not braided, his bushy white beard is brushed out for maximum effect, see-through-able to the vulnerable pink skin beneath. Somehow that's a good thing—that in this place and time, people are still knowable, that even behind the hairy wall of a heavy beard, you can see straight through to what someone is made of.

Clay smiles with approval. "That's right, pardner, let go of the reins. Get the story you come for."

My shoulders relax in a way they haven't in months.

"Fate and fate and fate," Clay says to no one in particular, before turning his attention back to me. "You ain't eaten in days, am I right? See, that's mistake number one right there—men not taking care of ourselves, thinking we don't deserve the goodliness, to use your word, or we need a wife to do it for us 'cause we're not capable of sparkin' it ourselves."

Grub is ladled. I take a bite and the angels sing. Turnips that have been soaking in gravy! Hidden onions, and those bacon slabs both crisp and juicy at once. It's the perfect accompaniment to more of Clay's words that also seem to hit the spot.

"The truth is, women don't corner the market on goodliness, any more than men do on muleheadedness. We dump it on them 'cause we ain't taught to see it in ourselves, when the fact is we got all the goodliness we need for a lifetime, jam-packed right inside us!"

Doctor Tom moseys over, sliding a bucket to sit on beside me. Across the barbecue fire, Bird Brain swats at a fly again, even though we're outside. Hap Hazard is moving his lips, silently engrossed in a book titled *Kittens for Dummies*, but everyone else is listening respectfully.

"Come right down to it, what are you missing?" Clay asks me.

"How do you mean?" I ask.

"What is the emptiness? If it ain't the goodliness, 'cause no one can take that from you when they go, then what is it? Your home? That's just a thing. Your real home, you carry that on your back like a turtle."

"True that," puts in Hap Hazard, blinking with both eyes. "Clay's got hisself a nice little trailer out by the river, everything neat as a pin."

"My boys," I answer Clay, "that's what I'm missing most. Forecast calls for fourteen inches of snow tonight, and the idea of them shoveling the driveway without me . . ." I shake my head, out of words.

"Yeah, but who taught 'em how to shovel?" Clay asks.

"I did, but—"

"Well, hell, old son, that's the family you built! If my family could shovel along without me, I'd take it as a compliment to how well I done my job. So straighten up and stake a claim to all that's yours! Don't sit there regretting whatever you did wrong—help someone else do something right. That's the best lesson you can ever hope to teach your boys."

Grunts around the barbecue—soft groans of sympathy. This is my therapy group, I realize, tailored with baffling precision to my needs. From some of the hardest faces I've ever encountered echo the softest.

"Don't look to her for justice. Look to yourself! Be your own wife!"

"Men think they lose all the sweetness and light, when truth is we make our own, just as nice!"

"You don't lack for nuthin'—you got everything you need right in there with you under your shell."

"Whatever," Clay says. "I've done my preaching for the day. Keep your bedroll rolled and your gas tank full. Sermon under the shadow of Turtleback Mountain."

The kittens wrestle each other in a clump of rolling fur as the group shares a common sigh of satisfaction, circling the grill. Clay rolls a fag and lights it, causing ashes to fly about his face in the wind. Raydeen reaches over and takes a deep, needy drag off it, loosening a spark that lands on the back of a kitten, causing it to screech and jump. Just as suddenly, Roy Joy screeches, too, with a burst of words like a blast of bacon breath in my face.

"But what in the devil's name are you gonna do, boy? I'm worried about you now, truly I am! How you gonna find that blond, and when you do, what then?"

"Don't know. I've looked everywhere."

Doctor Tom looks up. "Including the hospital?" he asks quietly.

"No," I say. "I figure it's too long ago, and privacy laws . . ."

Doctor Tom grasps me warmly on the knee, smiling with the simplicity of it all. "Tell 'em Tammy sent you."

CHAPTER 12

IT'S CALLED BEING TWENTY

NEXT MORNING I'M drawn to a badly a neglected woodshed behind the desert castle, where I find a girl's bicycle, caked with cobwebs and about as graceful as an old burro. The pink vinyl pouch, cracked with age, is cheerfully glued with daisy petals and the legend "Flower Power." I fill its two flat tires from a rusty hand pump hanging on the wall, and the air holds. This'll do nicely.

As I bike toward the hospital at the far end of town, I'm consumed with that desert-sand urgency again, as if this is my last chance to grasp the past before it's gone forever. When was the last time I rode a bike with no gears? The tires are the fat kind I remember from childhood; anything daintier wouldn't hold up against the roadway glass and goat weed burrs. I have to stand on the pedals to get any speed, especially going up the steep hill to the hospital. I park and push the glass doors of the emergency entrance: No Guns Knives Weapons Allowed. Inside, the ER has been refurbished beyond recognition. All I remember is lying on my back, trying to convince everyone I wasn't the crazed druggie they assumed I was. Forty years older, I don't have to account for myself to the young nurses dressed in regulation hospital garb. I walk through the ward without being questioned, making my way to an elevator that opens onto a back wing of my past.

This I remember vividly. Everything is tinted dim green—walls, floor tiles—like a cut-rate Emerald City. These are the rooms for the patients, unchanged since 1970. I remember coming up here after they'd released me and sitting all afternoon by Tony's bedside. He was unconscious, his skull wrapped like a mummy. Surreal how still he was, hour after hour. It was a bright day, but inside the ward the twilight was grass-stained, as it is now. By evening he was coming out of it enough to make weak jokes, and by the next day to berate me for sticking around.

Back on the first floor, I wander past an antique switchboard with old-fashioned plug-ins, no longer in use, then past a—wait, did that door just say Records? I back up. Yes, it must be the central filing office.

"Good morning, ladies," I say, entering. "You're gonna wish you'd locked this door today."

"Why is that?" they laugh, looking up. There are five clerks, two chewing gum. It's unclear from the way the desks are arranged who's in charge, so I continue addressing them as a group.

"Because I'm about to hit you with a nutty request."

It's seventy-five degrees in this office, and they're wearing stockings inside their sandals—a kind of Western prim. But they're game. "Try us," they say.

"My friend Tony Wilson and I were patients here a long time ago after a car crash, and I'm wondering if there might be any kind of record."

"How long ago?"

"When we were twenty."

They laugh. No telling when those documents crumbled to dust.

"This is the same hospital from the summer of 1970, right?"

"No longer Catholic, but sure is. And we're still takin' care of crashes. Had us a beauty this morning, didn't we, girls? Coming off the interstate, flipped right off the ramp."

"Any fatalities?"

"We'll know soon enough."

Sometimes the best way to get what you want is to make a conscious decision to enjoy the opposition. Not sure you'll prevail against someone? Deliberately admire them. Go out of your way to appreciate them. And mean it. For some reason it seems to trigger all kinds of helpful signals between the parties. Fortunately, it's easy to do with these five because they're already appealing, each in her own way. "You're a lively bunch," I say, truthfully.

They laugh some more. "We're a regular little family in here. We know way too much about each other."

To prove it, they share the information that Paloma over by the window is married to the son of Rosa, who sits one desk from her. But even though Paloma's in the middle of divorcing him, the friendship between these two remains strong as ever. "I'm tossing the dead weight but keeping my mother-in-law!"

This arrangement delights everyone. Rosa blows Paloma a kiss to underscore their deal.

"Does the name Tammy mean anything to you?" I ask.

"Doctor Tom? We love Doctor Tom!" they exclaim.

"It was Tammy who sent me here," I say.

Amid the general festivity this promotes, Paloma excuses herself to slip into a back room out of sight.

"Tammy's one of the best things that ever happened to this hospital," the one with rose-colored stockings says. "His spirit."

"And not just in the hospital," adds another with tan stockings. "In the whole rinky-dink town."

"Rinky-dink, huh?" I ask. "Why d'you live here, if that's how you feel?"

"'Cause I love this rinky-dink town!"

I'm not much of an office person, but it occurs to me that I've never seen one I'd rather work in. For ten minutes, anyway. One of the ladies has spied the torn notebook in my back pocket and has taken it upon herself to repair it with a paper clip. "Seems like we're always stitching you back together," she says, winking.

In the middle of this repartee, Paloma the daughter-in-law comes back from the room of Dead Archives holding an index card. Here's what it says:

Charles Anthony Wilson
Sept 5 1970

The admission card is as white as the day it was filed. No card for me because I declined to be admitted. But the date shows we were looking for a newspaper in the wrong months: it was not June through August, but September.

I'm speechless. There's only one person who can summon my voice from me. Maybe my phone still works? It does, and the ladies get a front-row seat to a live episode of the Tony-Danny show.

"C'mon, let us in on the fun. Put it on speaker!"

I do so, just in time for the connection to be made.

"Dan? Danny, turtle dove?" I hear Tony's half yawn of relief on the other end of the line. "Thank God. I've been worried sick I was winning my bet with Patty, that you'd gotten trapped in quicksand by now."

"Since when is your middle name Anthony?" I ask. "I knew about Charles, but Anthony? Why didn't you ever tell anyone?"

"Right, Asa. That's exactly what I'd want to share with a class of sadistic sixth graders. Your reaction even now as a more or less grown-up proves how right I was to keep it under wraps all these years."

The ladies are eating it up, watching us have our little fun. I stage-whisper to them: "He's just sore 'cause I never let him join my detective agency, but that was only because he called it babyish!"

"Didn't mean I didn't want to join!" Tony shouts, twanging the souvenir ukulele he must have smuggled home with him from the desert castle, as out of tune as ever.

The women titter with enjoyment.

"OK, ready for this, Tony? Big news. I'm standing here at the local hospital with these nice women from the Records Department. Say hello, ladies—"

"Hello, Anthony."

"Que te pasa, calabaza?" Tony says, suavely getting his cool back.

"They came up with your actual hospital admission card. And guess what? We were looking at the wrong months! It wasn't June or July or August. It was September. That's why we couldn't find it! The September 5 issue."

"Holy shit, I wish I could fly out there to give you ladies the biggest hug you ever got!"

"Promise?" says one of them, giggling at her nerve.

"Soon as I bust a few more things off my desk," Tony says. "Believe me, I'm champing at the bit to get back there."

"But do you realize what this means, Tony? We can go back to the newspaper office and totally track her down!"

Everyone's worked up, not least of all me. "I told you ladies you should've locked your door today."

They're cracking up now, as if we're all involved in something risqué, possibly even French.

"In any case, party's over," I tell them. "You've just been privy to a private conversation between me and my best friend."

"Best friend *forever*!" Tony exults.

"Say bye-bye to Anthony, ladies."

The room erupts. "Bye, Anthony!"

"Bye, Asa!"

"Bye, Paloma and Charles and Danny and Rosa!"

With everyone off the speakerphone, Paloma hands me a xerox of the hospital index card. She and her mother-in-law walk me outside the glass doors, where I spy a row of four mature yew bushes growing against the brick foundation. I must have seen them at the beginning of their life span as junior yew bushes forty years ago, lush with shiny berries, but now they're at the end of their run. None of them look in the least appealing to sleep behind, as they managed to seem back then.

I'm visited by a memory. "Didn't there also used to be a white statue somewhere around here?" I ask.

"At one time there was a statue of an angel with both arms outstretched," Rosa confirms. "But it must have been moved somewhere when the hospital went nonsectarian."

I pick up my bike, hating how corny the symbolism is—an angel lifting her arms heavenward. I guess things have to be at least a little corny sometimes to fulfill a quota of corniness in the world, but I change the subject so I don't have to dwell on it. I look over the desert beyond instead. The sand dunes surf on endlessly, punctuated by cactus.

"From here I hitched home last time with two-and-a-half bucks in my pocket," I tell Rosa. "The whole continent on two-and-a-half bucks."

Rosa and I shake our heads with smiles both sad and happy in equal measures.

"It's called being twenty," she says.

CHAPTER 13

IT'S ALL HERE

IN BLACK AND WHITE

JUDI THE NEWSPAPER editor is not pleased to see me.

"Crash dummy back to aggravate my life," she says, flicking her fingers in front of her to shoo me out of her way. "I've already given you way too much of my time."

"Yeah, but I've got an actual date this time," I say, flashing Tony's admission card. "It wasn't June through August; it was September."

This stops Judi in her tracks, her reporter's curiosity getting the better of her. "Well, that'd be a different bundle, then. Let's take a look."

She leads me back to where the newspaper bundles are stuffed into a flimsy file cabinet, opens the drawer, and loosens the string to riffle through the September headlines.

Front page one week before: "Las Cruces Man Injured When Pinned under Truck." "Car Overturns on 1-25 When Driver Falls Asleep at Wheel."

Our week is missing.

"Hmm!" Judi snorts. She keeps going.

Front page one week after: "Semi-Trailer Smashes into Bridge, Killing One." "Motorists Find Accident Victim Unconscious."

Still no trace of our week. Judi turns to me with cigarette dangling. "Three strikes, you're outa here."

"Something's not right—"

"What you're not comprehending, see: this is an omen," Judi gloats. "If you can't find it, you weren't meant to find it. We got every issue nice and neat the way they're supposed to be, September 3, September 17,

September 24, down the line—so why do you suppose September 10 isn't there? God doesn't want you to find it!"

"Yow," the cat chimes in. Judi triumphantly slams the cabinet drawer shut . . . but it bounces back an inch, like something's stuck. I put my hand in.

"What're you doing? Get outa there!"

I feel a lump of newspaper jammed against the back. I get a grasp and slowly coax it loose . . .

And there it is. September 10, 1970. I smooth the paper out flat on a nearby desk so we can see, dead center of the front page, a giant photo of our crash, the leading wreck of the week: our Land Cruiser crumpled up hard against a battered truck. Complete with misspelling in the headline: "Two Injured When Vehiciles Collide."

Judi is dumbfounded, choking on her smoke. "Well, I'll be."

How obviously real it is, now that we have the evidence before us. How concrete and irrefutable. It was a serious crash. Both vehicles are clearly totaled. The front of the truck—a two-ton pickup, incidentally—not a Mack—is demolished. The entire side of the Land Cruiser is mangled as if—well, as if hit by a two-ton pickup. Everything around the passenger compartment is caved in, the bare steel glove box shoved down straight into the seat.

"But what's that in the middle of the road?" Judi asks, too inquisitive for once to be skeptical. "A sleeping bag?"

Riiiiiight. Now I remember. The Land Cruiser was so bumpy without shock absorbers that Tony and I kept sleeping bags under us as seat cushions. The rolled-up one in the road must have been Tony's. Mine unfurls from my seat onto the street.

"Shut it, Bite-Size," Judi says, kicking the cranky cat aside. Everything pisses Judi off today, for some reason. Chubby Checker's "The Twist" comes on from somewhere, exasperating her even more. "I keep telling my nephew I don't need him to download any more ring tones for me," she says, muting her cell so she can read the article aloud.

> Two college students from Connecticut were taken to St.
> Ann's Hospital Saturday morning (continued on page 3) . . .

Judi opens the paper to continue reading.

> . . . after the vehicle in which they were traveling was struck by a pickup truck at Broadway and Austin Streets. Charles A. Wilson, 21, was admitted for treatment and his passenger, Daniel A. Rose, 20, was dismissed after emergency treatment. Wilson was driving a four-wheel vehicle and was traveling east at the time of the crash. A pickup truck driven by Mary Louise McLaughlin of Caballo—

"She *is* named Mary! Holy shit, Tony was right!" I interrupt.

> —failed to stop at the stop sign at the intersection, according to patrolmen Ronald Kenny and John "Babe Ruth" Porter of the city police department. . . .

"As in *the* Babe Ruth?" I ask.

"As in big."

It's all right here in black and white, the breakthrough I've been hoping for. Caballo is less than twenty miles south of here, if I'm not mistaken. Everything seems within reach.

"Mary Louise McLaughlin! Ever hear of her?"I ask. No one replies. Judi and I stare at each other for a minute, amazed that a mystery has been halfway solved, opening up new mysteries. But it's too intimate a moment for her; she shakes it off. Her effort now is to pretend her momentary enthusiasm had nothing to do with my quest. "Will you look at that," she says, leaning in closer to the paper. "This was back in the days when we did everything on a typewriter. See here how the letters don't line up? We hand-counted the spaces."

She goes back to her judgment pose, letting the smoke curl in and out of her nostrils.

"Mary Louise McLaughlin?" I try again.

"Nupe."

I do a quick Google search on my phone, but no such name turns up. "Would you mind letting me take a look at your phone book?"

"Unbelievable," she complains, shoving over the county phone book, about the size of a manual for a microwave oven. I run through the pages and determine there are no McLaughlins in Caballo, and only three in the entire county, none of whom include any Marys, according to Judi.

"You positive?" I ask.

"You're questioning my knowledge base now? After all these years in the editor's chair, you don't think I'd know every face fifty miles around and his uncle?"

"But what about other counties? Do you know any—"?

"Mr. Rose, if it doesn't upset your grand plan too badly, I got a few other duties today besides being your fetch-it girl."

I know I'm being pushy, but this is too important to let go. "Judi, I realize the next couple days are big ones for you, getting out the paper and all. May I possibly come back when you're not so much under the gun, say Friday?"

"Got my granddaughter Friday."

"How about Monday?"

"I'm meeting the Queen of Sheba. Why do you want to come back, anyway?"

I shoot for some charm, if possible. "Basically to sweet-talk you into letting me buy this copy, when you're under less pressure. I mean, if you're just going to pulp it anyway in a few years—"

"No way, nohow, nyet, nada."

"What if I steal it when your back is turned and leave a fifty-dollar bill on the counter?"

She takes a drag, using her cigarette for punctuation. "You'll go straight to hell."

"What if I—"

But I'm pushing too hard. Her face is screwed up like she's dangerously close to her limit. "Ain't gonna happen. Have I not made myself abundantly clear?"

A burly middle-aged customer comes in, slaps a classified on the counter. He's just off a customized black short-bed truck; his bodybuilder's neck muscles are made of titanium.

"This is the troublemaker you may have heard me complaining about," Judi tells him. "Obsessed with something that happened forty years ago."

"Joe," he says, jutting out his manly hand to shake. But it's not friendly. It's more like, "I'll get rid of this for you, Judi." It's as clear to me now as it was forty years ago that I'm not much liked in these parts.

"You already got the cops' names," Judi says to me. "And look here, their snapshots on this other page—both of 'em. I don't know what more you're hoping for."

"All this is a huge help, thank you," I say. "But at the risk of being even more of a pain"—she snorts at the understatement—"can you just tell me if those cops are still on the police force?"

Judi treats me to one of her favorite gazes, like I'm a high-functioning goldfish. "See, this is it," she tells Joe. "Prince Charming here thinks that once he left town, everyone else was locked into place, like *Bad Day at Black Rock*. Here's the bad guy, here's the good guy. Life stands still, and he's the only one movin' through it." She lets out a little shriek of exasperation in my direction. "Boy, do you have a good wallop coming. Maybe that's why Ms. McLaughlin hit you in the first place, that ever occur to you? To knock some sense in?" She cocks her head at me, raising her eyebrows. "No, they are not still on the police force, to answer your question. This was forty years ago. Cops get paid so low here that no one lasts more than three or four years before they turn to other things and then turn to other things after that. See how it works? Everyone's life keeps moving on, just like yours?"

"Moving on, that's the key phrase," Joe says, squaring his powerful shoulders threateningly.

"OK, I get it, but is either of them still in town?" I persist.

"Kenny I couldn't say for sure, but the Babe's easy. You're likely to find him at his home up in Butte."

"Thank you, truly," I say, preparing to take my leave after getting his number from the phone book. "One last thing. You'd probably charge me an exorbitant amount to make a xerox of the front page, wouldn't you?" I ask.

She stubs out her cigarette with more delicacy than I would have credited her for.

"Got that right," she says.

. .

Outside, I take a photo of the xerox and shoot it to Tony, then call to tell him he was right about Mary's name.

"Shit," he says. "Shit shit shit shit."

"It doesn't have to mean there are otherworldly forces at work, Tony. I'm as wary of that stuff as you are. We can still be hard-asses."

"Yeah, but this may force me to rethink things," he says. "I hate rethinking things."

"One more point," I say, "though I hate to admit it. It wasn't a Mack truck after all. It was what you always said: a pickup."

"I'm not gonna hold that against you, Dan. Instead I'm gonna be magnanimous in victory and tell you that memory plays tricks on everyone, young and old. You douche nozzle."

"Gotta go."

"What's next?"

"I've got the phone number of one of the cops who was at our crash. Remember the big scary one, the Babe Ruth of anti-hippies? I'm looking at his picture right now."

"You're killing me here! That's like looking at Darth Vader!"

"You can rejoin the fun anytime you choose."

"Every hour brings me closer, Danny boy. Just a few more things to get out of the way, then I'm all yours. Definitely by the weekend . . ."

CHAPTER 14

BIG MAN DYING SMALL

WITH SOME TREPIDATION, I call the ex-cop's number and state my business to the robust-sounding woman who says she's his wife. "Well, if this ain't the strangest," she says, then raises her voice to call for her husband. "Lovey, it's some fella says he was in a crash forty years ago, you were officer on duty, and he wants to talk to you."

A minute passes before I'm greeted by the man himself. I'm relieved that he doesn't sound prone to despise me as much as I'd assumed. "Can I come over sometime? Is now a good time?"

"Come own."

His wife gets back on the phone to give me directions that sound like they could apply equally well to anywhere around here. Left at the sanitation plant. Straight past the propane gas outlet. My route takes me into the neighboring town of Elephant Butte, newer and less beat up than T or C: a resort town with vacation homes overlooking the forty-mile-long reservoir that features watersports of every kind. The main drag boasts amenities its poor sister town of T or C couldn't imagine: marine supplies, camping sites, playgrounds, nature trails, family-friendly restaurants. Eventually I arrive at a brick ranch house with someone's gaunt grandfather smoking on the porch. Gulp. Am I short-winded because of the ride or because I'm nervous?

I approach the porch. "There's a John Porter expecting me?"

"Have a seat."

I do so. The gaunt grandfather is not well. He sits there with a tube in his nose, respiring with effort in a bathrobe barely held together with a loose knot. After a while he catches his breath enough to ask, "What can I do for you?"

Wait, *this* is John Porter? This old warhorse, with almost no teeth in his head and brown spots on his grizzled cheeks? Babe Ruth is buff no more, his voice a pitiful strangulation. "How you doin'?" I ask.

"So good I shoulda been twins." He forces out a smoker's laugh, which makes his joke kind of valiant.

"Glad to hear it," I say, still recovering. What could have reduced this bruiser to a fraction of his former size?

"Lung cancer," he says, almost as if he heard me. He runs a feeble hand over the sparse quills of his chin and jaw. On the porch table in front of him a glass ashtray is heaped with cigarette butts.

Involuntarily, I take a breath. "You're still smoking, though."

"Uh-huh," he says, rolling the ash off his cigarette into the ashtray. "It's called dirty smoking, on oxygen." He snaps ten feet of tube in front of him like a lasso, but wearily, a rodeo star down on his luck. "You say you got some paper to show me?"

I unroll the xerox of our crash and he cranes forward, staring hard. "Well, I'll be dog tied," he says at last.

"Something, isn't it?"

"Ten cents, the whole paper. It's at least a quarter nowadays."

"Yes, but—see the picture?"

Wearily he returns his attention to the page, inhaling with effort. "Oh," he says, "she smack you good. I'm glad to see you up alive."

He looks me over, then looks at the picture again. "Tell you what, I faintly remember that old Land Cruiser."

"You do?"

"I'm fixin' to. It's just beyond my recollection. Reason is because my daughter was T-boned like you at that very spot a few years later."

"She was?"

"Can't say I remember any details of yours, but it's the damnedest thing, my daughter . . ." He shakes his head, his eyebrows turned up to give him a quizzical look, like he's puzzled by this and a lot more besides.

"What about the name Mary McLaughlin?"

"It blinks in my mind," he says, mulling. "Light-colored hair? Plucky little thing? But that's all I got."

Maybe it's not that big a deal, but I'm amazed to be sitting here with the only person I've met so far who has even a faint recollection of Mary. Plucky! Now we're getting somewhere! In forty years I've never been this close to her before—only two degrees of separation and getting closer.

"Must seem like a very long time ago," I venture.

"No sir," he says. "Seems like just about yesterday."

Since when did I become a *sir* in his world? It seems not so much a promotion for me as a demotion for him. I want to shake him by the shoulder. *I'm just a spoiled hippie!* I want to say. *You're the intolerant pig and fucked-up authority figure—I'm the stupidly rebellious kid!* Forty years ago he'd have no sooner called me "sir" than I'd have called him "faggot."

He chuffs a little, catching his wind. Something in his windpipe whistles as he reaches to crush out the cigarette and falls back in his chair, weary. "Hand me one a them Luckys, will ya?" he asks.

I feel guilty handing him one—even dying, only the deadliest brands will do. Also a little embarrassed because our fingertips touch, and I cast about for a neutral topic.

"I guess the potholes make for hazardous driving too," I venture. "Think they'll be fixed by Fiesta, like they say?"

He doesn't bother to answer, limply snapping the coils of his cord to get the kinks out.

"How's your daughter, meanwhile? She survive her accident OK?"

He ignores this question, too, huffing between little sips of his cigarette. I find myself staring at the figure of a smiling bunny eating a carrot on the chest of his bathrobe. He's clearly fatigued by the effort he's made. Cars drive by, and I smell the different kinds of dust they release from the road: the fine white powder crushed under their tires, the little gravel pebbles thrown up when one of them pulls a U-ey. After a while I notice there's a pinprick of wetness in the sick man's eyes. Then I decide I'm mistaken—it must be a drop of moisture from his meds or a reaction to the dust—anything but what I know this truly is: a tough ex-cop crying in front of me, not making a sound as his gray bristles quiver. Top of his game in 1970, Babe Ruth sits here a ruination of himself in 2010, a big man dying small in the dry desert air.

"You all right?"

"Dyin', no big deal."

I don't know what to say. Nor does he necessarily want me continuing a half-assed conversation that will rob him of even more of his hard-earned breath. "LSMFT," he finally says.

"Pardon—?"

"'Lucky Strike Means Fine Tobacco.' Shit, those old ads really had us going, didn't they?"

No longer stony-faced, he wears a confused, beseeching aspect, like he can't figure out what became of him, and it would frighten him as much to know as not to.

"Wish I could be more help, but I'll tell you what, the one to see is the best detective I ever knew, my old partner Kenny."

"I was hoping to talk to him, too, but I don't have an address."

Laboriously, the Babe scrawls out something about Moose Lodge, then hands it to me in a gesture that also serves as a half goodbye.

"Thank you, sir," I say.

CHAPTER 15

ENEMY TERRITORY

CONFESSION: I'M AFRAID of Moose Lodges. Along with old-time VFW posts, they've always seemed the ultimate other for someone who picketed against the Vietnam War, who voted against Nixon his first time at the polls. If New Mexico could sometimes feel like enemy territory, the Moose Lodge was its commissary. So as uneasy as I was about meeting the bully cop on his home turf, I'm even more nervous about meeting his old partner at the Moose, where he serves as director.

Outside the warehouse-type structure clothed in dull metal siding, I call Tony and offer to put him on speakerphone, warning him to stay quiet in my pocket.

Inside, the Moose is instant midnight. Stale smoke blasts me before my eyes can adjust to the cavernous space, empty as an airport hangar but for a few tables by the bar in front, coated with multiple layers of heavy-duty shellac. Illuminated beer signs abound. There's an air of resentment, at least from the bartender with the nametag *Doris*, who makes a point of not responding when I say hi. Or maybe she didn't hear me.

"Is Kenny around?"

Doris takes this opportunity to plunge suds-stained glasses onto a vertical scrubber. It feels personal, this grudge she seems to be harboring, as if she holds me responsible for anyone who ever burned a draft card anywhere. Or maybe I'm projecting and her bad mood has nothing to do with me. Why do I always think everything does?

"Who wants him?" she says at last.

"What is this, *The Wizard of Oz*? I'm someone who wants to thank him for something he did a long time ago."

"Oh, that's good," Tony says, from inside my pocket. "That's a winner."

Doris wipes her hands on a towel and steps around the bar. "I'll see if he's in."

Looking around while she disappears into an office in back, I notice an abundance of ashtrays—glass ones, plastic ones, even rudimentary wooden ones that look like they were chiseled in shop class years ago. Filled or empty, makes no difference. They all contribute to the reek that I feel is aging me with every breath. Smoking is legal at the Moose because it's a private establishment, and the place boasts an impressive collection of cigarette burns, especially on the console of an old pinball machine. Trudy, Rest in Peace, reads a sort of shrine next to the cash register. Below the makeshift plaque, a waitress uniform is neatly folded with nametag in place.

"Yeah, she bit it on her wedding day," says the only other person in the room, a youngish veteran down the bar with one and a half arms. "Ejected from her vehicle after eloping with her phys-ed coach. He was driving like a bat outa hell when they hit an emu." Scores of emus graze the land hereabouts, he tells me, courtesy of Ted Turner, who lives nearby and owns a good portion of the state. With his arm stub in a madras short-sleeve shirt, he's pointing at various cinderblock walls, but I get the picture.

"Ted loves it here," the vet continues. "I shouldn't talk up the competition, because we have pretty good meat right here at the Moose, but he sneaks into town now and again to feed himself a Big-A-Burger down past Candy's. Claims it's the world's best burger. Damn shame what happened to the owner."

I don't ask.

"What do you say, try a little pasta cake this morning?" he asks, offering me a plastic forkful of the lasagna before him in a silver foil tray.

I'm game, but Doris returns before I can take him up on it. "He says to come back later," she tells me.

Ignoring this, I excuse myself from the vet and walk to the office Doris came out of. There sits a Sean Penn lookalike with a headful of scraggly salt-and-pepper hair and more than a bit of bad boy about him.

Before he has a chance to throw me out, I work my new approach a little more. "Hello, Kenny, my name's Daniel. I want to thank you for something you did forty years ago, when you were a proud badge-carrying member of the local police force."

Despite himself he enjoys this, as if he knows he's being buttered up and wants to see how thick I'm going to lay it on. He torches up a fag and allows himself a tight smile. "You got my attention," he says.

"First of all," I say, "how you doing?"

"Takin' it one punch at a time. Got back this morning from a cross-country road trip, got caught speeding and I was, too, but they found my .357 under the seat. Cuffed my wife while they put me through the wringer."

"Even though you used to be a lawman yourself?"

"They don't care." This said matter-of-factly. "So now's we got the politeness out of the way, what can I do for ya before I gotta get back to work here."

He's the skinny cop with the yardstick in all those photos from Judi's crash box, I realize. Time has filled him out so he's less squirrel than weasel, alert with cunning. With that crafty face, he could have been a thief in another life, but he devoted his wiles to catching thieves instead. Maybe they're two sides of the same coin? Anyway, it's time to get down to business.

"Forty years ago, on a cross-country trip of our own, my friend and I were ambling through town bright and early one morning and got hit by a Mack truck."

"Not a Mack," corrects the voice in my pocket.

"Right, not a Mack, but a pickup, out on Broadway and Austin."

Kenny nods, but not because he thinks there's anything odd about a voice coming out of my pocket. "Bad intersection," he says.

"Well, it was bad for us," I say. "We got T-boned, and you were the cop on the scene who took care of us, despite whatever reservations you might have had about us. I'm here to say thank you."

Kenny angles his head down and affixes me with a shrewd look through a veil of smoke, sussing out any ulterior motives I might have. "All right, I appreciate that," he says.

I spread out the newspaper copy on the desk in front of him. "That's our vehicle on the right," I say—pronouncing the *h* in *vehicle* the way folks do around here. "What do you say," I ask as flatly as I can. "Jog any memories?"

Kenny studies the paper while I take in the room. There's a urinal out the side door, but it may as well as be in here with us, with the overpowering smell of piss pucks filling the air. The sound of a police monitor squawks in the background.

"So you're tryin' to locate this McLaughlin gal, I take it," Kenny says after a minute. "Can't say the name fires any circuits."

"Anything else strike you one way or another?"

"Right off the bat I should tell you I'm what you might call a skeptic," Kenny says. "Things don't tend to impress me much. I've seen every kind of crash and the strange things that happen. Seen a three-hundred-pound woman sucked out of a tiny side window one time. And a lot of other things we don't believe in till it suits us. Seat belts that save lives, and seat belts that take lives, for no reason other than you got up on a certain side of the bed that morning."

"Would you venture any thoughts?"

Kenny stares at me a minute with a neutral gaze. "You sure you're not here to stir up trouble?"

"Scout's honor."

He inhales hard, making the cigarette paper sizzle. "First off, as you must have noticed, the headline has one typo and the caption has two. Two Injured When *Vehiciles* . . . As for the caption: 'Two person were injuried Saturday when these two vehicles collided.' Singular *person* instead of plural, and again an extra *i* in *injuried*."

"I only noticed the headline typo," I say.

"Well, Dan'l, you better get on the stick if you're gonna fulfill that childhood dream of being a detective."

"How'd you know?"

"Plain as the nose on your face," he says. "Next, judging by the shadows, it was not bright and early, as you claim, but midmorning, say around 10:30."

"Huh!" I say. "Well, 10:30 would have been bright and early for a couple of lazy college kids like us."

Kenny doesn't care for my attempt at humor. In his life, 10:30 was never bright and early. Nor has lazy been much of an option.

"That there she's driving, that's a '67 or '68 Ford pickup, traveling I'd say forty-five miles per hour, to judge by the damage. They built 'em like tanks in those days, and this one's mighty messed. Plus, you see those dents bashed into your side? If I'm not mistaken, the gas tank was under the passenger seat in those Land Cruisers, couple inches behind where she hit you. You're lucky you weren't blown up, sittin' on a powder keg like you were."

"Why d'you assume it was me in the passenger seat and not Tony?"

Kenny doesn't need to look me over because he's already taken me in, every inch. "You strike me as the delegating type," he says evenly, holding my gaze. "I'm not sayin' that's bad or good, only that you let your pal do the heavy liftin' while you enjoyed the passing scene."

Tony can control himself no longer. "Busted!" he explodes from my pocket. "Looks like he's got your number, squash blossom."

"Not necessarily, sugar plum!" I explode back. "I offered to drive at the beginning of the trip, and you said no way!"

"'Cause maybe I didn't want to crash and burn on the Garden State Parkway!"

If Kenny sees anything strange about my bickering with the contents of my pocket, he doesn't let on. "Tinker Bell's your bodyguard, I take it? You didn't want to come into my domain without some sort of protection?"

"OK, what's the deal?" I ask Kenny. "You some sort of genius cop or something?"

"Look over here," he continues, ignoring my question and pointing to the center of the photo. "What's got me wonderin' is this little doodad right behind the left doorpost—"

"Wait, I'm enlarging it on my end; here it comes," Tony says. "Oh my God, I completely forgot about that! We were carrying an extra five-gallon an of gas on the other side, directly behind my back seat. We were like a rolling A-bomb waiting to blow a mile high."

I can't bear hearing this and shut off the phone. In the sudden silence, Kenny maintains a fixed expression. "Not a mile," he says steadily. "Woulda been a medium-sized firebomb at best."

The only sound in the room is the police scanner, to which Kenny cocks his ear. Something about Milepost 92.

"Another damn vehicle traveling the wrong way up the interstate," he comments.

"Any theory why that is?" I ask. "Why the general climate of crashes?"

"Not my zone of expertise," Kenny says. "But if you're looking for pure conjecture, I believe the desert may have something to do with it."

"How's that?"

"Seems to draw people who've got a measure of chaos in their lives, who need the quiet to silence the demons in their heads. Or try to, anyhow."

My phone rings. I put it back on silent.

"I'll tell you what I do know, from my stint doing accident reconstruction," Kenny says. "T-bones are the worst kind of accident, counting for 90 percent of all fatalities. If you'd have been wearing your seat belt, you'd a been trapped, no ifs or buts. Sippin' Grape-Nuts through a straw the rest of your life."

"So how did I escape?"

"You finish high school? Remember the definition of *inertia*? 'An object in motion stays in motion.' When this here Ford moves forward and stops against the Land Cruiser, the energy is transferred to your vehicle so the passengers are thrown forward at the same speed—but in the opposite direction. Tinker Bell here was stopped by the windshield, but both of you were thrown forward at the same rate the pickup was traveling."

He casts an eye toward the police monitor before refocusing his attention on me. "It's all physics and math, called vector analysis." With his right hand he picks up a stray beer cap and places it on the groove between his left index and middle finger. Then he tilts the fingers of his right hand and hits his left so the beer cap flies several feet away at the exact opposite angle.

"The beer cap's me?"

Kenny squints at me from under his brows. "One fortunate beer cap, better believe."

"But when did I escape? That's what I can't figure. Did I jump? How would I have had time? My whole side of the Land Cruiser was pushed in from the hood of her truck blocking my exit."

"Not right away, it wasn't."

He sees the blank look on my face.

"What you got to understand," Kenny explains patiently, "is that a crash is not a static event. It's not an instant in time and then it's over. She doesn't just hit you and stop. When she hits you, that's when you fly out the empty door space. But the crash continues to take place over tiny units of time. It's all fluid. Over the next microseconds she continues to intrude into the space of your doorway, causing the damage you see here before eventually backing off."

So now I know. I didn't jump. I was catapulted out before she had a chance to block my exit. But still I'm in a state of denial for a minute longer, like I have one last chance for a reprieve before Kenny's official pronouncement. "So if I'd been wearing my seat belt, I would've ended up in a wheelchair the rest of my life?"

"You're not hearing me, Dan'l. No wheelchair for you. You'd a been sawed in half before being mashed to death on the spot. And that's not mentioning the double fire potential we already discussed."

That's that, then. His words put an end to something in me, some youthful omnipotence that should have expired at the scene of the crash but hung on through decades of stubborn denial. I'm also getting the sense of a bigger picture. Something about time, the passage of time, tiny units of time adding up to great big sweeps of time . . .

My phone stops vibrating at last. Tony's given up. But then it starts again a few seconds later, furious as a bee in a jar. When it stops again, Kenny resumes.

"What I figure," Kenny says, sharpening his toothpick. "Austin was a dirt road in those days, with a steep gulch before meeting Broadway. She must have gunned it out of there, which is why she hit you so hard. Or another possibility, those clutches were loose in the '68 Fords, if memory serves, so she may have had to hammer the pedal to get any action out of it. Either case, she figured she could beat you out. Unless there's one other option. She didn't see you at all."

"But with all that visibility?"

"Sometimes that works against you. Sounds strange, but in the large expanse of landscape out here, you don't expect things to be close up. Then again, what if she had a drink in her? I'm not sayin' she did, but when you're imbibin' you tend to lose your side vision, so she might not have been able to see you quite as well."

Imbibin'? That doesn't fit my picture of the Angel. "But wouldn't the police have cited her for drunk—"

But oops, I stop myself in time to imagine his reply: *You want the extra paperwork for drunk charges?* Kenny takes a full drag of his cigarette, an expression of watching me without watching me on his not-thief face. When Tony calls again, I put him back on speakerphone and he jumps right in.

"But how does any of this get us closer to Mary?" he asks. "Would it help if we directed your attention back to 1970?"

Kenny and I look at each other, both caught off guard by the strategic new tack Tony is taking.

"Like, for instance, I'm curious what it was like for you officers back in the day," Tony goes on. "I bet they worked you guys plenty hard . . ."

"Matter fact they did," says Kenny, warming to the subject. "Made $395 a month, all that time raising four kids. We worked so hard we forgot we had kids. Worked two jobs to make ends meet, a full day in uniform followed by ten to daylight, and that's not countin' when a fellow officer took sick."

Tony mines the vein he's hit. "How old were you in 1970?" he asks.

Kenny calculates. "Twenty-seven," he says, shaking his head. "All of twenty-seven."

"I'll bet you weren't thrilled at the sight of a coupla rotten brats joy-riding through. What'd you make of us?"

Kenny is enjoying the interrogation but measures his words closely. "Not much."

"I'll bet not," Tony laughs. "Long-haired scumbags dirtying your pretty little town."

Kenny says nothing for a minute, computing how far he can let himself open up. "You was the hippies, and we was the pigs. That was the drill, right? No love lost."

"Pretty much open warfare, as I recall," Tony says.

"Culture clash, what they called it."

"So you wouldn't exactly have minded busting us for drugs, right?"

Kenny smiles carefully around his cigarette. "Innocent until proven guilty," he says cagily.

"Oh, c'mon, Kenny, you can't kid a kidder," Tony laughs. "We were red meat for you guys."

Kenny smiles wider, but he's not about to give away the store.

"C'mon, tell the truth, you sly dog," Tony continues. "You woulda loved to throw our butts in the cooler. In fact you probably raked our car over with a fine-tooth comb, didn't you, just dyin' to come up with a nickel bag."

Kenny takes another puff. The rolling paper sparks down at the bottom, where he's sucking it through.

"You've stopped answering, but I'll bet you've got a twinkle in your eye—right?—remembering how you were tempted to plant a little something of your own, just to see what mischief you could cause?"

Tony's right. Kenny does have a twinkle in his eye. He's amused by this cat-and-mouse and clears his throat. "Tell you what," he says. "You coulda been from Pluto for all we knew. Skipping across the landscape fancy-free—we were jealous. We mighta liked to try that ourselves. But we were trapped down by circumstance. Then again we didn't know what sort of threat you posed. Revolution? Anarchy? I guess what we felt most was what you might call wary. Scared, even."

"But we were scared of you!"

"Well, then, we're dead even," Kenny says.

This feels like an important milestone in our conversation. In our lives, even. Something evident from a distance of forty years that wasn't evident before. The three of us old men admitting that what was motivating us as young men was not hostility. Not anger. It was fear. Fear and fear and fear, as Clay from AA might say. This feels like an important discovery.

Almost shyly, Kenny rubs an ash into the knee of his denim. "Later on we mellowed a bit, come to see how some hippies might be decent in their own right, just different lifestyle, was all. Some were a little strong on the pot, but hell that didn't turn out to be no big deal. I myself never had the heartburn against hippies. Posted bond for two of 'em personally, never lost a dime . . ."

Something incongruous strikes me. I catch it before it gets away. "Wait, Kenny, what you just did with your fingers, meaning *two*. You made a *V*! Just like the *V*s we hippies were sending back and forth to each other on the highways that summer!"

"Guess I did, didn't I?" Kenny says. "Whyn't you send one to ole Tink there too . . ."

Roger that. Tony gets it a second later and crows. "There you are, Ken, you rascal lawman. We'll make a dope fiend out of you yet!"

Kenny enjoys this. "Well, ain't this cozy," he says. "There we were on opposite sides of no-man's-land, and forty years later we're on the same team, havin' ourselves a little powwow as we try to track our Mary."

God help me, but I feel a burst of love for Kenny when he uses the word *our*. Is he going to partner with me in this endeavor?

"Now that you're ticklin' my brain, she does glimmer a bit in my memory," he goes on. "Could have been a waitress at one of the old watering holes—Silver Slipper or the Buckhorn—but those places are long gone. Or if we could track down the owners of old Ford pickups, but there'd be thousands." He lowers his head to concentrate, furrows his brow. This is what cops dig, apparently, even ex-cops decades off the job—working all sides of a problem. "I'm running this thing as hard as I can, just can't figure what the angle is."

"Could this help?" I ask, showing him the admission card from the hospital before.

Kenny examines it, letting the smoke escape out of his mouth slowly. "Well, here's something. See those three initials on the bottom, *J. J. L.*? That would be the admitting doctor, Jack Lapp."

I didn't notice that before. "Can I speak to him?" I ask.

"Only if you have a hankering for overpriced coffins," Kenny says. "But his colleague Doc Studds who ran the local morgue was a car buff who might remember who Mary was, if he'd talk to you."

"Why wouldn't he?"

Kenny cocks an ear toward the police scanner, listens for a minute, before returning his attention to me. "Dr. Donald Studds, at one time the county medical examiner, delivered half the babies in town, even operated on golf pro Lee Trevino when he passed through town and had his appendix act up. He ran into a bit of controversy a number of years back."

"Controversy?"

"Had his license yanked for selling a few more prescription drugs than he should."

So how do you like that? All the time on my stretcher I was trying to convince the doctor I wasn't a druggie, yet he was the one who ended up the stoner.

"Still a good man, though," Kenny says, in his defense. "Ran into some trouble is all, had a Karmann Ghia that accidentally killed the woman beside him, not his wife. Always did have an eye for the ladies. Now whether that's what knocked him off his game or something else did the honors, I couldn't say, but he did have a stack of bills to pay. You go give him the third degree like you just did me, he might just link you up. You sure got me to yappin' this morning."

We shake hands but I catch his palm wrong and it's off-kilter. I wish we could have a redo but . . . awkward. Instead, I turn at the door before leaving. "Mind if I check back to tell you how I'm making out?"

A barely perceptible nod as he speaks while holding his breath. "I'll be here," he says, using two different fingers to pinch the base of what is certainly not a reefer, most certainly not a reefer. "But then again," he smiles, letting a blue plume float out across the room, "I might just make like smoke and blow away."

••

"Been thinking much about mortality these days?" asks Tony as I wait to meet Studds outside the lodge.

"Not particularly," I reply with fake nonchalance. "Why? Anything special on your mind?"

"Nothing much," he answers. "Just how we're all mostly clumps of energy floating around the universe, having our chance to see what the racket's all about. Don't laugh, Dan. But do you ever think about shit like that?"

I'm not laughing. I'm astonished. This is the kind of exchange I've been wanting to have with my sidekick since man first peed in a spacesuit.

"So, what's the deal?" Tony continues. "I mean, am I ready to come out of the kiddie pool at last? Don't tell anyone, but I think this whole experience is starting to make me . . . what's the word? *Deeper.*"

I refrain from saying the obvious: "It's about time," "Better late than never," and so forth. I can imagine Tony half yawning with embarrassment, taking every precaution not to look at me.

"Reason I'm bringing all this up," he says. "We're sixty! Have you taken this in? That's nuts! How could two postadolescent jerk-offs be boomers, for Pete's sake. Boom boom! What a fuckin' rip! Here we are roaring into old age, and I keep wondering when I did something wrong by getting older, as if I let my guard down or something. It's not just that I didn't live up to my dreams for myself, which I guess comes with the territory. It's more that life has let me down somehow. Or I let life down. I'm not even sure what I mean by that. Is it all right that I don't even understand what my own questions are about?"

"Maybe it's better than all right," I say. "Maybe it's extremely all right."

In the middle of these overheated thoughts, up rolls the Sunbeam Tiger convertible from the fifties. Out from the driver's seat unfolds a tall, creaky figure in shorts and short sleeves, fragile with a curved backbone. His skin is cadaver-white, but his Bermuda shorts are red, which sort of fits what I'd expect of an old man who collects antique sports cars and dispenses more pills than he should.

"Sorry, I had to run downtown to get a battery," he says, extending a long, cold hand. Why he thinks he has to apologize to a complete stranger is unclear. Nevertheless, I accept his invitation to step inside his nearby house, which is muggy and smells of dog. The drawn curtains are half off their hooks. The white wall-to-wall is stained here and there by what looks like brown trails of . . . let's say root beer.

Studds tries to settle into a beige recliner, but he tips off sideways. I help him up to try again and he tips off the other way. It's not an alcoholic imbalance, I think—more neurological. Two boxer dogs in the corner under a shelf of gold sports-car trophies raise their heads to watch me take their master by the armpits and secure him in the chair.

"Thank you, who's winning?" he says, turning his attention to the tennis game playing on the flat screen propped crookedly atop a massive dead TV console.

"Not sure," I say, "but I found my way to you through Kenny the Cop."

"There's a fella who hasn't had an easy time," Studds says. "Lost two stepchildren, one to a heroin overdose, one falling out a tree. Just ten years old. Came home to find the boy pinned through the chest with a garden sprinkler."

He looks dissolute, delivering such horrible news while slumped there like that, and I'm glad I remained standing because I want to make this visit as brief as possible. Especially since Tony's call has somehow been disconnected.

"Reason I'm here: you stitched up my cheek after a car wreck back in 1970, Broadway and Austin."

"Didn't leave a candy wrapper inside, did I?" he jokes.

"No, you did a good job. But I'm wondering if the name Mary Louise McLaughlin rings any bells."

"That's a long time ago. Got anything to jump-start the old memory bank?"

Is he asking for a bribe? I feign innocence and carry on. "You were joking to put me at my ease. You said, 'I hate to carve up your hippie beard.'"

"Sounds like something I'd say, all right."

"The nurses got a kick out of it. You did seem to have a way with them."

"They'll save you, the nurses will. You treat 'em right, and they'll treat you right when it's your turn. In my case I had a crash not long after yours, if I'm counting correctly. Lady bent on suicide came out of oncoming traffic. I was boxed in and hit her head-on. Eight busted ribs, fractured hip. I was laid up for months, and those nurses, I'll tell you what: Want to talk about some sweet hand jobs?"

"Out of curiosity, were you wearing your seat belt?"

"The only thing that saved me. But the person next to me, the minister— he wasn't and he died."

"It was a minister sitting next to you?"

"That's right," he replies, unblinking. "Didn't make it. Though the woman who hit me, she survived and we became good friends afterward."

Really? I think. Why did he lie to me just now, and so smoothly? Why tell me it was a minister who died in his car instead of a woman "not his wife," as Kenny had said? And how interesting that he befriended the driver who crashed into him, as I'm trying to do with Mary.

"Well, I'm fixin' to go down for a nap, if you'll excuse me," Studds says, dizzily attempting to lie back in his recliner.

"But that name? Mary Louise McLaughlin?"

A frail white hand floats up to his brow. "Can't help you. But you know who might: the towing outfit less than a block from your crash. Husband's dead, poor fella, but Ada's still around, I believe, though I haven't spoken to her in years. She woulda jumped to the sidewalk soon's she heard the impact. She kept records on everything, so she might have a bead on McLaughlin's whereabouts. Go see Ada, lives out by the Geronimo Tree, so called, where the great chief used to have his powwows, according to legend. Ada Martin, your best bet to find this Mary person."

A little more life comes into his face as he adjusts his hips slightly, adds a touch of roguishness to his smile. "By the way, you do see Ada," he says with a wink that's downright lewd, "tell her Donny Junior says hey."

CHAPTER 16

FLUKES AND HUNCHES

FULL DETECTIVE MODE: all the sleuthing I ever wanted to do as a kid, and then some. Having the propulsion of all these people behind me—the Assholes, the hospital ladies, the two cops, Doc Studds—gives me the adrenaline thrust I need. It's like I'm gathering power-ups, those packets of energy my son Spencer collects in his video games. Each one surges me forward as if I deposited a few doses of youth here at age twenty, when I had more than I needed, and I'm back to pick them up now when I can really use them. The Crash Site, the hospital index card, the newspaper photo—each power-up fuels me with a surety of purpose I haven't felt in ages. So to find the so-called Geronimo Tree, I just ask a succession of strangers on the street until I'm standing before a venerable old cottonwood deep inside a trailer park on the banks of the moribund Rio Grande. There are no historical markers, but its size tells the story—its trunk is so massive it would take three men to encircle it. A polished aluminum Airstream trailer is nestled under the hefty lower limbs. When I ring the bell, the sound of a cough eventually approaches from the dim interior.

"Are you really keeping dangerous snakes?" I ask, referring to the sign on the door that says Caution Snakes.

"No, but it works better than a guard-dog sign. How can I help ya?"

Turns out that in his three years here he's never heard that this could be the Geronimo Tree. But he allows how this would be the perfect spot. "See how the river curves out so they coulda seen enemies coming from all directions?"

He never heard the name Ada Martin either, but it doesn't matter: Door to door I go, flashing my newspaper xerox. It's amazing how much credibility that single piece of paper gives me. It's like my personal "open sesame." With evidence of my crash in black and white, I'm not just a nosy Yank but someone who tangled with this town well before most of them did. And now I've also got Kenny's name to drop whenever a little extra authority is needed. Only one woman in the trailer park fears that I'm an unsafe character and spanks her children into the RV when she sees me coming. "Git inside!" Most everyone else racks their brains to see if they can help. At last one resident, opening a paper bag to feed her hungry Saint Bernard, says she has indeed heard of Ada Martin. She tosses a cheeseburger for Smiley to wolf down in a single gulp. "Heard she died."

One way to find out. I pedal to Kirikos Family Funeral Home, the only such business in town. In the otherwise empty waiting room an agitated woman named Zita, tanned from the wind as much as the sun, rushes over to stand too close to me. "I was running away from a mean man five days ago," she confides, "but I picked up two mean hitchhikers and they robbed me of everything. Now I got to find someplace to pilfer." Wordlessly she opens her palm to drop a tiny crucifix into mine.

Zita is an acid casualty from my generation, a living example of what our elders used to warn us about, with unkempt dreadlocks that match the untied shoelaces on her ancient desert boots. "No, that's OK, but thank you," I say, putting the crucifix back in her palm. She steps back and regards me suspiciously, like I'm suddenly a mean man too. "You better give me a dollar for gas," she demands.

Nothing can slow me down, not even the presence of more lost souls than usual. I take a seat and adopt a mid-distance stare until the nattily dressed funeral director, Mr. Kirikos, comes out and asks Zita what she's doing there. She informs him she's related to Amelia Earhart. "I'm going to have to ask you to leave," he informs her politely. When I show Mr. Kirikos the xerox, he assures me that he has no record of anyone named Mary McLaughlin dying in town. But Ada's alive and kicking, so far as he knows. She moved East, he thinks, not sure where. "You know who might know, though? Jose the barber, very well-liked individual, I'd even say beloved, whose shop is right across from where Ada's use to be."

..

PLEASE DON'T LET
YOUR KIDS TEAR UP
MY BARBER SHOP

says the sign on the bathroom door of Jose's Barber Shop. Below it, like a running haiku, hangs another sign that reads:

OR YOU WILL BE
ASKED TO LEAVE
THANK YOU

And below that is another sign:

IF IT DON'T
BELONG TO YOU
DON'T TOUCH IT

All of which might lead the casual observer to imagine that Jose, purveyor of nine-dollar haircuts, could be a prickly fellow. But a minute's conversation reveals why this classic-looking barber—gray, gentle, avuncular—is so well-liked. "We may not know exactly what brought you back here," he tells me after listening to my story while snipping a customer's cowlick, "but what we can say is that a lot of people, their hearts would be filled with hate for Mary—"

"But I wasn't seriously injured."

"Regardless, they would. But you are not filled with hate. You are filled with love; that is what we can say."

"Jose, I can see why you're beloved in this town."

"Well, I have some very favorite customers, I'll tell you that, and now you are one of them too!" He lays his scissors to rest in a glass of blue liquid and turns on an electric clipper. "Now as to Ada, you'd think in a small town, people would keep better track of each other, so I'm a little ashamed to say I can't help you there. We can ask the town's oldest citizen, though." He indicates the man in his chair, one-hundred-year-old

Fred "Freckles" Pitch, whippet-thin in jeans and black suspenders, sipping from a Sprite can.

"Dan here was almost killed by a woman forty years ago, and he come back to it," Jose tells him. "Got any idea where Ada Martin run off to?"

"Who?" He puts his hand before his ear like an old man out of *Lassie*. "Ada Martin?"

"She killed him? That's news to me." Freckles points to something with the thick rubber base of his cane. What he's pointing at isn't clear, or maybe he forgot.

"Freckles used to be a champion jitterbugger back in the thirties," Jose explains to me, "and after that a brakeman for the Santa Fe Railroad, weren't you, Freckles?"

"That's right, 1942 to 1974," Freckles confirms. "I tell you, when that old girl got to the top of a mountain, we'd stand on top of the engine and ride 'er down."

"Was it beautiful up there on top of the engine?" I can't help asking.

"Beautiful?" Freckles sips his Sprite, considering this question as if for the first time. "No. Just a job."

"Tell him your secret for living so long," Jose prompts, buzzing the little hairs around his customer's ears.

"My secret? Whiskey and women," he laughs, showing little boy teeth and a rascally tongue. "That and toting my Smith & Wesson since it weighed more than I did. Had my heart attack a few years back—they put a speedometer on me and I've been goin' ever since. Take life as it comes, saves a lot of wear and tear. Do my own cookin'. They try to get me to eat at that senior center, but the problem is, you have to eat what they want you to eat instead of what you want."

"Tell him what you've got planned for supper tonight," Jose prompts.

"Chicken fried steak, mashed potatoes with gravy, canned pears," he says, self-satisfied. He almost drools at the prospect.

"Tell him where you're from."

"From Maine," Freckles says. "The Maine part of Kansas, ha ha!"

Freckles has the old-age smell of anchovy coming out of his mouth and a small burn spot at the tip of his sharp nose that is most likely a souvenir from his dermatologist. No doubt he's a selfish bastard who's committed his share of minor atrocities over the course of his lifetime, like everyone else, including me, I guess. But I'm eager to hear what else he has to say.

"Were you around when this town was called Hot Springs?" I ask him.

"That, sir, is none of your business," he replies. Then breaks the puzzled silence that follows. "Only kiddin'! Of course I wasn't around. I was somewhere else, like everyone else was. Sorry if my breath stinks. I'm a hunret!"

"A what?"

"A hundred. In my spare time. The rest of the time I'm just a kid like you!"

Jose snaps the sheet off him, and Freckles jitterbugs to the exit, all sharp elbows and knees.

"Where you off to?" I say.

"Do my own cookin'!" he says, starting to recycle his material. "Take life as it comes. Don't do nuthin' wrong, but do break the law on occasion."

"No, Daniel here is asking where you're heading," Jose clarifies.

"Gittin' to my girlfriend's!"

"Freckles, you're my hero!" I exclaim.

"Yup. I like to chase the ladies. But remember, just 'cause you chase 'em don't mean you catch 'em," he counsels me. He tap-dances to the sidewalk, then holds up a licked finger to test the wind before crossing the street.

One final sign for me to read before I leave:

**IF YOU
LEAVE THE SHOP
* YOU *
LOSE YOUR TURN**

But I had my turn and got my clue—the senior center that Freckles mentioned. With its treasury of historical memories, someone there's bound to help move me forward. I have so much energy after the power-up of Freckles that I feel not twenty again but eighteen! Or the hell with it—sixteen! I hop on Flower Power and zip around town like a big-city message courier, only instead of cabs I'm dodging potholes and tumble-weed. Didn't I used to take naps around this time each day? That's like something from a lifetime ago.

In the entranceway of the senior center there's a community white-board listing hobby rooms for the various clubs: tai chi, wood carving, square dancing. The whiteboard's question of the day is "What would you like your last words to be?" Someone's answer: "Here goes nuthin'!" There's also a notice for a lecture on Reverse Mortgage Strategies for Retirement—"another civic service brought to you pro bono by the King"—and an announcement for a patriotism luncheon sponsored by the Sierra County Republicans, which likely explains the festive sounds coming from the central dining hall. I poke my head in, and sure enough the various clubs have broken from their hobby rooms for lunch: the wood carvers here, the quilters there, the square dancers off to the side in full Western flounce.

"That'll be five dollars," says one woman in a star-spangled bonnet, stamping my wrist with a purple star as I get in line at the food table.

"Like some lettuce?" asks the next lady behind the table. Lettuce is exactly what it is; iceberg lettuce as opposed to salad. Pork ribs are added to my paper plate, and an ice cream scoop of brown beans that leak into the lettuce. At the end of the table an old-timer dressed as Uncle Sam squirts a dollop of Cool Whip on my cupcake, then sprinkles red, white, and blue jimmies on top. There's a four-inch American flag at each place setting, but I choose to eat standing up, watching the stage where six blue-haired women have their backs to us, shaking their bums to "God Bless America." Some members of the audience are inspired to get up and shake their bums, and damned if I don't feel moved to shake mine, yodeling with the best of them when the song's done. Hey, it is a great country. Where else could a complete stranger come into an unfamiliar senior center and wave his arms for quiet so he can ask a question?

"Just one question," I promise, when the commotion dies down. "It'll just take a minute."

"Louder!" someone shouts.

"Quieter!" someone else shouts. They all laugh. After dancing like they did, the whole room's in a frisky mood.

"Use the mic!" someone shouts. I hop up on the stage and look over the gathering, imagining it's the great-grandchildren of Apaches sitting cheek by jowl with the great-grandchildren of the cavalry who came out to fight them.

"Happy Republicanism, everyone!" I shout. "I have a quick question, if you don't mind. Anyone happen to know the whereabouts of that great American patriot Mary Louise McLaughlin?"

"No, but we know about you," says someone from the retired farmers group, dressed in denim bib overalls. "Riding your girlie bike around town like a daredevil fool!"

"Ha ha!" everyone laughs. "I seen him do a U-ey in front of Family Dollar 'bout an hour ago," says someone else. "Nearly hit him with my Chevrolet!"

It's like the roles have been reversed. I'm the youngest in the room yet have been assigned the adult role; the seniors are the naughty kids cutting up. I'm the lunchtime amusement, the substitute teacher they can pick on to their heart's content. Happily for me, however, I've recently had practice standing my ground with my colleagues at AA. Go ahead, ridicule! I'll kick ridicule's ass! I don't even mind taking a bite of my meal right in front of them onstage—enjoying it too—while I wait for them to settle down. That I'm comfortable enough to chew my food onstage appears to have a sobering effect on them, for some reason. It brings them into line. The cupcake tastes a little beany, but even so has a pleasing texture.

"Or if not Mary," I say, "next best is Ada Martin, if anyone knows what's become of her."

"Dead," volunteers someone from a table by the window, his face a mix of sawdust and sunburn.

"Ain't dead. I checked over to Kirikos," I say, automatically taking on my drawl again.

"Went to live with her daughter Kathie in Ohio someplace," puts in someone from the wood carvers club.

"Hell, to that matter, her son John-Johnson's still in town," says a woman from the tai chi group. "When Ada left he tried to run the towing operation. Run it into the ground is more like what he done. He'd be knowing if she's alive or not," she says with a wink to the room, "'cause ole Ada's got a mattress said to be stuffed with cash money."

This raises a general guffaw, but an appreciative one, as if we've got a common enemy.

"John was a hell-raiser, all right," someone else continues, waving gnats off his coffee. "He'd raise hell his way. And if you didn't like it, you was in some kinda trouble!" They laugh with fond memories that require only a few key words to keep it going: "Crashed his Harley through a plate glass window," "Married a semipro lady hockey player," "Got hit by lightning twice—"

"We tried tellin' him, you're not supposed to hold your fishing pole straight up in a thunderstorm," one offers.

"Or your pecker!" adds another, to a burst of catcalls.

I adore Americans, I find myself thinking. Such an unlikely thought for me to have.

"Time's up. You got what you come for?" asks someone else.

"Reckon so, thank you, one and all!" I say to light applause, and leave the mic in place as instructed, since the King is scheduled to give his lecture any minute. There's his booming grizzly bear voice now, in fact, coming down the hallway as I exit the building and jump on my bike.

··

J&J Towing is not far, as it turns out. Or maybe nothing is far, in the mood I'm in. The garage with big block letters—J&J—is chained up, with some form of broken-down shelter behind it. I holler over the metal fence, and out sashays a creased-up woman in plastic curlers whose dried-out face betrays years of 30 percent humidity. "Ain't seen him since last Tuesday," she volunteers. "Probably him and his flunkies off on a drunk. I'm glad he's gone, tell the truth."

"Heard he was quite a character. And you too," I add.

"Well, I'll be goddamned," she says, with a slow smile.

I'm feeling the effects of the cupcake. "Hey, you wouldn't happen to have a Beano in there, would you?"

She likes lifting her fingertips to a curler and causing the copper bangles on her wrist to ring. She's sultry, like the singers in those girl groups of the sixties, the Ronettes or the Shangri-Las—the hair done up in a poodle cut, the shapely figure in skintight pants, the eyes that know their way around in the dark.

"You're welcome to come take a look," she smiles.

One thing I don't need to do is flirt with John-Johnson's partner. He'd raise hell his way. "Maybe another time," I say. No sooner has she gone back inside than another woman steps out from a neighboring trailer, beaming cheerfully.

"Here's your Beano," she says, placing two pills in my hand. "A Beano from Bonita. But as to where John's at, he put his tow truck in a ditch last week, then went to jail a couple of days ago on an old warrant."

"Wonder why his wife didn't tell me that," I say.

"Well, I wonder about things too," Bonita says. "How do we get mixed up with the people we do? Why do we bump into the things we need sometimes, and sometimes we can't find 'em for all the tea in China? I don't know. My aunt used to call 'em flukes: flukes and hunches. And how come everything seems to come full circle, if you hang around long enough? Everything round goes square and then back to round again, ever notice?"

"What was the old warrant for?" I ask.

"Crushing a car without the owner's permission to sell for scrap."

"Couldn't that have been an honest mistake?"

"Three times in a month! No, John's got hisself an overactive crusher. Best bet he's still in the joint."

..

To the joint I go. The outdoor kennel cages are empty this afternoon, no orange-suited inmates pacing back and forth. I can't find an entrance to the building until I locate some sort of locked metal door off the parking lot in back with a black surveillance camera beside it. Apparently the jail is too poor to provide a proper entranceway with a reception area—visitors have to stand outside on the tarmac and wait to be received. I touch the bell—getting a shock from the dry air—but don't hear it ring inside. I knock on the door, but it's made of such inert material that the sound stops where it starts, not traveling where it needs to go. I dead-knuckle it a few times more until eventually a voice crackles out of an overhead speaker I hadn't noticed.

"State your business."

I state my business.

"We're closed for lockdown."

I'm shameless enough to state my business a little more, that I'm hoping to meet John-Johnson so I can ask him if it's possible to reach his mother, Ada. I'm not expecting to prevail, exactly, but I'm making it clear I'm not going away soon. After a while the door opens a few inches and a guard's furrowed face appears. "You the new bond bailsman?" he asks.

"Wow," I can't help saying, "that's a first."

"Better adjust your attitude if you want any protocol from me."

I wait in silence until my deference is established. It's only now that I see the guard has a skinny black braid snaking down the middle of his back. The trenches in his cheeks are so deep they look edged by a chisel.

"Got any warrants out on you?" he asks me. "Any outstanding arrests?"

"No."

"What is it you want, clearly this time?"

I ask him if I can speak with John-Johnson regarding his mother, Ada.

"No can do, guy," he says. Apparently, they had an escape yesterday: One of the inmates was doing yard work when he took off running. Marshals picked him up ten hours later in Las Cruces, and now all the inmates are being punished with a general lockdown. But even as he's telling me this, I see that once again my xerox is serving as my open sesame, sparking his curiosity to the point where he comes fully outside on the tarmac and we get to chatting. Turns out Maxwell is fifty-one, half Cherokee, born on a farm in the Midwest, grew up to be a cop in Las Vegas, came here because his brother lived outside of town. His brother had a drinking problem, but he licked it.

"Good for him," I say.

"Yeah, stuck a twelve-gauge in his mouth. He licked it all right."

Maxwell's mother died just last week, his sister's going in for a liver biopsy next week, his four kids are living more or less productive lives. "I tell them the same thing I tell these clowns in here," he says. "You

Flukes and Hunches • 139

show respect for me, then I'll show respect for you, but these jokers in here . . ." Bitterness is seeping out of the cracks in his face. "Fuck it, I'm just in a bad mood," he says, looking down at the curlicues on his cowboy boots. "Last night one of these clowns throws his dinner juice at me, my uniform's sopping wet. I tell him we're stepping outside. Clown says, 'There's a rule book.' I say, 'We're gonna rewrite it, you and me.' I put his face on the con*crete*."

The bitterness is spewing from everywhere now, like he's draining an oil filter on the tarmac. "For $9.97 an hour, I'm not in a mood to hear them complain all night through the intercom, which the rules say I gotta keep on night and day . . ."

"There's no way you can turn it off?"

He hears that I'm taking him seriously, focuses on me with soft brown eyes.

"We do turn it off, now and again," he admits. "It just upsets me to see them taking advantage of the system like they do. I say let 'em drink and drug themselves to death. Reduce the number we have to pay for."

With that final venting, he rubs the butts of his palms into his eyes for a minute, a vulnerable gesture, and when he's done he actually looks lighter.

"Hell, tell you what I'll do," he says unexpectedly. "Can't let you in, but I'll see if I can get a message out. What you want me to ask him, exactly?"

And in five minutes he comes back with a piece of paper upon which John-Johnson has grimly scrawled his sister's name.

Kathie johnson West Chester ohio.

Could Kathie help get me to Ada? I start Googling on my phone right here in the parking lot, sitting against the jail's outside wall. In half a sec I've tracked her to a newspaper site out of Plainville, Ohio, which links to her praising the TV show *Extreme Makeover* for some reason and talking about the part-time work she puts in at some Christian academy's day care. The academy's front office, when I reach them, won't let me talk to her without her permission, but they promise to give her my number, and before I can even stand to stretch my legs I'm talking to Ada's daughter like we're old friends.

"I myself had already left T or C by 1970, so I'm afraid I wasn't there for your wreck," Kathie says. It sounds like she's expressing regrets for missing a party. "My husband was in Vietnam, and I used to have panic attacks waiting for word, because in those days of course there were no cell phones or email. I had to wait to get word by mail."

"But during that summer, Ada was in the shop right there on Broadway, right? According to Doctor Donald Studds—who says hey to your mom, by the way—if anyone would have been first on the scene, it would have been her. And if she has files—"

"Oh, no, all those files got tossed when Father died of bone cancer, must be ten years already. It goes so fast!"

"Or maybe some memory of the woman who hit us, Mary McLaughlin?"

"Well, about memories," Kathie says, "I've got good news and bad. Mother's still with us, thank the Lord, but her brain's sketchy since she got hit in a crosswalk right there on Broadway, life-flighted out by helicopter. It'd be unlikely she remembers, but I'll go ask her." A minute later she comes back to report that Ada didn't spark to the name Mary McLaughlin.

"Oh," I say, discouraged.

"One thing she did remember, though—the name of that doc you mentioned. Mother must have been sweet on him at one time 'cause she said to give Donny Junior a big kiss. Her face hasn't lit up like that for a long time, I'll tell you."

Great, so I've abetted an ancient flirtation. But I'm back to where I started—full circle to a stop.

"I don't mean to meddle in your affairs," Kathie says, "but you've tried the obvious, right? Talking to the county clerk right where you're at in T or C?"

Lucky thing I kept my day job because, holy shit, I suck as a detective. I reached all the way to Ohio when the answer, as any part-time day-care teacher could tell me, was right here a few dozen yards in front of my face. I leave Flower Power in the jail parking lot and jog across the street to the county clerk's office, where the first thing out of the clerk's mouth is the suggestion that McLaughlin might have been her married name, in which case all we need to do is see if there's a marriage certificate that sheds light on what her maiden name was. Immediately she's on her hands and knees before the shelves of a back room—pulling out one of those oversized ledgers that look as though they date from the 1760s but are just from the 1960s—and locates a copy of the marriage certificate.

"Doesn't list a maiden name but does have a date and place of marriage," the clerk says, slapping dust from her palms. "Mary and Tommy McLaughlin were married on August 16, 1967, in a place called Stilwell, Oklahoma. It's an hour later there, but if you hurry you may still have time to reach the district court's office before they shut down for the day."

Where's the afternoon gone? The first thing that pops up on the Stilwell website is a bulletin from the National Domestic Violence Hotline titled "How to Get a Protection Order." Evidently Stilwell is the seat of another dirt-poor, violence-prone county, this one in northeastern Oklahoma, seven miles from the Arkansas border. It's 4:54 already, central time, and the line is busy. I keep getting a busy signal and assume they've unhooked the phone so they won't have to work after 5:00. But at 4:59 a woman named Christie picks up and tells me the only way I can access the information is by snail mail, three days minimum.

Rarely do I resort to the journalist's stock-in-trade three magic words. But I've journeyed too hard to give up now. "I'm on deadline."

Why these three words produce urgency on the part of people who needn't give a damn, I'll never understand. But they almost always do. It's like saying, "I'm bleeding!" People jump to, even if it means working a few minutes overtime. At 5:04, Christie comes back to the phone. "Name on the marriage license is Mary Louise Greene."

Three magic words of hers to match three magic words of mine. Mary Louise Greene, born May 24, 1945—which made her twenty-five at the time of our crash. With an effort I manage to contain my elation.

"Thank you for the overtime, Christie."

"Pleasure's mine."

·•

I should have enjoyed my high while I had it, because soon enough the trail goes dead. There are simply no Mary Louise Greenes anywhere

Google can find. Not in the records of high schools within a fifty-mile radius. Not in—oh, the hell with it, not anywhere. To be so close and yet let Mary slip through my fingers is too dispiriting for words. And to keep forcing my will on all these unassuming people and still fail at finding the object of my quest . . .

The sun is going down when I wander back to the jail's parking lot, where I left Flower Power. It's one of those sunsets with daubs of pink clouds so unrealistic that if you saw them on a painting, you'd say, *Come on, no way.* I squat in a patch of dwindling peach light, not far from the prisoners' cages. They're in lockdown, and I'm in lockout—no way to move forward. All my power-ups are depleted, and I'm drained. The high lonesome of the alpine desert, as Clay from AA put it.

On my wrist, the purple star from the Patriotism Luncheon at the senior center has faded to near nothing. A little girl drags an empty plastic bottle along the sidewalk by a string around its neck. A strange bird stares at me, not moving. It's a roadrunner, I guess. I've never seen one outside of Saturday-morning cartoons. Then a fifties-type hot rod drives by, trailing haplessly jaunty music, the trumpets wobbling as though on a warped vinyl record, all of it punctuated with a wild falsetto whoop—*yeeeeeee-ah-ha-ha-ha!*—that can come only from having eaten the worm at the bottom of a tequila bottle.

I shiver—no more patch of sunlight. It's getting dark. My prospects have dimmed even more. I'm as blue as blue can be. But my face is lit white by my phone as I try to think whom I could call. Illuminated like this, I wonder if the prisoners can see me from their cells. On a whim, I activate Google Earth to see if I can locate my home. It must have been summertime when the satellite snapped its image last year; the lilies are in bloom, the elms thick with leaves. On the street, four people with bare legs are riding bikes. I zoom closer. Wait, is that me in front? Are those my sons between me and my wife? It's not us, on closer examination; it's just another ordinary everyday happy family. But it's similar enough. How did I manage to lose that?

Foolish, foolish, miserable man.

Just then my phone rings.

"C'mon over to Candy's," comes the voice of Kenny the Cop. "I got someone you need to talk to."

CHAPTER 17

HIGH LONESOME

STATE LAW PROHIBITS smoking in the public bars of New Mexico, with fines up to $500. Try telling that to anyone at Candy's. The smoke is so thick I can barely make out Kenny at the end of the bar. But that's him all right, shielding himself with an extra smoke wreath of his own making.

I take a stool beside him and share a handshake, though it's another botched one, like at our first meeting. Why can't I show him I'm a good handshaker? It's how a lot of men gauge each other's masculinity; mine must keep failing because I'm over the falls in a rowboat with no oars.

Without a word he gestures to the guy on my other side. He's the one I'm supposed to talk to.

But can he talk? The man is so drunk his head is nodding slowly on its spine like a faulty bobblehead. His cruddy shirt has several slices across the back and shoulders, as though it was rescued from a shredder. On the saggy upper-arm flesh is a tattoo so runny as to be unreadable, like it was rained on before it dried. But what stops my breathing for a second are the eyes—the color of spit in ashes. They're blurry and viscous—the light entirely gone. Altogether he could be a museum piece out of Madame Tussauds. *Tragic Drunk*, New Mexico, 2010.

"Name's Frank," he says. "Can't see what good it does you." And with that, he reaches his stiff, earth-thickened fingers past four empty cans of Icehouse Beer toward a wet saucer containing the remnants of a hard-boiled egg.

"Howdy, Frank. Nice dog," I say, referring to the little shit-nipper he's got leashed too tight to his stool. "What kind is he?"

"*D-O-G*," Frank says. "Problem with that?"

"No siree, not me. Is he going to bite me?"

"She liken to dig a hole outa your leg," Frank says, taking a sip of Icehouse before closing his rheumy eyes. When he opens them again, he doesn't seem happy to see me. "What are we doing here?" he asks.

I look at Kenny, who nods patiently, like, *Keep going, stick with it.*

"Well, first I'm wondering: Can you and I be friends?"

Frank looks hurt. "Why can't we?"

"I'm one of the Jews you got that emblem against," I say, smiling sadly. I'm referring to the trucker's cap he's wearing that features a Jewish star with a diagonal line through it. Frank is as alarmed as an Amazonian tribesman would be, seeing a Hasid twerk on YouTube. "You Jew?"

"Only on my parents' side." But I'm being cocky—unease brings that out in me. I immediately repent, especially when I see how much this throws him. He tips his head to focus on me, his eyes rounding and narrowing on my face to keep his balance. "Maybe you're black Jewish like I'm black Irish," he concludes, somewhat ingeniously. "Frankly I don't give a shit. I just wear it for decoration."

"He found it by the dumpster, tell you the truth," says someone on the other side of him, a faded mouse of a woman named Linda, with a blond wig so thin you have to wonder why she bothers. "He don't mean nuthin' by it." I'm reminded of how Americans will rarely embarrass themselves by insulting you to your face, if they can avoid it. Unless they're in a group. Then all bets are off.

The shit-nipper snaps at the air four inches from my ankle with little teeth that look sharpened to piranha points. Her beady eyes seem pressurized like they're going to pop if she can't bite someone soon.

Frank comes to a decision. Squishing his cigarette into a gnarled sardine tin, he launches into a tale about how his truck broke down one night on the interstate outside town. Linda fills in some of the details as Frank continues squishing. This was back in '98 or '99. Frank's then-wife, Lenora, told him to stay with the truck, and she herself lit out across the highway to fetch help for a breakdown. But then she got run over by a Cadillac. "They drug her down the road, then turned around and drug her back," Frank says. "Some hot-shit lawyer, head honcho or like that. The wife was driving 110 miles per hour, got off scot-free."

"No one went to jail?" I ask.

Frank stops squishing and rears up, almost in slow motion. "Why'd I go to jail for?"

"Not you. Him."

His eyes blink at my stupidity. "Head honcho!" he repeats. And with that he kicks down hard on the leash to yank the dog's head to the floor, where it makes strangling noises.

"Cut my hon's body in four pieces. Never did find her right foot. Might still be stuck inside the grill, for all I know."

The image almost makes me gag, but it passes. Instinctually I take my phone out and lay it on the bar, something to remind me there's a bigger world out there beyond Candy's. "What was the upshot?" I ask.

Frank makes a throat-slicing gesture. "They give me nine hundred dollars to shut up. God's honest truth. I got the papers."

This initiates a throaty cough and expulsion of smoke from Linda. "Honest truth," she confirms.

"Unbelievable," I say.

"Believe it," Frank says, wheezing into his hand. "Weren't married but twenty-three days, neither."

"You were newlyweds?"

But Frank has stopped trying to calculate me into his consciousness. He sits back on his stool wearing a look of stupefaction, as still again as a wax figure. So lifelike, right down to the line of moisture rimming the underside of each eye, as though a small candle had melted in each socket, the flame drowning itself in a mini-puddle of wax. He claws the cheek of his face up high, a way of wiping his eyes without appearing to.

"She was studying to be a, what do you call it?" Frank makes a whirling gesture near his head. I'm thinking, *Studying to become a crazy person?*

"Psychologist," he says. "Getting her master's. Another one in archaeology."

Words I didn't expect. I check his eyes again, where the moisture is gelling. He can't help but swipe at the tears directly now with the back of his hand.

"That makes me humble," I tell him.

"'*Humble*, that's the word," he says. "That's my humble right there," he says, gesturing to Linda, who squeezes his hand and looks gravely down, then gravely up again. It's not a smile, exactly, but it's full of dignity, whatever it is. Seeing this, being privy to this, also feels like an important discovery.

There's the pop of a cigarette lighter on my other side as Kenny fires up a fag. "Enough with the pleasantries," he says. "Tell him what you were telling me, Frank."

"'Bout what?"

"'Bout you know."

Frank claws blindly at his cheek in confusion.

"Never mind, then," Kenny says. "Dan'l, show him the xerox."

Frank barely glances at it before concentrating on his Icehouse. "Yeah, that's the one," he says.

Kenny winks at me.

"The one what?" I ask Frank.

"The one I seed."

"What do you mean? You've seen this paper before?"

Frank looks at me like he can't believe he's still talking to a person of such an abysmal IQ. "Not the paper. The wreck. I seed it."

"You seed it? Holy shit, an actual eyewitness?" I turn to Kenny. "How'd you find him?"

"I'm picky where I choose to drink."

"Me and Daddy was coming over the hill," Frank explains. "Traffic backed up on accounta there was a fuss going on. Word was one of 'em flewed out the car."

"That was me flewed out the car."

"That was you?"

"That was me."

Frank looks me up and down, to the best of his ability. "How'd you live through it?"

"That's one of the things I'm trying to figure out."

"Want my theory?" Frank offers. "Don't do it anymore."

"Thank you. But you're sure it was this wreck you saw, not some other?"

"This one, 'cause it was in the paper." And I said, 'Daddy, that was the one we seed!' I musta been six or eight . . ."

Which would put him at forty-six or forty-eight today. I took him for sixty-five, easy.

I'm dubious but excited. I have an eyewitness. He may wear a fascist cap and an unreadable tattoo, but he's all the eyewitness I need.

"Did you know the person who hit me?"

"All my life!" he says. "She and my uncle went to school together. That's Mary . . ." His face blanks out. "One of the colors."

"Greene," I say impatiently. "Yeah, that much I've heard. Her name's Greene."

Kenny nods once to show admiration for the way I've been pounding the pavement. "That's some decent police work right there," he says. "We worked two different directions and come to the same end point."

"But we're still stymied," I point out. "I've checked everywhere. There isn't a single person around named *G-r-e-e-n-e*."

Snickering quietly to himself, the ex-cop hunches down deeper over his cigarette to hide his amusement. From my phone on the bar comes a coughing sound. Kenny picks it up. "Kenny here. Is this Tinker Bell trying to eavesdrop on me again?"

"Howdy, officer," says Tony. "Bust any hippies lately?"

"Tony?" I ask. "How'd you get here?" It seems miraculous that he's on the phone in this hellacious place.

"You must have butt-dialed me, smart guy," Tony explains. "I'm just minding my own business with Patty here and two minutes ago my balls started buzzing. Sounds like you found a nice new playmate, Asa. Hey, Frank, how's it hangin'?"

Frank groans something that sounds like "cogsuck" into his latest can of Icehouse.

Kenny addresses Tony. "I was about to tell Dan'l that he may have made a little error, on accounta being a half-step too smart for his own good."

"Kenny, you're my man!" Tony says. "That's what an old teacher of ours used to say! 'Danny, with that brain of yours, be careful not to make things harder than they have to be. Sometimes they're just as simple as one plus one.' Oh, Kenny, you'n me, we'll knock some sense into this cowboy yet."

Kenny's a natural diplomat. "I'm sure it's something he already thought of, but maybe sped right by it on accounta having a tendency to overthink things a little."

"Frank, what do you have to say about this?" Kenny asks.

Frank raises his head slowly, like it's on a broken crank, and fixes me with soggy contempt. "You a moron?" he asks. "Don't know how to spell *green*?"

OK, so I'm having a spelling contest with Frank now? Frank who probably thinks there are only two *e*s in—

"Oh my God," I say, as a full-body blush starts to rise from my tailbone. "Uh-huh."

Oh my God, how stupid of me, how oversmart, not to assume the easiest spelling. I just assumed it was *Greene*, like all my points of reference—Graham Greene, one of my literary heroes; Brian Greene, the theoretical physicist; Fort Greene in Brooklyn; plus all those cutesy grilles and shoppes in this wannabe tourist towne . . .

Oh my Goddde . . .

"'Cause if there's no final *e*," Kenny is saying, ignoring the mounting cackle from Tony, "there's a Green clan not too far south of here. Sandy Green down in Caballo is a member of the lodge, comes up to play bingo with us Monday nights. Matter fact, ole Sandy has a niece Karen James who's pretty high up in the US Postal Service, might be able to point you to Mary."

"'High up in the postal service?'" I ask. "You mean in DC?"

Kenny allows himself to snicker openly at his hopelessly overthinking junior partner. "No, Dan'l," he says, shaking his head. "At the post office branch five blocks from here. Brick building on your right."

. .

Clang! go the cowbells against the glass door of the post office as I burst in, not a minute to lose. It's after-hours, but they haven't gotten around to locking the door.

"Is there a Karen Green on the premises?"

"No Karen Green but a Karen James," replies an attractive brunette woman seated behind the counter, cordial but reserved. "Green's my maiden name."

Blood rushes to my head as I stride to the counter with my hand out-stretched. "Karen, you may be my missing link. Do you have a relative by the name of Mary Louise Green?"

"I'm a niece of Mary Louise Green," she says, standing to shake my hand a little warily. "What's this about?"

As I lay it out for her, dates and all, Karen stands there like a rabbit that's just spied a fox. Stock-still. Not moving a muscle.

"September 5, 1970? I wasn't but a month old," she says.

I show her the newspaper. She studies it and studies it and finally lifts her face from the page with tears in her eyes.

"Tell you what," she says. "I feel like I'm not at liberty to say anything. But I can tell you who to talk to."

"Who'd that be?"

"Her son."

"Mary has a son?" It never occurred to me.

"Scott Trumbull," she says. "We're not close by any stretch, but last I heard he was working at the Cozi Inn right off the highway exit. Might still be there."

She takes a sticky pad and draws a street grid to show me how close it is. "It's lucky you found me here," she says. "I transfer to Silver City in four days."

··

The urgency is almost unbearable. The blood pounds in my head as I pump my bike nearer. Karen was just what I was hoping for—a regular person with an appropriate amount of caution. Seeing her official post-office shirt made me feel I was steering into a safe harbor of nice at last. No more defrocked doctors or people carrying railroad spikes. I've paid my dues.

I stand outside the vestibule of the Cozi Inn for a minute, taking stock. Heart: calm. Hands: steady. I step into a dun-colored lobby and zero in on a forty-something man in sharply creased khakis and tailored blazer, primping a bouquet of cactus flowers in the center of the room.

"Scott Trumbull?" I ask.

"I beg your pardon?" the man says in a thick Italian accent, looking embarrassed as he steps back from the bouquet. Oh, he wasn't primping but touching it to see if it's as plastic as it looks. So he's a . . . tourist?

"Over here," calls a Hells Angel at the receptionist's desk: black clothes, slicked-back blond hair. I approach, wondering what a Hells Angel's doing behind the desk. Unless, that smile—he's too agreeable to be a Hells Angel? And that voice—too high for a Hells Angel? It's a musical tenor that doesn't square with three hundred pounds of muscle. "We having fun yet?" he asks sweetly, giving me a perfect fist bump by way of greeting.

"Scott?"

"That'd be me."

"Sorry, I'm just . . . you surprised me, is all."

"You're still surprising me, buddy. How'd you know my name?"

"Karen Green, down at the post office?"

"I'll try not to hold that against you," he says good-naturedly. "Only kidding, I wouldn't recognize her if she was in a line-up all by herself. Got my own little fam—don't need the extended one. What can I do for you?"

He's a big boy for sure, wide and strong. Laid-back. Likable, now that I'm over my surprise. About thirty years old with a gentleness I find appealing. With that high voice, he's a cross between a gangbanger and the nicest kindergarten teacher you've ever met.

"OK, I'm going to say something strange now, Scott, but don't be alarmed, it's all good. You and I are connected, in a way, through a car crash."

"OK," Scott says immediately, like he's caught up and ready to hear. "That'd be my mom, Mary, I'm guessin'?"

"How'd you know?"

Scott chuckles to himself. "Let's just say it wouldn't be her only crash."

The desk phone rings. "Cozi," he sings into the receiver. The Italian tourist is deciding whether to register for the night as he pretends not to eavesdrop. "Let me connect you to housekeeping," Scott says, hitting a button and turning back to me with a guileless smile on his round face.

"First off," I say, "I want to assure you I'm not looking to blame anyone or point fingers or anything like that. This was way back in 1970, and she was like an angel to me."

"Angel, huh?"

"Happened midmorning on the corner of Austin and Broadway. She cradled my head and told me I was OK while we were waiting for the ambulance."

Scott doesn't react. "What'd you say your name was?"

"Daniel."

"Listen, Daniel, you seem like a nice guy, and the last thing I want to do is burst your bubble, but she's not anyone's angel, not even mine, and I'm her son."

Scott says his words so simply that there seems no harm in proceeding. "So she's had more than this one crash?"

"So many she not only stopped countin', she stopped noticin'. I hate to say it, but if no one got killed in yours, I doubt she thought twice about it."

It takes me a minute to process this, as if things are on a three-second time delay.

"It's why I don't dare get behind the wheel to this day," Scott continues. "I don't even feel safe gettin' in Sarah's car. Mostly I pay Rocky to taxi me anywhere I need to go, and even that makes me nervous 'cause he can't afford to replace the headlight that burned out last year."

I try to keep up, saying the first thing that enters my mind. "But, I mean, don't all those crashes throw her husband for a loop?"

Scott chuckles again. "Oh, about husbands? You're better not knowing."

"What do you mean?"

"I mean, especially back in those days? Let's just say she was missing the fidelity gene."

The Italian tourist is joined by his wife back from the women's room, both of them craning to hear us while pretending not to. My head's growing muzzy, trying to reconcile Scott's good-humored tone with the crazy meaning of his words. Missing the fidelity gene?

"None of this jibes with my impression of her," I say. "I mean, you just met me, Scott, so please don't think I've gone off the deep end, but when I was lying on the street looking up at her, she seemed to have a glow around her head, like a . . . halo. Don't laugh," I say, though he's not laughing. "I'm the first to say it wasn't real, but doesn't the fact that I got such a positive impression say something about—"

"Probably *was* a halo," Scott interrupts genially.

"How's that?"

"1970? That's about the year she broke her neck the first time. Her head was in one of them halo braces, like a metal gizmo round her head to immobilize it or whatever."

Wait—so that was the halo I saw?

"Listen, it's nice that you're interested in Mary and all, but I don't know how much more I can help. I never knew her, not since I was one and a half when she lost custody. I don't have anything from her or about her, just a few details comin' down thirdhand. My dad never let me see her face or hear her voice or anything. I've never even seen a photo of her. Sorry."

"She lost custody when you were one and a half?"

"On accounta her drinking, from what I hear. She was so bombed for one of her doctor visits, fell clear off the examining table."

"She had a drinking problem?"

"Drinking condition, more like. The custody judge was so disgusted he plain walked out of the courtroom. I don't want to use a bad word, but in this case I have to. What we're talking about is a drunk whore."

This is delivered so matter-of-factly—the mildest voice saying the vilest syllable—that I'm slack-jawed. His genial delivery is a defense mechanism, I see now, a way of distancing himself from the terrible import of his words. The Italian couple tent their mouths to whisper to each other.

"I mean, I could sugarcoat it for you, but I figure you want it straight, feeling related to her and all. Or maybe you want to rethink that, now that you know the truth."

My mind is in a floating space, comprehension draining from me and panic taking its place. This was the woman who told me I was OK, yet apparently she was deeply not OK herself. A desperate need flares in me to be in touch with Mary right now, to see her for myself as I feel her slipping away. Maybe it's not as bad as her son says. Or she's reformed. Or I could help her. Or—

"Can you at least tell me where she's living?" I ask.

"Oh, she's not."

"Not what?"

"Living. She's been dead going on—what, twenty years now? Something like that. Killed."

"Dead," I repeat. Dumbstruck that I hadn't even considered the possibility. And then, "Killed?"

"Murdered." He lets this soak in a minute, gauging my reaction. "By her seventh husband."

I have stopped understanding the language. I don't know what *murdered* means. What *seventh* means. But the dun-colored walls look dirty. I feel like pointing a rifle at the tourists gawking at us. Get back on the highway, rubberneckers! Stop finding us losers colorful!

"If he even was her husband," Scott goes on affably. "I don't know whether they were legally married or not; it's hard to tell."

It feels foreign for my mouth to say these words. "How was she murdered?"

"Basically beheaded." Scott makes that chuckling sound again, the sound of a disconnect being filled with empty matter. "Stabbed so many times her head was barely hanging on. At least that's what I heard. He roped her to the toilet over in Arizona somewhere and kept hacking to get her to say where her unemployment check was at. Used a bowie knife—them suckers is eight or nine inches long. The neighbors complained about the stench after a while."

The tourists have fled the lobby for the parking lot. Through the plate glass I see them starting their car, gabbling excitedly to each other. I'm not making a lot of sense to myself, asking questions that are very stupid, even for someone stupid enough to have idealized a drunk whore.

"Have you ever visited her grave?"

"On my to-do list. I got the directions in my head: down in Hatch, 'bout forty miles. Fourth row under two cedar trees. Don't ask me how that got stuck in my brain 'cause I do not know."

The housemaid comes in to ask Scott a question. The voice with which he addresses her—"How can I help you, princess?"—is so soft and placid, I am undone. How could someone with a mother like his come out so mild? And inside that Hells Angel body? Which may be protective padding—a fearsome outside to cover his tender inside. I stand before Scott like a naked idiot, envying his defenses—his girth, his wadding, his ability to chuckle it off like it doesn't matter, keeping his inner self child-soft.

"I think I got it figured out, what happened," he says when the maid has gone and we're alone at the reception desk. "This was a daytime crash, you say?"

"Right. Saturday morning."

"So what I figure is, she was still finishing up Friday night." He sees my confusion and explains. "She must have spent Friday night at Candy's. Getting drunk as a skunk. Finally passed out. Then when she come to Saturday morning, she saw she was late getting home, hopped in her truck, ducked down Austin there, and shot straight out Broadway. No time to stop and clutch it."

"You think she saw us and decided she could beat us out?"

"Doubt she bothered lookin'."

Doubt she bothered lookin'. Doubt she bothered lookin'.

"But she was wearing her halo brace. Wouldn't that have slowed her down?"

"Doubt it slowed her in the bar."

"What do you mean?"

"Well, not to speak ill of the dead, but she was kinda famous for takin' all comers, halo or no . . ."

He sees my reaction.

"Pretty crazy, huh? I wish I could tell you more, but that's about the size of it. I can take your number in case anything else comes up."

My stupid politeness is so ingrained, it functions through my shock. "Sorry to add one more crash to the mix," I find myself saying.

"Oh, that don't bother me none, just an extra hell factor. Anyway," he says, giving me a fist bump goodbye as some new tourists waltz through the lobby doors, "that's your angel for ya!"

CHAPTER 18

HER BEAUTIFUL MOUTH

THERE IT IS, that painting. That painting on the wall of my trailer. Drunk Virgin Mary with her beer-blitzed eyes and creepy smile-curse. She was here the whole time, silently mocking me. I should have taken it as a warning—the truth about Mary right in front of my face. Now it taunts me as Tony vents over the phone, saying terrible things I know he doesn't mean. "A slut, Danny. A tramp. The fantasy girl's a floozy."

On and on. Vile things. Tony was invested in Mary, too, after all. He needs to say violent things for a while to get them out of his system.

For my part, I have only one thing to ask Tony: "You any closer to getting back here? I could use the company."

"OK, about that: it's taking me a little more time to iron out the wrinkles," he says. "But never fear: in my mind, I'm already halfway there."

The events of the past few hours make me direct. "Actually, you're not halfway here. You're nowhere near at all," I say. "Know what I think, Tony? I think you have no intention of coming back, and never did."

"Well, that's an interesting thesis," Tony says. "Let's examine that for a moment, shall we? Suppose I find coming back problematic for a variety of reasons having to do with the preservation of my own marriage. Suppose I'm deciding I don't want to find myself in the same boat you're in, with the woman I'd actually like to grow old with, if that's in any way possible. Would that be so awful of me? Would the fact that I was willing to get you out of your house into a diverting new environment, but not quite willing to go so far as to put my own blessed union in jeopardy—"

"I can't believe it. You're finking out on me."

"Now there's a word I haven't heard since '62."

"You're ditching me. You're stranding me out here."

"I mean, do I want to come back? Yes, a hundred and one percent. But would that be a smart thing for me to do, Patty-wise? That's a question of a different order."

"You fuck."

"That's good, Danny. You're feeling good enough to be pissed."

"You fuck!"

"'Cause here's the thing, my best friend since sixth grade." He speaks more seriously than usual. "I know this is gonna come as a shock, but I'm a real, live person with issues to deal with just like you. For instance—and I may have mentioned this if you check your notes—I've got a long-lost daughter who wants to see me, and I'm trying to get my mind around that as fast as I can, even while my wife is flipping out that this could threaten our whole family infrastructure. So I'm real sorry your prom queen turns out to be a porn queen, but I've got problems, too, and have you spent even one second thinking about what that must be like for me?"

"Yeah," I say apologetically, "how's it going with the daughter?"

Too little, way too late. "Oh, Danny, why even pretend you give a flying fuck."

And with that he hangs up.

..

OK, you know what? I don't need to be here either. I don't need to waste one more second in this trailer, in this town, on this woman in the painting whose beery eyes taunt me. With the sharp point of a corkscrew, I slice an X through the canvas. "Wholesome"—slash! "Trustworthy"—slash! Then I lift the shredded rectangle off its nail and fling it across the room. I hurl other items too. I dent walls. I yank curtains. Finally I stash clothes into the pack on my back. Out the door I fly.

I don't even know where I'm going—I just bike and bike. Thank God it's night and I'm a danger only to myself. *Ha!* for all the close calls I ever had—fourteen, if truth be told. *Ha!* for all the close calls I never had, as well as those that—never mind, it's enough that I'm in beautiful danger now, a dark figure darting through even darker streets. No streetlights, no bike lights, just an occasional twitch of distant lightning as I ride and ride with no idea where I'm going. My muscles ache from pumping around town all day, and I'm glad they ache. My lungs gasp at the thin air, and I'm glad they gasp. Before I know it I'm out of town at a fateful junction. To the left is the highway and home. I could ditch the bike and hitch home as I did forty years ago. To the right is the way to the Jornada del Muerto death stretch of the desert. Is there a choice? Home? What home? I bang out a right.

Reeling, I ride breakneck through the treacherous pass toward the desert. Silent lightning zigs as I zag, snaking through the mountains with hairpin turns, passing at least one wooden cross where a car went over the edge. Hazard awes me; I'm close enough to death to thrill at its rank breath roaring up from the canyon bottom below. In the blackness I can barely see where I'm going, then for a time I can't see anything at all . . .

Finally, from the level expanse of the Jornada, I take out my cell phone and tap out the numbers. The connection is made.

"Can we just stop this madness and let me come home?" I hear myself beg.

The desert ticks in silence. Between us, twenty-four hundred miles, every meter of it alive and listening, the entire vastness of the country seeming to pulsate with anticipation.

"Look, I love you," Polly says at last. "But you've worn me out. It's like I don't exist as a real person for you most of the time, except as an offshoot of you."

I listen. Out there in the endless expanse of desert, I listen. Why haven't I always listened like this? I make out crickets, some in the brush around me; I make out a catch in her throat. "Where do I start to say how sorry I am?"

"But it's not just that," Polly says. "It's everything, who you are, what makes you wonderful in some ways, but it would be nice if you realized other people's pain was as real as yours—"

"I've given up driving, if that's any consolation."

"It doesn't matter, Danny. What's done is done."

"I know that, but—just come out here!" I say, suddenly emboldened. "Totally do it! Bring the boys! I'll show you a guy who's been stoned since '71 but can recite the whole history of the town in one fell swoop. There's another guy who carries a Raggedy Ann doll but may be kind of a genius, a lama who practically glows with wisdom, and a motorcycle momma who—"

"You're not hearing me," she says.

"You're right," I say. "Guilty on all counts! Now will you take me back?"

A sigh of sixteen years' duration, born of long-suffering exasperation. But not without affection. I press my advantage. "What're you sucking on?" I ask.

"Nothing. A Good 'n' Plenty."

"From the box I got you at the airport on our honeymoon?"

"A new box, you crazy man! That's what I mean! It's not about you all the time! Don't you think I'm capable of going out and buying my own—"

"I'm joking, sweetheart."

"Oh!" she laughs. "You got me."

"See? I can still make you laugh."

She is silent a minute. "I can hear you smiling," I say. "I can hear it in your voice, see the corners of your beautiful mouth turning up . . ."

She breathes, faintly. "Oh, there's so much I adore about you," she says. "How you . . . so many things!"

I want to make a harmless little joke about my inner mensch, about both our dinner plates being too full. About wanting a happy ending. Two happy endings! Ten! Like the stories her father told her when she was growing up. But I don't dare. Instead I listen. I listen like my ear's on fire.

"It's strange," Polly says. "While we're talking, I keep reverting back to a memory. That time the four of us biked along the beach path in Florida for miles? Remember? The boys and I were so exhausted you had us all lie between your arms, right there next to the path, with our heads on your chest. You stayed awake while we closed our eyes and slept. You sheltered us. You weren't off somewhere in your own world for once. You were completely there guarding us as we slept. If only there'd been more moments like that—"

"Then let's try again with me being that way more often. It proves I have it in me."

"I can't," she says simply. "I just wish I believed I had a real partner who was like that more of the time." She chokes back a snuffle, like it's important to her pride that I not hear her cry. "I don't mean to sound unkind. I hate how this is hurting you, but it's what I have to do. I wish I could say, *Sweetie, come home to us right now, be with us again and don't ever leave . . .*"

"Then say it!" I plead with sudden abandon, wild with optimism as in our earliest days. "We'll fix our family, and all of us will—"

"I can't!" It's a scream I've never heard from her before, and it frightens me down to my bowels. Then she gains control of herself and speaks with a deliberateness that frightens me even more. "After sixteen years, I can't give anymore," she says. "I've given and given and I'm worn down to almost nothing. I have to save whatever's left of me and try to start building it up again, without constantly giving myself away."

Crickets sing like mandolins in the brush. A charged silence ensues. It sounds like ship-to-shore radio with far-away static, but at the same time it's intimately close, like she's breathing in my ear. How can she be so far and so close at the same time? Is she warding off tears? Is she struggling to accept me with all my millions of flaws, reigniting her belief in me one final time?

But no, what she's doing is letting go at last.

"I just can't," she says finally. "Maybe six months from now we can be friends, or six years, when all this is behind us . . . but in the meantime, you've got to find your own way without calling us. It only upsets everyone to hear your voice. If you truly care about us, you'll stay away. Wherever you are, in that New Mexico place, or wherever you've gone from there, I just want you to stay there, or anywhere, but please just don't contact us for a while."

. .

I'm alone in the desert, making strange noises with my mouth and strange steps with my feet, stamping the sand and flailing my arms. I want to draw down lightning to strike me hard. I want to conjure quicksand to swallow me whole, rouse rattlesnakes to bite me again and again, blacken my body, make me writhe in agony and die right here on the desert floor—slow or fast, it doesn't matter, so long as it gets the job done. I want to be finished.

Soon I'm lying flat on the sand. There is no thought, no sound or movement, only the emptiness, which might be vast or not: I don't care. This feels like the final horizontal of my life, the ultimate horizontal for which the earlier ones were merely dress rehearsals. I have, gratefully, reached the end.

Almost. First I have to have one memorial thought. Later on that afternoon in Florida, after the bike ride, we all took a swim. My wife and boys were happily frolicking with a sea lion and her pups on the shore, but I swam out far enough to encounter the family patriarch, a sea lion dying alone. There was his family, like mine, frolicking back on the shore, and here he was twenty yards away, dying without them—a once mighty leviathan floating insensibly on his back, powerless to stop the sea from doing with him what it wanted. The sea wanted to roll him over, and roll him over it did. The sea wanted to roll him back, and roll him back it did. The sea lion seemed at peace, since he had no choice. He couldn't fend off death, so he was letting it come. I was struck by how provisional it all was. You're alive until you're not. Time is on your side until it isn't. And not even your family can save you. Odd that my final thought on the desert would be of the sea. But the world worked that way, apparently: wet unless dry, alone when not together, yes until no. Before we can grasp it, it's gone.

But maybe not quite. Eventually there is a flicker of light at the horizon. At first it's almost unnoticeable and it goes away. Then it comes again—not a lightning flash but a tiny beam like a firefly on my brain. Against my better judgment I stand and am illuminated by the light whose source I don't comprehend. I know it's not heaven-sent but think maybe it's one of those UFOs they're always spotting out here, winking closer. The beam gets brighter until I have to shield my eyes. When it's so near it's almost paralyzing—a cyclops eye of blinding light—it slows to a stop ten feet away. Through the glare I see it's the single headlight of a taxicab, driven by a man in tie-dyed PJs whose name I vaguely recollect is Rocky. The back door opens to reveal a second man, a wide man, in the back seat.

"Buddy, I been looking for you everywhere," Scott chuckles. "Hop in. It's time to meet the fam."

PART III

TWO MONTHS LATER

CHAPTER 19

HAVING FUN YET?

THE DESERT: AFLAME with carpets of crimson poppies, stripes of emerald fuzz on the sand hills, splashes of Indian paintbrush so orange they make even the most garish litter look pale by comparison.

Ready? the desert asks me.

The Rio Grande: truly grand, after all. Since the March dam release, it's no longer a sluggish, shit-brown creek but a sparkling green swash of energy, sloshing headlong between banks of thirsty red clay.

Ready now? the river asks.

It's springtime, two months since the devastating phone call with Polly. Since taking a rain check from Scott in Rocky's taxi that night, I still haven't readied myself enough to meet his family. I've been recuperating. Watching spring happen. In two months, the single-wide trailer on the double-wide street has become framed by color as the dead mesquite trees turn out to be not dead after all but explosive with lemon-yellow flowers. In two months, I've learned to luxuriate in my backyard hot tank, sporting a cowboy hat and Wyatt Earp mustache, listening to the radio playing the florid music I've come to love.

Inevitably, it's time to rise. I enter my castle, festooned now with antique road signs and strings of chili-pepper lights draped through new curtains. The repaired portrait of Drunk Virgin Mary occupies a place of honor on the newly painted wall, looking different from when I first got here. Her eyes aren't scary any longer but scared. Her arms aren't crossed in defiance but in self-protection. We had her all wrong. She's not creepy. She's hurt.

Two months can be a lifetime.

I dress, stamp into my pawnshop cowboy boots, and hop onto Flower Power, which I've pimped out with red, white, and blue streamers. Feeling like a regular member of the community, I exchange greetings with Roy Joy, as well as with the two junior-high-school girls necking as usual. Pedaling down Broadway under a faux-innocent sky as blue as a pretty little blue jay carrying parasites, or as a country pond glowing with blue cyanide, I look for all the world like yet one more homegrown T or C character, approaching a brand-new destination beneath a pair of drunk-driving billboards with a single question on my mind:

Am I finally ready? To meet the fam at last?

And there it is, Scott's house, one of three I unkindly called "hovels" my first night driving into town. Actually, it's a decent little structure made of cinderblocks painted dark brown. Two white PVC pipes snake out from its foundation across the dirt yard, giving off a suspicious dribble. The front door is nailed shut with a rectangle of particleboard upon which the painted letters *K-Bob* are flaking off. I drop my bike and make for the back door, but no sooner have I rounded the corner than I gape at one of the most majestic views of Turtleback Mountain I've seen, blazing in the sun like a giant red oil painting. It's such a monumental vision, it almost takes a physical effort to pull my eyes off. I mount the back porch to knock, stand beneath a cobwebby yellow lightbulb I suspect is never off, and am soon greeted by the sound of three locks turning, one after the other. The door is swollen shut against a warped floor and opens only partway, despite the efforts of the two strong women pulling at it.

But wait, I've seen these women before. Yes, the goths from the gas station our first day in town, the ones with the stuck accelerator.

"Sorry, wrong address," I say. "I was looking for Scott Trumbull."

"Hey, Dan buddy," comes that surprisingly high tenor from the dark inside. "We having fun yet?"

Well, he's having fun of a sort, lying in the middle of the wall-to-wall beneath two little boys who think he's their trampoline, jumping all over him.

"How're you doing, Scott?"

"Happy as a pig in you-know-what," he says, brushing back his hair as he rises with the boys attached, as if with Velcro. One of the goths triple-locks the door behind me, plunging us into twilight as the mountain brightness is replaced with the blue-red of TV cartoons. "Dig your 'stache!"

"Sorry I couldn't make it here before now," I say. "I needed a little time to process things."

"Oh, we understand that," one of the women assures me, smiling despite the obvious pain I remember from the gas station. "Some burdens take longer to work through than others."

How lucky, I think: a sympathetic spirit.

Scott readjusts the boys on his backside while clinching both women around the waist. "Dan, this is my wife, Teresa, and our best friend, Sarah. Ladies, this is the man I was telling you about, got smacked by my mom forty years back."

"Nice to meet you, sir," says Teresa, ducking her head in a gesture of hospitality, but with her stiffness it comes out like a lopsided curtsy.

"Wait a minute," says Sarah, offering me her plump hand to shake. "Ain't you the guy got our car to settle down that time? Remember I was telling you, Scott? We wanted to say thanks but got flustered?"

"Not a problem," I say.

"My 'gurrls'!" Scott chuckles beneficently. "Yeah, we all live together, one happy family. I love wonderful women with low standards."

Both gurrls are guarded with me, like they're careful to contain their feelings behind a concrete dam, letting as few trickles of emotion seep over the top as possible. As for those black jeans and T-shirts, they're probably less a fashion statement than an attempt to budget visits to the laundromat. Everyone's barefoot except me, their arms and faces the kind of pale that hasn't seen much sun lately.

"Cute kids," I say, because they *are*: towheaded and bright-eyed, clinging to Scott like koalas.

"What, these monkeys?" Scott says, reaching around to tickle both squirming bodies. "They're ornerier than heck!" he says as they squeal with delight.

"What'd you call them?" I ask, but am drowned out by Sarah swatting their bums and saying, "Well, get off and say hey to the man!"

One by one, they drop from his arms like miniature primates. "Hey," says the bigger one, handing me a plastic Happy Meal insect. "Hey," says the other, putting up his arms for his father to pick him up again. In a second they're both squiggling over Scott's neck but managing to stay on despite one of them having his wrist in a comic-book cast, twine holding it in place. I do believe Scott would piggyback them around the world if he could.

"Yeah, we love 'em to death," Scott says. "How could we not? Just look at 'em. I mean, they're a pain in the butt but can't never get me mad."

Both boys are bare-chested, wearing holsters that tug their bathing suits down. The little one's got a runny nose, so he keeps pulling up his suit or wiping his nose, unable to do both at the same time. Puppies in a pet store: the more you give, the more they want.

"The biggest, he's four and he's Draike," Teresa says. "We spelled it with an *i* in the middle so it wouldn't be like a duck. And the two-year-old here is Vaughan with an extra *a*."

"I have two boys at home," I say. "But I never thought to give them such original names."

"Her folks hated the names," Scott says. "Said we were too high and mighty to use regular ones, but we did it so they'd stand out from the general craziness of life. Same reason we gave 'em each other's names for middle names, so it's Draike Vaughan and Vaughan Draike. That way no matter how far life yanks 'em from each other, they still gotta know they're brothers."

"Was that your idea? It's beautiful," I say.

"Teresa's got their phone numbers plotted out, too, don't you, sweetie pie?" Sarah prompts.

"When they get old enough to carry phones, we're going to give 'em numbers the reverse of each other, like 343 and 434," Teresa says. "Get it? So even if it's bad trouble they get tangled in, they can't never get lost."

I'm incredibly moved by this. In this land of deep disconnect, where so many people are doing their best to cut themselves off from their past, this family is planning ways to stay in touch over the long haul. Scott himself is so disconnected, he wouldn't recognize his cousin Karen at the post office just a few blocks away, yet he's inventing ways to make his nuclear family last.

"See, it shoots arrows!" says the bigger boy, shooting projectiles about four inches out of his McDonald's wrist weapon.

"Which'll come in handy for the career he's picked out," Scott says, upending the boy and squeezing his head into his belly. "Tell Dan here what you want to be when you grow up."

"Parole officer," comes the muffled reply.

"I don't know where they come up with these things," Scott chuckles. "Glad it's this side of the law, at least."

As my eyes adjust to the semidark, I take in a setting so primordial as to be dreamlike, the couch and chairs huddled around the TV as though around a fire in a cave. Tucked over the couch is a sheet that used to be white. The only windows are two pieces of plexiglass at ceiling height, cemented directly into the cinderblocks so they don't open, in front of which SpongeBob curtains are drawn tight. It's dark and airless, yet the mood is good. Teresa manages to keep a smile on her face as she lugs herself about.

"We're raisin' 'em right," Sarah offers. "Never cuss in front of the boys. Nothing sweet to eat neither, except for Christmas and happy occasions."

This cheers me—knowing they're health conscious. They must disallow smoking too—it's one of the few places I've been recently that doesn't assault my lungs. I let myself be ushered to a seat on the couch—a spring's broken so I sink lower than I expected—and look around at a room that's surprisingly spacious. The walls are painted the same brown as outside, a warm brown that matches the wood grain of the TV. A synthetic Christmas tree stands behind a pool table covered with a vinyl shower curtain, under which sit a couple of antique computers bulky as air conditioners.

"Yeah, looks nice 'n' all," Scott says, watching me take it in. "But there are serious misgivings to this place. Water pours in when it rains, causing mold to grow so the kids always have allergies. Soon as Draike gets over one cold he gets another, seems like. When you turn on the light, the socket smokes, and I'm a fire paranoid? That gate going into the kitchen is to keep the kids out 'cause the floor is caved in on account of the old well. And see that Mickey Mouse pillow in the corner? That covers a hole that drops down to the dirt. You don't want to reach your hand down in there, never tell what might bite up at you."

"Like what?"

"Put it this way, Vaughan trapped a scorpion the other day, six inches long and mad as could be. And we got our share of those, though they're not much worse than a bee sting. Thing we got to watch out for is brown recluse spiders: they crawl into bed with you to get warm, and when you roll over they bite you, but you don't feel it 'cause they got a way of numbing you right out."

For some reason these details fail to creep me out. I feel safe in the hospitality of my host and hostesses, like this is exactly where I need to be, sitting with the family of the woman who crashed into me forty years ago. I can't explain why.

"And for safety?" Scott continues. "We keep the doors locked night 'n' day 'cause this here's the meth-making neighborhood."

"Meth's a problem here?"

Like droplets of water spilling over the dam, a round of giggles erupts at my naïveté. "You didn't know T or C's the meth capital of the Southwest? Used to be, anyhow, till a few years ago. Lots of murderous activities associated with it. Matter fact, when we moved in there was crime tape right here in the living room. You can still see the dark patch on the rug next to the pool table. That's where they found the last guy who lived here."

"What happened to him?"

Sarah mimes a pistol to the head. "Bang," she says.

"Yeah, we got the murder discount," Scott says, with a wink. "Only way we could afford it. But the house next door? Supposedly that's a meth house to this day. We sometimes catch that weird, awkward smell, like after a gas leak but it don't have that burn."

"Sweet?"

"Nasty!" Scott snorts. "Plus their son Tyrone? Four years old and weighs 110. Poor kid's teeth rotted out 'cause they give him a lollipop to keep him quiet when he goes to sleep. The good news is the dad's going back to the slammer again soon. Every time he goes, Tyrone's weight comes down."

As before, Scott manages to say these words without sounding judgmental: accepting what's what without needing to render a verdict.

"Long and short, too dangerous to let the boys outside," Scott says.

"If we had a chain-link fence, that'd be another story, but them things are expensive on the salary I make."

He sees I'm curious and goes on. "I see ads saying forty thou is poverty level? Heck, I'd give my eyeteeth for forty. I work thirty hours a week at the Cozi and make less than ten. We're fixin' to move as soon as disability comes through, hopefully near the river so I can teach the boys to fish."

That word "disability" sticks in my ear. "Disability for what?" I ask.

"Teresa's wreck," Scott says, planting kisses on the ladies' necks. "She was idling at a stop sign couple blocks over when a muscle truck with no insurance rear-ended her, twisted a disk into her nerve."

"Seven years," Teresa says. I wait for the word *ago* but she doesn't say it, maybe because it's not altogether in the past. The effects of the crash are still with her.

"Ouch," I say.

"Pain don't never shut up," Scott says. "One day it's like knives stabbing in her back, the next her whole side's numb. Drives her out of bed every morning before 4 a.m., tears running down her cheeks." As at the Cozi, he chuckles to mitigate the effect of his words.

"And she's no wuss when it comes to pain," Sarah says, gathering the boys off Scott's shoulders and giving them back after he's had a chance to realign himself. Amazing how seamless the operation is, how well everyone operates as a unit. "I mean, she didn't take a bit of painkiller when they were born in case it was harmful to the fetus. Didn't even yell 'cause she heard yelling can make newborns go deaf."

"We got a whole cabinet of pain meds, but they could be Tic Tacs for all the good they do."

Throughout all this Teresa keeps half-smiling in a way that also looks like crying. Her face is like one of those upside-down drawings: right side up it's happy, the other way it's not.

"She's a little love muffin, is what she is," Scott says, planting a kiss on her nose and making her giggle through a grimace.

"Shouldn't she be in a wheelchair?"

Teresa raises her brows in a way that conveys she can't afford a walker, much less a wheelchair. "I'm getting around pretty good today, but on bad days I use a hillbilly wheelchair," she says. "Otherwise known as a chair I can push ahead of me when I walk," she elaborates, seeing my incomprehension.

"What else does the doctor say?"

"Well, the doc situation around here ain't great," Teresa says. "They come 'n' go. I've seen six over the years, and none two diagnose the same. Even Doctor Tom over at the hospital, he threw up his hands, too, for the life of him. The doc I have now comes up every few months from Alamogordo, says he knows I have a disability but he won't write it down as a diagnosis."

"Why not?"

"We have no clue," Scott says. "He says she has two out of five symptoms of MS but two don't count. And he can't find another disease to pin it on. Rheumatoid arthritis? That didn't check out. Other ones too: one disaster after another. Getting the runaround from disability, except I'm not 100 percent sure it *is* a runaround? Maybe they're doing the best they can? But sure does seem like a long time for nothing: seven years."

"How could that be?" I ask. "I mean, it's obvious at a glance that if anyone ever deserved disability, it's her."

"Well, see, that's common sense talkin' right there," Scott says. "But the disability folks, they're not too big on common sense. She already been rejected twice."

"Part of the problem was I had two kids since the wreck," Teresa says. "They said if I'm well enough for relations, I'm well enough for work."

"Which is why we got our little 'procedure' last year," Scott says.

"Yeah, but that's another horror story," Sarah points out.

I breathe in through my nose, steeling myself.

Scott chuckles. "Let's not get into that one. Good thing we got bad luck, otherwise we'd have no luck at all!"

"That ain't quite true," Teresa reminds him. "We did get that big settlement in the beginning. Seventeen G's!"

"That's it, for all you've been through?" I ask, astounded.

Teresa nods. "And from that we had to bail out my parents—my dad's brother suddenly dying of AIDS and then miraculously gets better after we sent the money. So we were broke again. And then the lawyer died in a wreck of his own, and since then nobody's been in a hurry to help with the rest of the disability—the monthly payouts or what have you."

"Have you had a good lawyer since then?"

"The King!" Teresa says proudly, like saying she got her wedding gown at Bergdorf's.

"How come it's taking so long?"

"It's in the lawyer's hands," Teresa says flatly, as if saying "the Lord's." His ways are mysterious to mortal man.

Sarah is carrying a chair from the pool table over to Teresa. "Rest now, sweetie pie," she tells her. But no sooner has Teresa sat down than the kids make a beeline for her, starving to be on their mother's lap. Sarah scoops them up and places them in Teresa's arms.

"She can't even hold her kids unless we help, which has got to be some sort of hell for a mother," Scott says, "and even that's only for a few seconds."

As if on cue, the boys tire of being unable to budge her and wriggle off to watch *SpongeBob* on the floor before us. The giddy music is like a frantic soundtrack to Teresa's pain.

"So I already know about your mom, Scott," I say," but is your dad in a position to help?"

"My dad's a pretty good drinker," Scott replies by way of saying no. "Always screamin' at me, my whole growing up. He was a dairy hand goin' from farm to farm, so I was never in the same school more than a year. But I gotta say to his credit: he never abused me like his wives did."

"Talk about evil stepmothers," Sarah says. "One of 'em took a metal dog brush to his hand so bad he couldn't hold a pencil for a week. He got scars on his scalp to this day from where she tore out his hair."

"Did you say something to make her do that?" I ask Scott.

"Asked for a raisin."

"How did all that affect you growing up? If you don't mind my asking."

"Nothing fazes me; I really don't get mad," Scott replies in that placid way of his. "I don't generally like to touch people, not even shake hands. Never hug. I mean, I hug my family, but not nobody on the outside. I'm going on thirty and still don't have my driver's license, 'cause you know why. It's a joke around here, driving drunk. At my driver's ed class all the teacher taught us was which breath mints would disguise our breath so it wouldn't reek of liquor. He was just tryin' to get in the girls' panties, but still."

Scott runs a pudgy hand through his slicked-back hair. I feel a quiver on the back of my neck, knowing he's afraid to drive, too, same as me.

"Now that I'm thinkin' about effects, though?" he continues. "I don't drink, of course—just the smell makes me want to spew. But maybe the worst effect is I can't stand anyone being hurt. Like last night at the Cozi a man called to cancel his reservation and he wanted his money back, but I told him we had a twenty-four-hour cancellation policy. He was beggin' so bad I went to the manager and asked if we could make an exception. He said, 'No way!' I went back and told him my hands were tied, he was crying on the phone, but that dude is evil. My chest hurt all day."

"Still and all, Scott's put up with him longer than anyone else: six years," Sarah points out.

"He's a saint," Teresa concurs.

Scott lowers his head, blows them both a kiss.

"But still, you haven't got a bigger community to speak of?" I ask.

"We had us a church for a while," Scott says, shaking his head. "But they kicked us out 'cause they decided we were demons. We dressed in black, and there were six letters in each of our names. The preacher's wife said Teresa was the devil's child."

All three adults share a laugh at the silliness—a pleasant laugh free of bitterness. "I don't want to say I don't get along with people," Scott says. "Because heck, I've got a front-desk job dealing with people all weekend long, two fourteen-hour shifts. It's just—" He opens his arms to encompass everyone in the room. "This is all the community I need."

I look at the back of the boys' heads, so handsomely reminiscent of my own boys at home, watching *SpongeBob* as their parents hold hands without even knowing they're doing it.

"You're a loving man, Scott," I say.

"One thing I can do is love!" Scott concedes. "Easiest thing in the world when you've got people like this to do it to!"

I sit there smiling, past envy, just in a state of admiration.

"Matter fact, now you got me thinking, here's a thought that just popped into my brain," Scott says. "What if you, Daniel, were to go see the King yourself to ask how the case is coming along?" He sees me hesitate but goes on. "I'm just thinking out loud, but if the King tends to take his local clients for granted, maybe it would take an out-of-towner to light a fire under his butt."

I consider for a second, appreciating Scott's resourcefulness. "I think that's a smart idea," I say.

But Teresa has her doubts. "That'd be nice and all, but the thing is, if the King really is trying his hardest, it'd be a kick in the you-know-what for an outsider to be doubtin' him."

"I wouldn't be doubting him exactly," I say, warming to the idea. "I'd just be asking for a progress report, like lawyers are used to giving every day. Maybe we can speed him up, in case he's been dragging his feet for some reason. I mean, I'm sure you've gotten as much out of him as anyone could, but the addition of an extra person might do the trick."

The idea still makes Teresa nervous. "What if he's just building up a head of steam slowly, though?" she asks. "'Cause he might drag his heels even more if he thinks we're yanking his chain."

"He's your lifeline, I get that," I say. "But asking for an update shouldn't jeopardize that. Especially if we assure him we think he's doing a great job."

"Well, if you do it that way, sure, go ahead," Teresa concedes. "It ain't been fun waiting all this time, I'll grant you that."

"While I'm at it, maybe I could speak to some of your extended family to see if they're aware of your situation." I watch Scott, wondering if I've gone too far.

"I can't say I love the idea?" Scott says. "But heck, why not. Maybe they'll come up with some angle we haven't thought of yet."

"One thing, though," Teresa asks me. "Who'd be paying you for your time?"

"You kidding? I should be paying you for taking my mind off myself," I say, hoisting myself up from the couch. Sensing departure, the little one tearfully reaches out his arms for me to pick him up.

"Vaughan, you can't always be crying when someone leaves, you monkey," Sarah says, scooping him up and giving him a tickle under his arms.

"Thank you, Mister Rose," Teresa says.

"I'm not a mister," I say, squeezing her hand. "I'm just Dan, OK?"

"OK, but don't get hurt setting your hopes too high," Teresa warns me. "Good things generally don't happen to people like us."

"Except for the monkeys!" Scott reminds her.

"Except for them," Teresa agrees.

CHAPTER 20

GOES WITHOUT SAYIN'

BECAUSE HERE'S HOW I see it. I was chugging along in the train of my marriage when suddenly the engine blew. All the ardor I was carrying for my wife got halted midway. But as it happened there was a train alongside me on a parallel track heading in a new direction. That was the Mary train, as driven by Tony. So I offloaded onto the Mary train and went chugging along there for a while, until that engine also blew, at which point I offloaded again—onto the train of Mary's family. So all the zeal and energy I originally had for my marriage is still here; it's just chugging along on a new track. Same devotion. Different recipients. Make sense?

Meanwhile, I'm cooling my heels in the waiting room of the King's office. "Am I any closer to seeing him?" I ask again. "It's been over forty-five minutes already."

"Like I say, he's a busy man," says his high-efficiency secretary, clacking away on his keyboard.

The room is a dazzling display of cowboy kitsch. Loops of lariat ropes are shellacked and mounted between watercolors of bucking stallions. Profiles of mighty miniaturized buffaloes are bronzed in bas-relief. Antique stirrups merit pedestals of their own. It's a marvel— all the outlaw passion of the unruly frontier commodified into cutesy nostalgic collectables. Triumph of the Fake Wild West.

By the time the yodeling songs of Gene Autry, "the singing cowboy," begin looping a third time, I hear the bullhorn voice of the King reverberating toward me down the hall. "Howdy-howdy," he says, ushering me into his office with a large sweep of his arms as though hustling a cow onto a truck. "I hope you've brought written permission to speak to me," he says as he tumbles into his Ben Cartwright throne and yawns enormously.

I hand him a paper Teresa signed before I left their house. Beneath the Scooby-Doo logo, my scrawl reads: "I, Teresa Trumbull, give Daniel Rose permission to talk about my case with the King." I redid the s in *case* to ensure it didn't look like an *r*. The last thing I want is the King to think I'm questioning his "care."

"Looks good, amigo. What can I do you for?" The first thing to know about the King is this: He really is kingly. Up close he is matinee-idol handsome. Not only the sheer bulk—there's also a largeness of life emanating from the man. A snappy dresser, literally—his cowboy shirt has pearl snaps for buttons. He's one of these immensely likable fellows, mostly by dint of how much he likes himself before it spills over onto you. Just being in his powerful presence makes you feel more good-humored and charismatic than you normally do, like you might want to try wearing a cowboy crown yourself, topped with costume jewels. I have to resist being swallowed by his magnetism so I can ask the hard questions I have to ask. Still, I can't help thinking: Could I pull off having a throne like his, cushy with layers of rainbow-colored lambswool?

Luckily there's plenty of vanity, too, his obvious soft spot. I decide to lay the flattery on extra thick.

"Right off the bat I want to say I've been hearing great things about you all over town," I begin. "That you're not only a crackerjack lawyer but also civic-minded."

"OK, you got your first minute free," he says. "To what do we owe the displeasure?"

"Brass tacks, I'm wondering where we are with Teresa's disability case."

As congenial as he is, it would be a mistake to think the King's a pushover. Behind the ole-boy conviviality there's a slyness in his eyes that bespeaks a razor-sharp intelligence. In the manner of many small-town dynamos, he's too smart to actually hold office or serve any sort of public function, preferring to be the power behind the local ruling council, where he can get more done with less exposure. He swivels to the small fridge beside him, extracts a purple slushy, and takes a manly sip.

"You figure 'cause it's taking a little longer than a New York minute, you're going to hold a match to my backwoods balls."

"Honestly, I'm not jumping to any conclusions," I rush to say. "I'm just trying to help the family get a sense of how much longer it's going to take. I mean, you're the King, so tell me if I'm wrong, but it seems like not much progress has been made since the settlement seven years ago."

"All seventeen thousand worth, as I recall."

"Which seems kinda low for someone who can barely move."

The King smiles sadly, casting his gaze out the window across the street to where the orange-suited prisoners are pacing between their chain-link traffic cones.

"Damn shame what happened to their first lawyer in that Honda Civic of his. With my schedule I never should have rushed in to pick up the pieces of his caseload. But I'm a softie, did it out of respect for a dear departed colleague."

"And of course concern for the Trumbulls," I say with a smile.

The King masks his expression by taking another sip. "Goes without sayin'," he says.

That was a bad move on my part. "Sorry, I don't mean to seem over-anxious," I say.

The King waves it off, no harm done. He picks up a photo of his handsome family from the desk, its rustic wood frame ornamented with tiny Colt .45 pistols, and seems to calculate a minute. "Tell you what, champ. Which you want first: good news or bad?"

"Let's get the bad out of the way."

He nods. "To be frank, I'm not entirely sure we're gonna win this thing. New Mexico's such a poor state, with everyone and his uncle looking for disability, that there's nowhere near enough money for all the deserving people who need it. Then there's her youth. The last thing the government wants is to carry a person her age the rest of her hopefully long and happy life. So that's two strikes right there. Plus we're up against a judge in Texas, because El Paso is the administrative hub for the region. And they're hard-ass over there. You ever hear the expression 'hanging judge'? Judge Smith, he's one of the worst. Short and sweet? The odds aren't pretty."

"Can I be of assistance?"

"You hot and heavy to help?" he asks. "Tell you what. If you've got the nose for it, you could hunt down some doctors' opinions, because we're not as strong as we'd like to be in the medical department. We could use some letters testifying to her medical condition."

"That's gotta be the crux of our case, right?"

The King nods. "Problem is, the docs can't put their finger on exactly what's eatin' her. Without a firm diagnosis, they don't like to sound airy-fairy. But if you can find a bona fide MD to vouch for her condition, that'd be worth its weight in gold."

"Is there specific wording you need?"

"We need a statement, on letterhead, stating she can't lift anything over ten pounds. She is down-for-the-count disabled based on her condition. *Can't sit or stand more than ninety minutes* would be a good phrase, but I'm not expecting miracles. Anything in that neighborhood would be gravy."

I'm writing it down. "She also seems depressed," I say, thinking of her upside-down smile. "How about a letter from a psychologist attesting to her mental condition?"

He fires his index finger at me as if to say I've got my thinking cap on. "Unfortunately, the town's only psychologist is showing his Dobermans over in Germany for the month. Closest we got is a fill-in shrinkologist with a part-time office down by the sewage plant. But all this has to be done fast, 'cause here's the good news I was getting ready to notify them about: we got a court date in two weeks."

"That's great!" I sputter. "So do we have time to get what you need?"

"You get your East Coast in the groove, you might just!"

I'm elated, stammering about how good it is to be in good hands, given how much this case means to everyone concerned.

The King accepts my gratitude magnanimously. "So you see you didn't need to be gettin' your pointy head in a vise," he says, notching what look like handcrafted ostrich boots against the desktop and kicking back in his throne. "The King's got all the bases covered!"

"I apologize if I came on too strong; it's just so crucial to the Trumbulls."

"All good," he assures me. "Fact is, it's healthy for us shitkickers to get goosed by a Yankee know-it-all every now and again, show us how it's done. With you leading the charge, we'll see just what kind of fortune we can rustle up for dear disabled Rhoda."

"Teresa," I say, uncertainly.

"Goes without sayin'," he says, flipping me a business card with his knuckles, expertly, like we used to try to do with baseball cards in the schoolyard.

I rise from my chair, feeling mostly good. A little handled, but mostly good. I only wish I hadn't lost my home keys so I could feel a little more secure in the world. "Oh, one more thing," I remember to say. "We were thinking that I may be able to get some background from the larger family too. You know, to give the judge a sense of the big picture? I mean not just Teresa's background but maybe look into her mother-in-law Mary's life, too, while I'm at it? How rough their lives were, that sort of thing?"

"That's the Mary got herself beheaded all those years ago? Hell, if you got the stomach for it, the more the merrier. We'll play the sympathy card. Assuming the whole scenario was a snake pit, as I can almost guarantee you it was, we'll feed the judge a sob story and open the floodgates of charity!"

"Well that's great, then. Let's you and me go out some evening and grab a drink together."

"I sure would like that, pardner, but see I don't drink."

"Neither do I! We'll have a nondrink together!"

"No can do, compadre. Wish I could, but there are just too damn many—"

As if to underscore the point, he takes a finger and gives his spurs a twirl.

Briiiiing-briiiiing!

Nice touch: time's up.

CHAPTER 21

JORNADA DEL MUERTO

WAS I JUST given the bum's rush? Kind of, but who cares, so long as the King's on top of things. I feel pumped, almost literally, like my tires are rock-hard with new air—ready to get medical testimony and go meet the rest of Mary's family. I call Mary's older brother Sandy to tell him of our odd connection and invite myself over. Then I hop on my bike for the thirteen-mile ride, past the usual roadside crash markers and a vanished racetrack with an old hand-painted sign of cars cheerfully tumbling into each other, down to the Green family homestead in Caballo.

A snake pit it's not. It's a tidy trailer park under the lip of Interstate 25, with trucks and SUVs roaring along just out of sight. Six thousand vehicles a day, did Tony say? That's a lot of traffic to be hearing night and day. But the panoramic view in front is commanding: Caballo Lake and the mountains lit up like a jumbo drive-in movie screen—not unlike the view of Turtleback that Scott could enjoy from his house if he chose to open his curtains. A couple of gleaming motorboats are parked in the yard of Sandy's trailer, amid cheerful signs saying, Welcome, Friends! and A Hunter and a Normal Person Live Here.

A Roy Rogers lookalike, handsome and genial, lopes out the front door in a Stetson hat to meet me on the driveway. "Hey, that spot's reserved for the bartender! Only kidding, Dan, you park anywhere you like!"

Sandy gives me a warm double handshake: one hand to clasp and the other to cap it off on top. "Boy, you don't see many of these workhorses around anymore," he says, stepping back to admire my bike, then fingering a piece of black rubber coming off the end of my hand grip. "Drop of Liquid Tape would fix that right up."

"How you adjusting to our little corner of God's country?" asks Sandy's wife, an attractive lady by the name of Lola, stepping out of the trailer with ice water and a slab of pecan cake on a heart-shaped plastic tray.

"Tell the truth, I've yet to hear one unfascinating thing since getting here," I say. "Nothing has not riveted me."

"Well, good for us, I guess!" says Lola with a spirited air, cutting me a piece of cake. "This is from our sister-in-law's very own pecan trees up in Socorro. She has two of 'em right out the back door." We sit outside on ceramic patio chairs, and I'm grateful at how sunny and scrubbed clean everything is. This is the heart of where Mary grew up, and it's blessedly normal.

Sandy's left forearm is tanned darker than his right. About what you'd expect for a man who was a long-distance bus driver for Greyhound, his arm propped in the window for twenty-five years.

I take a chance on asking him something unexpected. "Do you consider yourself lucky?"

"I don't know. Rackin' up a total of three million miles, the equivalent of driving around the globe a whole bunch of times, and never had so much as a serious sideswipe? I guess that's lucky. Luckier than my sister Mary, I guess."

There, the subject has been broached. We transition to Mary, and he lets me take notes on the stories he tells that are horrifying and moving, both. I'm amazed at how candid he is, and gratefully fill out page after page of my torn notebook. One of the stories, about how Mary tumbled out of a car when she was a toddler, is so disturbing I almost can't bear to write it down.

"So she just kept repeating that all her life?" I ask, when he finishes the incident. "Getting knocked out of cars and knocking others out?"

"I don't know about 'repeating,'" Sandy says, "but I'm not surprised it was on Broadway that it happened, near where she hit you later. That's a bad stretch of road for our family right there. Not only did Mary fall out there at one and a half, but when she was nine our daddy died wandering over the center line and hitting a tobacco truck, never regaining consciousness. Then as an adult Mary had another crash where Broadway leads south from town, when she flipped her black VW into a ravine and nearly died."

"Enough about that," Lola says. "Who wants another slice of cake?"

"I got a fuzzy-duzzy theory why that is, if you want to hear," Sandy goes on. "Just a theory, but Broadway parallels that there death stretch of Jornada del Muerto right there, the so-called Journey of Death outside of town. Maybe they're both bad news?"

"That's a little over my head," I say.

"Or under," Lola says.

"Well, I warned him it was fuzzy-duzzy!" Sandy says calmly. "Anyway, it's a deadly road for our family, no doubt about that."

"Tell him something positive, Sandy!" Lola says, cutting me another slice. "Tell him about my side of the family. I had one relative who worked for BFGoodrich, and he thought up the idea of a spare tire. Or better than all this talking, let's drive him down to Hatch for the best green chili cheeseburger he ever dreamed of."

"I'd love that," I say, "but right now I'd give anything to see any family photos you might have."

Sandy disappears into the trailer through a side screen while I listen to the sound of the interstate overhead. Through the trailer window I see the stuffed heads of big game mounted on the living room walls. When Sandy comes back outside, he hands me a framed photo of himself as a kid: a good-looking redhead with freckles. There's something lovable about him, assuming it was himself I wanted a picture of.

"Not of you!" Lola says, amused. She smacks him on the butt to move out of the way and soon comes back with a photo album, opening it to a colorful family portrait where all the siblings are squeezed together arm in arm, circa 1965. But Mary's a little blurred, half smudged behind her brothers, so I can't really make her out.

"Hold on, we'll get you something to see better," Lola says. She snatches a pair of reading glasses off Sandy's nose and puts them on my face so I can lean in close. It takes four or five seconds for my mind to reformulate the memory, and then: *ping*. She is back. That was Mary, all right. I can see the truth of that moment when she cradled my head. She was sorrowful. She was capable of trying to comfort me.

One other thing's for sure: Mary did have sexuality in spades. By evidence of these pictures, she was like one of the eternally unavailable high school girls when I was in junior high, the sweater girls Tony and I beheld with awe. She's a throwback to my earliest fantasies, even before Farrah Fawcett. There's also a hint of something wrong in these photos: premature weariness. Mary's a little worse for wear already, and life hasn't even begun to show her who's boss.

I ask Sandy if I could make a copy of the picture, because Scott has no recollection of what his mother looks like.

"He don't?" Sandy clucks with concern. "That boy was always kind of a lost soul."

"Yet he's smart as a whip."

"But he won't hug anyone!"

"He sure hugs his kids, Sandy."

"I'm sincerely glad to hear it," Sandy says, shaking his head dubiously.

"I think Sandy reached out to Scott a buncha years ago, didn't you, honey?" Lola says. "But he resisted our efforts."

Shrugging, Sandy walks me around the trailer park to point out the little shop by the road out front and tell me more details about Mary's life. Over here she . . . out there she. . . . Overhead, the highway keeps up its rhythmic drone. The whole time he talks I'm thinking that Sandy is exactly the sort of man you'd want at the steering wheel of the long-distance bus ride when you wake up in the middle of the night not knowing where you are, and you look up past rows of snoring passengers to the front. Seeing him at the steering wheel, the daddy of the bus, perhaps the only one awake in that part of Iowa or Idaho or wherever you are at 2:35 a.m., with his hair neatly parted and an aura of deep calm, you nestle back into the seat fabric and nod off, secure in his hands.

A good man. Why should I be surprised?

Back at my bike where Lola waits, Sandy double-shakes my hand again, almost like lost family.

"You come back again, we'll take you fishin'!" he says.

"Even better, to a rodeo," Lola says, handing me the photo album to borrow. "How's that sound to you?"

. .

A rodeo it is. Next morning the extended family—minus Scott's unit, of course—has gathered at the rodeo grounds for a memorial fundraiser for a sister-in-law's nephew, a budding rodeo star who died of leukemia at the age of fifteen. Such is the clan's tight-knit support system that they've come to town from miles around. One truck even has snow still melting off its hood from the mountains up north.

"This here's Daniel," Lola says, making the intros as cowboys get ready by kicking up dirt inside the ring. "I haven't known him very long, but I feel like I have."

"Why, thank you, Lola," I say.

"Daniel's here to find out about sister Mary, who knocked him with her truck one time, and come to find out her story's a lot more interesting than his own!"

I trust my surprise doesn't show. But I guess it does because she adds, "You wouldn't put it that way?"

"Well, I guess I—"

She cuts me off to point out more family in the crowd. "That's someone's stepgrandma on the barbecue, frying up a storm. If she fixes you a burger, tell her you like it rare, or it'll come out like this." Discreetly she opens her burger to show its pearl-colored interior. "That good-lookin' fella over there, that's Mary's kid brother Owen—owns a butcher shop down in Arrey next to Stickem's bar. He's a little private but a fine fella. And over there by the palomino? That's Charlie Cox, the old sheriff from about your era. He could tell you some stories, if you ever cornered him alone."

"Is he family too?"

"Not that I know of. But he did arrest one of Mary's cousins once for shoplifting, so he's practically family."

The crowd cheers as two riders lasso a steer. "What're they trying to do?"

"The first cowboy ropes his head and the second ropes his foot. A header and a heeler."

"Do women participate too?"

She elbows me sharply in the ribs. "Bet your ass!"

I walk to the concession stand where Sandy's ordering coffee and a Snickers. "Breakfast of champions!" he says, before leading me to a select spot on the bleachers among Mary's brothers Roy and Paul, all with identical black Stetsons. More stories get exchanged as I take notes: how Mary did this . . . when Mary did that . . . never *why* Mary did anything because they never knew why. Her reasons were her own.

"When it happened, her death, how'd you find out?"

The trio of brothers watch the rodeo in silence for a while. Eventually Sandy clears his throat.

"We'd gone elk hunting, all three of us boys," he says, keeping his eyes on the action inside the ring. "Went on a Friday, found a sweet spot to camp. Saturday morning my friend drove up, gave us the news." He clears his throat again. "Happened in Phoenix. She was so far gone, it had taken a couple days to ID her. Her body had blackened in the Arizona heat."

I hate asking the questions I have to ask if I want to get the whole story. "What was your reaction?"

Sandy's countenance slowly changes as he continues watching the rodeo. I would have thought he'd cover his eyes, maybe put a hand up to keep me from seeing, but he pushes his Stetson a little higher off his brow, exposing them instead. A vulnerable gesture.

"All of us were crying. Next morning we hunted only half a day, didn't kill anything. So that year was not the best elk hunting."

One of the brothers slips his bandanna to another so he can dab at his eyes. The last brother takes the bandanna and blows his nose. Lola slides in next to me and lightens the mood.

"Roy used to rope right in this ring, didn't you, Roy? But Sandy never cared for riding much. He doesn't even like to ride a bumpy car anymore."

"I was always more interested in girls anyhow," Sandy says.

Lola smirks, looping her arm through mine. "Dan here's becoming a regular part of the family," she says. "Maybe he'd like to run up to the Legion post with us to pack candy boxes for the troops sometime? Next one's day after tomorrow."

· ·

Gummy bears. Chocolate Kisses. Bubble gum. Lollipops. We're in a line working our way around a long table loaded with two dozen varieties of candy. The idea is to stuff the American Legion boxes full with a few of each, which the troops can either keep for themselves or hand out to make friends with the Iraqi kids.

"You keep stepping into the back of Daniel's boot," Lola warns a pretty old lady behind me, wearing a pretty old-lady sweater she might have knit herself.

"I don't know what's come over me," the lady tells me flirtatiously.

"But you keep doin' it!" Lola says possessively, slapping the lady's hand from my collar, which the lady has reached to straighten out for me. "He's ourn!"

"I just want him to notice my perfume. Nice, isn't it?"

"Nice," I say.

"A heap nicer than the perfume Lola's sister-in-law Mary used to wear, I can tell you that."

"Really?" I ask. "What was *her* perfume?"

The lady waits a beat, then shoots a "take that!" smile at Lola.

"Booze!"

..

OK, I admit it. What I'm doing now is going way beyond helping with Teresa's case. But I feel I'm in this deep, I may as well go all the way. Another night I arrange to meet Sandy and Lola to play bingo and fill in more of Mary's history. I arrive back at the lodge, sweating nervously. But I'm relieved when I see them waving me in and patting the chair they've saved for me under the humongous moose head overhead. A burger and fries waiting for me under a paper napkin never looked so good.

"G-49!" shouts the caller.

"Yeah, she made friends easily, but enemies too," Sandy confirms. "Wives, mostly. They didn't appreciate having their men stolen out from under 'em. Jumped her more than once in the alleyway."

"B-14!"

I get ketchup on my notepad racing to keep up. Sandy's some kind of bingo prodigy, conducting not only his game but patiently helping Lola and me with our games too. "You missed that N-45 right there."

Bingo takes more mental concentration than I imagined. Sandy's cool in the clinches, but I'm flustered, green ink on my fingertips from rushing to fill in numbers.

"O-70!"

"Were you some sort of math whiz in school?" I ask Sandy.

"I'm pretty good with numbers," he says matter-of-factly, reaching over to daub something for me, a B-3 I missed three or four calls ago.

He's managing to keep up his end of the conversation even while retaining old numbers in his head to help out Lola and me. And then I notice he's doing not one game of his own but three! That's five games total, while squirting extra cheese on his fries and chewing at a leisurely pace. My burger sits untouched on its Styrofoam plate, cold as the slice of American cheese on top.

"Was Mary as smart as you?" I ask.

"Smarter."

• •

Probate court, judge's chamber. "Smart?"

"Yes, she was smart . . . as a thief," Josie Zamora is telling me. "Smart enough to wait for my brother Sandy to fall asleep before she broke into his trailer to steal arrowheads dear to his heart." Josie is not only T or C's part-time probate judge, she's also the sister of Mary's first husband, Braurio, so I don't expect to hear many good words from her. But in her other role as volunteer paramedic, she also happened to be first on the scene of one of Mary's bloodier crashes, and I don't expect to hear words like these either:

"She'd rolled her black VW into the ravine sometime during the night and wasn't spotted till nearly dawn. And there the poor thing was lookin' up at me saying, 'Please help me.' I remembered the professional paramedic pledge I'd made to do whatever I could for anyone, no matter who they were, and I worked hard to keep her alive. Her beautiful blond hair was tangled all bloody in the steering wheel, and I had to cut it off to get her free. She had broke nearly everything—and her neck. Mary almost died three times on the way to the hospital, and I revived her each time. But after that, the drinkin' got even worse, you know—a bad drinkin' woman. There she was, hobbling around with broken legs on crutches and that halo gizmo, and still she'd go running around in cars with guys. I used to see her driving off with them. I can only imagine what they'd do to her."

• •

Next day Josie's brother Braurio, Mary's first husband, has two simple words to say over the phone when I ask him why their marriage failed.

"She wandered," he says simply. "Took off whenever the mood hit. The first time it happened I put out an APB, but I came to understand that was just her way. After she did that a few more times, I wouldn't take her back. I was with the highway department and got myself transferred to the cliff dwellings up at Gila National Monument, surveying the road to get there. At that time it was mostly water through the upper canyon, and one night up she comes in her car. She drove all that muddy mule track to fetch me home. And there she is and I say no more. That was that."

"Have you had a good life since then?"

"Oh yes. Married thirty years to a *good* woman."

••

Another conversation takes place with a Native American elder I run into at a deserted Apache ghost town some distance away. Eddie Montoya is sitting alone in the open doorway of his car, exuberantly eating pickled sausages out of a glass jar, when I bike up and say hello. His face crinkles with good humor, telling me he had a feeling that today was the right day to meet someone in the village where he was raised.

"I'm interested in you!" Eddie exclaims, opening his door wide. "I don't know why, but I am!"

With so many connections coming out of the woodwork, I'm not surprised when we soon make the link to Mary. He turns out to be Josie's other brother, former brother-in law of Mary through Braurio. "I remember Mary Green," he says quietly. "She had one eye that was a little crossed. Most people looked at her for years and couldn't see it. But to me that said she had a troubled soul. She had a spirit in conflict with itself. She prayed not to be in trouble, but she wasn't up to the task."

"You remember well," I say.

"I have a good memory. My mother used to say I could remember things from two years before I was born. Funny that I can remember back, but I can't remember forward!"

He giggles silently at his humor, then takes another sausage from the jar and gobbles it down like it's the best food that ever was. "With you there is no friction," he tells me. "When you first cycled up I expected friction, but there was none. I knew I was supposed to come here today."

I'm starting to think there's something sacred about Eddie, like he's kind of a medicine man, but I'm trying to square that with how impish his face is. Maybe it's the impishness that makes him sacred? For his part, Eddie keeps trying to suss me out, a mischievous spark in his eyes. "Everything is connected," he says. "To me the biggest mystery is how it led to this. We met here in the place my family used to live, and we got talking, find out we're practically brothers, and now what is to happen? What is to happen next?"

Suddenly I'm ready to leave. It has been only a few minutes, but it's been intense. I put out my hand to shake goodbye, but Eddie informs me that my grip is too firm.

"With my tribe, we do it loose, so the heart of my palm touches the heart of your palm. If we do it hard your way, that doesn't happen."

I try it his way and he's right. The palms touch. I've never appreciated a loose handshake before, but now I see: loose can be more intimate.

"Before you go, I want to do something," he tells me. He extracts a beaten leather pouch from his vest pocket and a plastic baggie of loose tobacco. "We've been using up the spirit, so we have to give some back," he explains, sprinkling a small amount of tobacco on the ground between us. Then he opens a black plastic film container to reveal bright orange-yellow powder inside. "This is the pollen of the cattails," he says. "I was going to scatter it out, but now I want to give it to you." He takes a pinch of powder and smears it on my lips: sideways then up and down. "This means you will tell the truth and you can't lie. Not that you would lie anyway, but this means you can't, even if you wanted to. It is to tell your stories with truth."

CHAPTER 22

WARTS 'N' ALL

IT FEELS EERILY familiar, being at Scott's house again—almost déjà vu as I step over the PVC pipes in the yard, as I look at the drunk-driving billboards above the home of a man who does neither, as I stand under the cobwebby yellow porch light that never goes off. It's like I've been here many times, though it's only my second visit.

Once again three locks click on the door that opens only partway. Once again a good-natured man lies on the wall-to-wall while two pale-skinned boys in bathing suits treat him like their personal exercise machine. Once again the gurrls are a little reserved at first but quickly warm up. Is that meth being cooked next door? It smells a little like the inside of a rubber ball—a mix of mold and cotton candy. But I don't mind. Scott's house is furry-warm, like being inside a bear's den. I'm snugged into a primordial family unit that's making itself work.

The boys are no longer bashful with me. A distinctly mixed blessing. "Cowboy!" they scream, squiggling through my arms and legs, taking turns pulling on the back of the broken couch.

Draike Vaughan or Vaughan Draike. I still can't tell them apart, and frankly I'm in no hurry to. Beautiful as they are in their bright-eyed particulars, I prefer to see them as pieces of sheer protoplasm—Proto and Plasm, the fundamental, flesh-colored substance of life—as they snap off the plastic Scooter Bug's yellow head and thrust it in my face. "Can you put new berries in?"

"'Batteries,'" Sarah translates. "He has trouble with his *t*s."

"Still has his cast on, I see."

"No, this is his other wrist," Scott says. "How he sprained 'em both so fast, I do not get. I leave him alone for five minutes to take a you-know-what and he hurts the second one? Oh yeah, they're ornery as heck," he chuckles proudly. "Scram back to your project now and leave the cowboy alone!"

"They're doing a little house fix-up," Teresa explains. And so they are. The boys hop to the corner and busy themselves dripping water from a McDonald's cup onto the carpet, adding cement powder from a box and shaping it to fill the hole where the centipedes come out.

"We having fun yet?" Scott asks me, getting up from the floor and clearing a path for me to sit.

"Well, it was a good meeting with the King," I tell him. "He's a smooth operator, but maybe that's what we want in a situation like this. Bottom line is he's got a court date in under two weeks."

Scott's head rocks back. "Holy smoke!"

"But he's not overly optimistic," I caution. "I've taken the liberty of making some doctor appointments to beef up your case between now and then."

"Good going," Scott says.

"But first I want to tell you I took a few days to dig a little around your family history."

Scott squirms at this news and chuckles preemptively. "Hate to know what came crawling out from under that rock," he says.

"Some bad, some good," I say. "Want to hear?"

He's struggling. "I mean, I'm curious and all, if you don't think it's gonna mess up my head too bad."

"I think you can handle it, but only you can decide."

Scott picks up a boy's stray sneaker and tosses it in the corner, where it bounces like a tennis ball. "Heck, it's now or never. I'm bound and determined to learn this."

"That's a yes?"

"Let 'er rip."

I take a folded-up paper from my pocket that I've copied from the family album. "First off, you say you've never seen a photo of your mom?"

"Actually, no." He smiles a conflicted smile.

"Would you like to?"

He thinks a second. "Actually, I would."

Teresa and Sarah crowd in close. Scott studies the photo like it's a street map of Mars.

"Insane," he says. His lips are parted as he breathes softly through his mouth. Proto and Plasm have flocked over. Scott catches their cementy hands before they can touch him.

"That would be your great-grandma," he tells the boys.

"Actually, no—their grandma," I say.

"I guess you're right?" Scott says. "She's so far gone it seems like another step removed."

"I've got a whole album in my bike pouch, if you want to see more," I say.

Scott upends one of the boys and tucks him to his armpit. "Keep it comin'," he says. "In for a Peter, in for a Paul, whatever that expression's supposed to be."

I return from my bike and open the album before him to display sepia photos from the 1930s: a field of low-growing crops, a tidy little shop by the roadside. "Your mom's dad came out to New Mexico in 1936 to start farming," I continue. "He established the family homestead, I guess you'd call it, on a nice little piece of land near Caballo Lake not far south of here. He grew cotton, corn, alfalfa—"

"Where were they before?" Sarah asks.

"Texas and Oklahoma."

"But I mean, way back?"

"Scotland. Ireland. Though some of the Oklahoma folks intermarried with local Cherokee out there. So it looks like you may have a little proud Indian blood running through your veins, Scott."

"I'm not surprised," he says.

"That's where your mom was born, on May 24, 1945, one of eight children: three boys, three girls, and a pair of twins who died in childbirth. You with me?"

"All the way," Scott says, letting go of the kids so they can resume their cement work. "Easy with the water," he reminds them as they drip more on the carpet between them.

"After your grandfather tired of farming, he and his younger brother set up a nice little trailer park there in Caballo, renting out hookups for other trailers passing through and running a bait shop for people who wanted to fish in the lake."

"That's the snapshot there," Scott tells his gurrls, who nod.

"This is a rock-solid family, really devoted to each other. Caring, kind—"

"Not trailer trash?"

I'm startled. "No way," I tell him. "They're people to be proud of, Scott, like the backbone of America. Gentle. Thoughtful. Considerate. Your uncle Sandy—"

"Yeah, I heard Sandy's a good guy."

"Really good guy, Scott. Courteous, capable—the kind of guy I'd want around my Thanksgiving table. And his wife, Lola, a classy lady who makes the world's best pecan cake. You ought to try it sometime. Sandy himself was a long-distance bus driver. He drove to Alaska fourteen times and racked up a perfect safety record."

"Kind of ironic," Scott says, "that he'd be a boy scout behind the wheel and his sister was a crash addict."

"Right? Equally ironic is that the whole family has lived for a couple of generations right below the interstate, while all those drivers whiz by above, most of them with no clue of the complex family dramas they're missing right under their noses."

I tap my finger on one of the photos, a girl with blond braids and a pretty smile.

"Nor of the heartbreak either," I say. "Like something bad that happened to this little girl, your mom, one winter day a long time ago."

Scott sucks in his breath, girding himself. "OK, hit me," he says.

I decide to tell the disturbing story Sandy told me back on his patio, about baby Mary tumbling out of the car on the way back from the grocery store.

Scott winces. "How the—?"

"Things were different in those days. Most car doors didn't have locks, and of course no seat belts. Even worse was that the rear doors opened from the front to make it easier to get in and out. They were called suicide doors, because if they weren't closed all the way, they could pop open. Passengers were likely to get thrown out, especially going around a bend, which is what happened to Mary when she was one and a half."

"One and a half!" Scott cries. "That's littler than Vaughan!"

Teresa groans with sympathy, clutching her back that's seized up.

"It was a pretty nasty bang, apparently. They had to pick glass shards out of her forehead."

"Poor thing," the three adults coo. Scott has to expel extra air in empathy.

"She started having fits shortly afterward," I say.

"What do you mean, 'fits'?"

"Seizures. Your uncle Sandy recalls sitting at the supper table as a kid when she started having one, and Sandy said, 'Mary's crazy.' His dad nodded to him, which meant he should go out back with him, where he took a willow switch and—I consult the notebook in my pocket. "'And slapped the pee outa me.' His words."

"So you think that tumble mighta had something to do with the way she acted later?"

"It's certainly possible. From then on, she seemed different from her siblings. She was supposed to wear glasses after that, for instance, the only one of the kids who didn't have perfect vision."

"Mary wore glasses?"

"Supposed to." I repeat. "Clearly she wasn't the sort to do what people said she ought to do."

"Sounds like a regular wildcat," Scott says. "I kinda like that. Shows spunk."

"To a point," I say. "Cause's there's wildcat. And then there's wildcat. And this is where the story gets kinda rough. You still good to go?"

Scott looks at his sons patting the mound of cement with wet fingers. "Good to go," he says.

"By the time she hit her teens, Mary was wilder than anyone could handle. Boys and cars. Liquor. She was transferred to a home for wayward girls, up in Albuquerque."

"Like reform school for juvenile delinquents?"

"For troubled kids, right," I say. "But they didn't have much luck with her either, and when she was fifteen she stole a car and met a Native American named Braurio. These days his sister is the probate judge here in T or C, and she filled in the details for me."

"Man, you been doin' your homework!" Scott says. "Did you always want to be a detective or something?"

"Can we please not talk about me? So we can stay on track?" I say. "According to Braurio's sister, Mary fed Braurio a song-and-dance about how she couldn't leave the reform school till she was twenty-one unless she got married, so he did the honors and took her down to El Paso, where she proceeded to get into"—I check my notes again—"'a little mischief.'"

"Uh-oh," Scott says.

I pause. "Drugs, I have to say. And maybe a stint at a cathouse across the border in Ciudad Juárez. Sorry."

Teresa lays her hand on Scott's shoulder. Sarah does likewise. Scott blows out his cheeks. "Keep goin'," he says.

"But to hear Braurio tell it—"

"You found her first husband? And he talked to you?" Scott gapes in astonishment.

"I can give you his number if you're interested. He's happily remarried with lots of grandkids, so it's far enough behind him that he said it'd be fine to tell you."

"No, that's OK."

"Mostly I talked with his brother, Eddie Montoya. According to him, her soul was good. But even so, it didn't stop her from breaking into Braurio's trailer and stealing that prize collection of arrowheads he'd found in the mountains, just so she could afford to go to another bar."

Scott gnaws his lip while Sarah and Teresa squeeze his shoulders. "That's a little hard to hear."

"Should I stop?"

"Lay it on me, brother. Don't leave out none of the bad stuff."

I go down my bullet points. "This was during the Vietnam War, and one of Mary's brothers was stationed at Fort Bliss in El Paso, and he introduced her to a soldier named Tommy McLaughlin, who took her home to Stilwell, Oklahoma, where she became Mary Louise McLaughlin and tried being a housewife. But a year later she left Tommy to live with her mom back in the family complex, having various car crashes, one of which involved hitting a couple of Connecticut boys on Broadway in 1970."

"And the rest is history."

"Hardly!" I say. "Our crash wasn't even a blip on her radar screen. You were right—no one in her family ever heard a peep about ours. Not that they were immune to crashes, themselves."

"Drinkin'?"

I nod. "'I mean, I'm not trying to pretend the family didn't have their share of hell-raising. Because they did. It's just that Mary's behavior was on a different level entirely. Anyway, she divorced McLaughlin and two months later married a younger Mexican man by the name of Fernandez. Then there was someone named McCoy whose two sons from an earlier marriage ended up in prison, then some cowboy who took her to Montana for three years, and then your dad, who took her to Florida. The custody battle was pretty gruesome. I'll spare you the details."

"No," Scott says, "I need to hear it all. Only way I'm going to lay it to rest."

"Well, most of the evidence was about the drinking. They say, when she was drinking, watch out, 'cause she'd get in fistfights with women and men alike. Even when she was pregnant with you, Scott, she didn't stop. She *couldn't* stop."

Scott scrunches his face one way, then the other. Teresa tries to come to his rescue. "Didn't she never try AA?"

"Sandy took her several times, even put her in two rehabs. But she'd get out and try one sip and that'd be that."

I put my notes away, hoping I never have to open them again.

"So that's the story," I say. "I may have missed a few husbands along the way, but that's the gist. After that she married Richard Filip, the guy who killed her."

Instinctively, all three of us turn to the boys in the corner to make sure they're not paying attention. They're still engrossed in the challenge of filling the centipede hole. I hurry to summarize the rest, about how Filip was an ex–Green Beret with PTSD. How Mary finally broke free of his clutches and started sobering up, even going to church six Sundays in a row, but she went back and soon had him arrested for domestic violence. How he spent thirty days in jail, got out on Friday, murdered her on Sunday. Ultimately, he pleaded manslaughter and served ten years, being turned down for parole every time he applied.

"There's a document in here somewhere," I say, pulling out a piece of paper from the backflap of the photo album: a letter from the Arizona Board of Executive Clemency, dated July 12, 1998.

> In compliance with Arizona Revised Statutes (13-4414.C),
> this is to inform you that when the board met and consid-
> ered the above-named inmate, Richard Filip, they voted to
> DENY: PAROLE

We sit there, the three of us poring over the document in the cartoon-colored dusk, until I tuck the document back and open the album again to what I hope is a neutral page. There's a photo of Mary sitting at a kitchen table with three homemade pies in front of her. Then I notice that the way the photo is angled, the top of her head's cut off. Yikes. Quickly I turn the page, hoping Scott didn't notice.

"She died in 1989 at age forty-four," I conclude.

"Quite a life," Scott says. "The good, the bad, and the ugly, though I gotta say I'm hard-pressed to see the good."

"Oh, but there was," I hasten to say. "I've been saving the positive stuff for last. When Mary was sober, everyone adored her. She was a wonderful cook; she made apple dumplings, sometimes so many she'd take them around to give free to everyone in the trailer park, even people just passing through."

Scott adjusts his legs to fit Teresa on his knee, then turns the album his way to thumb through the pages of his mother at home. Mary lying back on a plaid couch with her feet propped on top of a box fan. Mary playing solitaire on a card table, the shelves behind her crammed with plaster figurines of ballet dancers. Mary lifting a casserole out of a yellowish fridge, the cigarette in her lips at a raffish angle, her hair teased up in a bombshell bouffant. The Farrah Fawcett of the trailer park.

"She made everything from scratch," I say, "oatmeal, grits, biscuits with gravy. She made the best Mexican food when the family bait shop got turned into a restaurant for a while. When she was a dinner guest at someone's house, she'd always be first to get up and do the dishes, even wash down the stove for extra measure."

"But the drinking—"

"—is what you've got to understand, Scott. She hated the drinking. She'd always say, 'Pray for me and this dread disease.' But it had such a grip on her. She knew her Bible and she prayed to God . . ."

Scott turns the page of the album to see Mary and her siblings outside with their arms around each other. Brown horses crowd in like members of the family.

"And so pretty," I say. "She had a weight problem off and on, which got her hooked on diet pills. But she had a good heart. Everyone said she'd love you to death."

Scott doesn't look up from the page, where he's studying a photo of his mother waving at the camera, wearing great big seventies-style glasses like she was trying to get used to them at last. He speaks with a catch in his throat. "So she really was kind of a sweetie pie after all, wasn't she, when she wasn't evil? One a them split-personality deals. Ain't that a kick."

"She'd give you the shirt off her back, she was so generous," I say. "And funny. She'd draw people to her, she was so lively. She had a sweet singing voice. She walked around singing a song that had been her favorite since it came out when she was around ten."

"Sweet singing voice? Guess it runs in the family," Sarah says, winking at Scott.

Scott smiles shyly. "Can you get it on the Internet?"

"Already did," I say, clicking my phone. "This here's the Louvin Brothers singing it back in 1956."

At first it seems like just another hillbilly song with a goopy rhythm and sharp pluckings. But then the words start to mean something eerie . . .

> I met a little girl in Hard Knocks Ville
> A town we all know well
> And every Sunday evening
> Out in her home I'd dwell
>
> We went to take an evening walk
> About a mile from town

I picked a stick up off the ground
And knocked that fair girl down;

She fell down on her bended knees
For mercy she did cry
Oh, Willie dear, don't kill me here
I'm unprepared to die

She never spoke another word
I only beat her more
Until the ground around me
Within her blood did flow.

I took her by her golden curls
And I drug her 'round and 'round
Throwing her into the river
That flows through Hard Knocks Ville

Go down, go down, you Hard Knocks girl
With the dark and roving eyes
Go down, go down, you Hard Knocks girl
You can never be my bride.

"Spooky," I say, turning it off. "Almost like she was predicting her own death."

Scott looks shook up. It's one thing for him to hear the old stories about his mother, I guess; quite another for him to learn new ones. "Talk about making your own reality," he says, shaking his head. "A sweet little waltz about bloody murder."

Teresa happens to know the song. "Think they got the name wrong, though," she says. "The right name's supposed to be Knoxville, not Hard Knocks Ville."

"Doesn't matter," Scott explains gently. "Anyplace could stand in for anyplace."

Teresa nods proudly at this wisdom from her husband. Scott lifts the album to put it aside, and a thick envelope falls out, something I haven't seen before. It turns out to contain a letter Mary wrote in pale blue ink to her brother and sister-in-law Roy and Virginia in Socorro.

Dear Roy, Virginia, and boys,
I hope these few lines find you OK. Thank you, for the Valentine's Card & pictures.
The pictures were really good. Thank you.
Virginia, how is your folks doing? We're OK, not nothing new. Here's ya'll some pictures of us we took in January. Ain't little Scott cutest thing you ever seen?
Bye for now. God bless you all.
P.S. I love you all & you're in my prayers daily. Y'all pray for me also.

Then a surprise: bundled in with the letter is a series of loose photos. We take them out and stare, all four of us. A fat newborn in a bassinet, in booties and a pointed hoodie. A fat infant with a straw ten-gallon hat on his head. A fat four-month-old propped on pillows in his crib, holding his head up like a pro.

"Look what a happy baby you were, Scott!" I exclaim at the tot grinning in a high chair, baby food smeared all the way up to his blond bangs. Mary is nibbling his fat arms, nuzzling his neck, nesting him in the crook of her arm as she feeds him a bottle. "Seventy-four days old," says the caption in the same blue penmanship as the letter. "Seventy-five days old."

"Look how crazy she was about you," I say. "Taking pictures of you every day!"

"Good morning," "Pretty baby," say the captions. The pretty baby is being a good sport about the kisses smothering him in shot after shot, a jolly old soul of a baby soaking up every bit of attention he was getting. Her very own sweet baby boy.

"You reckon they'd mind if I borrowed these a while?" Scott asks, staring wide-eyed at a picture of mother and baby lying together on plaid couch cushions held together by duct tape. "I might like to make some copies, if I could."

"Lola said for you to keep them as long as you like."

We turn our attention to the boys, putting final touches on their cement. They've managed to fill the hole so no more centipedes will come out. At least until the centipedes find a new place to come out.

"So was it all right that I showed all this to you?" I ask at last.

Scott doesn't answer for a minute, adjusting Teresa on his knee but keeping her close. "See, here's the deal," he says at last. "If you'd come in here sugarcoating everything, Dan, tryin' to make Mary out to be a saint or like that, I wouldn'ta given you the time a day. But because you trusted me, you respected me, enough to give me the real dope, warts 'n' all, I just wanna say—"

Scott takes a deep breath before trying again to urge the words out.

"Wanna say I get it now. She didn't want to be the screw-up she was. She wanted to be a good mother, but she couldn't do it. Maybe it was fallin' on her head, or maybe something else we don't know about, but if things had been a little easier for her, it mighta gone different. She'd be the Mary she woulda been if she coulda been—respectable like Lola there, or sweet like Teresa, who I'm just gonna have to be as good as I can to till the end of my days . . ."

Teresa wipes tears from her eyes. Sarah is breathing heavily, as though trying to help Scott breathe. No one seems to be able to find the words to say anything more.

So now you know it all! I want to say. And I know, as well. I want to hurl the windows open and let the light flood in—no more secrets, no more shame—but I know it doesn't work like that. It'll take years to process this history. It may take lifetimes. Maybe Proto and Plasm will be able to crack the windows open a bit. But in the meantime . . .

"In the meantime, Scott, we've got Teresa to take care of," I say, getting back to business. "I've got some doctor appointments penciled in for the next few days, if you'd like to confirm them. And speaking of Lola a minute ago, she said she and Sandy had the feeling you want to be left alone, but if you'd ever like to try a bite of pecan cake sometime—"

Scott fidgets uncomfortably.

"Or maybe a ride on his eighteen-foot fishing pontoon. Bet the boys would love that. Hope it was all right that I gave them your number."

"Dan, you just love the idea of this family being all knit back together, don't you?" Teresa says with a laugh. "You're just crazy to see us all stitched up right."

"It does make me feel good," I confess.

"You know what? I'll take a rain check," Scott says. He can't stop gawking at the album pictures. Mary washing a red car with the Caballo Mountains as backdrop. Mary in front of Caballo Lake, hoisting aloft a stringer of catfish. "For now we got our work cut out, gettin' to the doctors."

At this moment the junior parole officers come charging back, clenching me, pushing off from me, bombarding me with questions all at the same time. I'm literally holding on to my hat as they demonstrate their arsenal of playthings that shoot from the wrist and bang in the ear.

"Too many weapons," I yelp, managing to make for the door, abandoning Scott to their entanglements. They're already besieging him with new questions by the time I'm safely out on the porch.

"Dad, Dad, can we get a cathouse, Dad?"

CHAPTER 23

PERFECTLY PLEASANT, MODERATELY OBESE

DOCTORS AT LAST. The only medical people I know in town are also two of the least available. Studds, the emergency-room doc from forty years ago, had his license yanked. Doctor Tom/Tammy from AA, the current emergency-room doc, is in Manila having a long-awaited sex-reassignment operation. We have a little over a week before court to get a real-life doctor to write a letter on Teresa's behalf—plenty of time, I assume, given how obvious her distress is. I assume wrong.

The first appointment is with the primary-care physician at the local clinic who's been treating Teresa for several years. I call the Trumbull household and reach Sarah. "Shall I bike to your place, and you can drive us to the clinic all together?"

A whispered consult. "Well, thing is—wait a minute, Teresa's asking me something (What's that, sweetie? I know, I'm telling him)—thing is, Scott don't like nobody coming over when he's not here."

"Of course. I understand."

"Is it OK if Teresa and I meet you there?"

Sure it is. I bike to the clinic at the appointed time, stashing Flower Power out of the way against the glass vestibule. Sarah and Teresa are in the waiting room, looking especially dam-like in public: concretely self-contained. It's hard to see them so uncomfortable, coping with the world beyond the walls of their house.

"Good morning," I say, taking a seat beside them. "I'm not going to ask how you're feeling. I'll just say, 'Pain the same?'"

"Yes, pain is the same," Teresa says with a forced smile.

"We got here an hour early. Only three people ahead of us," Sarah reports.

It's a generic waiting room, what you'd expect in a clinic that's part of a statewide chain: bad colors, bad music. Among the people waiting with us are my next-door neighbor, munching from a box of fish sticks; Dotty from the museum; and Freckles, the hundred-year-old from the barbershop, pointing his cane at various objects in the room and laughing to himself. Old home week. Also a sprightly woman who bears a resemblance to some sweet old grandma on *Bonanza*, except she's handcuffed to a prison guard.

I look for a bathroom off the waiting room, but none of the doors have signs. I try one locked door after another until I find the right one. Inside, a piece of gum in the urinal is shaped like a tomahawk. But there's no hot water to wash my hands. It's like a gas-station bathroom that saves money by welding the hot-water faucet shut and keeping the towel dispenser empty. Soon after I reclaim my seat, one of the locked doors opens from the inside and a short, uniformed woman stands in the opening with a clipboard. "Fullerton!" she shouts.

The prisoner and guard are ushered into an inner sanctum. The door clicks locked again. After this happens a few more times with people who came in after us, I approach the receptionist behind a sliding window. She isn't moved to slide it open until I rap with my knuckles.

"Hi," I say. "I believe we have a 10:20 appointment with a Dr. Khadir?"

"His semiannuals are this afternoon."

I hand her a copy of the appointment slip, which says 10:20. The receptionist wears a neutral expression as she closes the window to search her records. While waiting I read a sign taped to the window saying, "Please allow 72 hrs. on prescription requests." Isn't it usually a couple hours, max?

At last the receptionist slides open the window again. "We have you down for 10:20 but it's supposed to be 2:20. Even so," she says to me, "you can't accompany them unless you're a relative."

"I'm her uncle."

"You'll have to get authorization from Ms. Trumbull to do that."

"Well, she's sitting right here. Can she give you authorization here and now?"

"In writing."

I scribble. *I, Teresa Trumbull, hereby give my uncle Daniel Trumbull permission to speak to a doctor at the clinic about my condition.* Before I can stop her, Teresa staggers over to sign.

"And you need it notarized by our office manager, Thurma."

"Great. Can you ask Irma to do so?"

"Thurma. Take a seat."

We sit. Each journey to and from her seat causes Teresa to grimace silently. Dotty gives me a thumbs-up and a silent "Good for you!" which the others mimic in one form or another. Camaraderie of the waiting room. A couple of familiar faces enter: one of the teen punks who called Teresa and Sarah names at the gas station our first day in town, wearing a bandanna from jaw to scalp with a bow on top like the classic cartoon of a toothache. He's in too much pain to recognize us. But Hap Hazard from Assholes Anonymous does, giving me an elaborate high-five routine as he enters, complete with tap-dance spin.

We sit longer. It's obvious that time has a lower value in this locale than I'm used to. We're on what could be called minimum-wage time: everyone's hourly pay is so low that a forty-minute wait has virtually no value. It's like how Walmart often has only one cashier for a line of eight customers. Causing people to forfeit twenty minutes here and there represents so few lost dollars that no one bothers to rectify it. But at last a different short woman stands in the locked doorway. "Trumbull!"

Teresa struggles to stand.

"Not you. Him!"

Oh, that's right, I'm Daniel Trumbull. Thurma blocks the doorway against my approach. "I'm sorry, I don't have time to notarize your authorization right now," she tells me.

"It'll take twenty seconds. I already have it written out."

"Even so, can't do it."

"All you have to do is stamp it. We can break the land speed record in ten seconds."

"Nope." Her eyes flash. Behind me, I can sense that my confederates in the waiting room are stunned by my impertinence.

"You know, in the time it's taken us to argue, we could have done it already."

"I have a procedure to follow and that's that. We're done."

I take a deep breath, try a new tack. This is not about me. This is about Teresa.

"Tell you what: If I leave it with you, can you try your best to notarize it before our appointment this afternoon?"

She's noncommittal. "If time permits."

As we're leaving, the receptionist raps sternly on her little window. "Mr. Trumbull!" she calls. "Next time you can't park your bike there."

"But—"

"Per management."

••

Next up is the shrinkologist the King recommended. "I'll follow on my bike," I tell Sarah. "Which car is yours?"

"The white piece-a-shit."

Oh yeah. I remember from the junker at the gas station. I follow the white piece-a-shit through the parking lot, down the slope toward the sewage plant. Teresa and Sarah take turns knocking tentatively at the shrink's door, but there's no response. They're shocked when I decide simply to open the door and walk in—the correct decision, it turns out, because it opens into an empty waiting room. Green Astroturf runs across a space filled with stuffed animals and wall posters to match. "Wanted, Kiss-Kiss the Kangaroo," says one, "wanted for giving too many kisses!" Beneath the wanted poster sits the receptionist, a rangy woman with long arms and an animated delivery.

"Gettin' to be near springtime already! Global warnin', I guess. Scary, innit? But you're lucky you got an appointment, he is book-solid!"

"Oops, I forgot to bring my wallet," is Teresa's response.

"You're good for the payment, I seen you around town."

Sarah pushes aside a stuffed red lobster hanging in front of a nearby seat so Teresa can sit. The velveteen claw, holding a sign saying I Love Lobster, keeps bopping Teresa in the face, which makes her giggle self-consciously.

"OK, first things first. Who referred you here?" says the rangy woman.

"My uncle Daniel," Teresa says. "He found out you're the only one Medicaid will pay for."

"Is it Daniel or Dan? I like to keep things short as possible. My name's Velma, but I go by Vel. I like three-letter words. Vel. Dan."

"My ex-husband's dad was the same way," Sarah says conversationally. "He kept marrying women with three letter names. May. Joy. Also he preferred the number ten. Kept having children every ten years."

"Ten, huh?" Vel says. "Can't keep that up for long. So what seems to be the problem?"

"I'm a little upset 'cause I'm in too much pain," Teresa says. "Feel useless. Can't cook. Can't pick up my kids."

"Can't pick up your kids? That's rough!"

Teresa shoots me a glance, giving me permission to add my two cents. "She needs a psychological evaluation for disability purposes," I say. "Ideally a letter attesting to the fact that she's psychologically unable to work."

"Disability! Well, OK. We can work you up a Personal Assessment Inventory, all the poop."

Vel rubs the point of a paper clip against the gumline of her front teeth and proceeds. "Occupation?"

"Helpless housewife," Teresa says. She pushes away the lobster claw, but it bops her in the face again.

"Education?"

"She was never a straight A student," Sarah says.

"But I did graduate," Teresa says, "even though I flunked my senior exam because I said Pearl Harbor was attacked by Japan."

"Pearl Harbor *was* attacked by Japan," I say, somewhat incredulously.

"Not according to my teacher. She said it was China."

"Wait," I ask, "you got an F because you correctly answered who attacked Pearl Harbor? What was the upshot?"

"I had my dad, my aunt, my boss at the grocery store where I was a bagger—they all came in and argued with the teacher, but it was a lost cause. Finally the principal stepped in and graded it himself."

"And what'd he give you?"

"Practically a C." This said with some pride.

"Any case," asks Vel, "you ready to fill out these here questions? Eighty so it might take some time."

"Yes, ma'am."

Teresa takes a deep breath and gets on with the paperwork, eight pages of mostly multiple-choice questions, while Sarah opens up like never before, telling me how she married her high-school boyfriend after graduation. Both of them joined a carnival and traveled through the small towns of Arizona and Nevada, sleeping on an air mattress in the big tent, showering at truck stops. She operated the inflated slide, he the bounce house, until after a year he ran out on her. "It was awful," she says. "When I saw his note, I just about had a stroke. I ran down the road . . . cried and cried . . . then I started going to bars."

"Question," Teresa puts in from behind her lobster claw. "It says, Do I know who I am? Sometimes I can't concentrate to spell my name, so does that count?"

"But you do know who you are, sweetie pie," Sarah counsels her. "So the answer is yes."

Teresa uses her eraser while Sarah tells me how she quit the carnival and took a job at the front desk of a motel down the street from the Cozi. "That's how I met Scott," she explains. "It was like a courtesy to call the other when either of us had an overflow."

"And how'd you happen to throw your lot in with them?"

"They gave me a place to stay during my divorce. And it saved my life, plain and simple. I used to smoke, but I quit cold turkey under their roof. Stopped drinking too. Little by little I started to feel myself become—like, nourished!—in my heart. Had pillow fights with the boys. Gave me a new life with a beautiful new family."

"Question," Teresa puts in. "Does thinking about being thrown down the stairs count as I 'keep reliving some past traumatic event'"?

"Sure does," Sarah says. "Put in about your nightmares too—all them cars skidding into the house." Teresa bats back the lobster claw and resumes her questionnaire, while Sarah seems to find a lower octave in herself, her voice evincing a tender quality I've never heard before.

"See, I'm twenty-three. Teresa's twenty-seven. That's the age my older sister woulda been by now if she hadn't died of SIDS. Laura Beth, born Christmas Day and died four months later. So Christmas is a bad holiday for my dad. He has to push all his emotions down. When I hear stories about Teresa's childhood, I get upset."

"The last time I weighed myself, what was it?"

Sarah snickers. Teresa snickers back and puts down a number that starts with a *two*.

"Do I panic easy?"

"When it's something bad for your boys, darn straight!" Sarah says. She rolls her bottom to sit up straighter and turns her attention back to me. She can tell from my face I'd like to hear more.

"When I think about Teresa's mother, I want to slap that woman silly. All through high school she never let her see a penny of the money she earned at the grocery. Never let her buy a stitch of clothes for herself. Just wore hand-me-downs from her brothers. Can you believe a mom like that?"

Sarah's face pinkens with the intensity of her sympathy. "It's like, you might not know it to look at him, but Scott is a very talented cartoonist. He should have gone to art school, but he didn't have a mom to give him confidence. So you can understand, when they met it was like, you know, match made in heaven."

Teresa stands, limps across the Astroturf a minute, tries to take a sip from the drinking fountain that has no water in it, then resumes diligently writing, her nose down by the pencil. "My relationships can't be classed as 'stormy,' can they?"

"Not with Scott they ain't," Sarah tells her, then turns back to me. "Scott treats her like a lamb. She ain't never been pampered till she met that lover boy. Which is a mystery to me, how he's so capable of it, given what he was brung up with. I mean, when his friend Glenn comes over, they go out and throw knives at each other, just for fun."

"Throw—"

"For fun, uh-huh. 'Cause that's what he was used to from his upbringing. Yet and all, here he is, letting the kids basically use him like a free-for-all. I ain't never seen such sweetness in a dad, even including my own."

Teresa looks up again. "Do I get exercise?"

"You walk around the pool table with the kids."

I approach Vel, who's reading a brochure on Christmas tree ornaments. "Wasn't our appointment supposed to be 12:30?" I ask.

"Hang around, baby, he'll get here."

"So that's my story," Sarah says. "Hope I didn't bore your ear off."

"It was beautiful," I say.

"My dad says that word a lot too. *Beautiful*. It's a good word." She plucks a Rice Krispie off her sweatshirt. "So what about you? What are you doing here, really and true?"

"Not quite sure," I say slowly. "I came here to get something, you know, but now I kind of want to give?"

Sarah reaches over and squeezes my hand. "See, that gives me a shiver," she says.

The door opens. But wait, where have I seen this man before? Oh, shit, it's Joe, the guy who didn't like me very much in Judi's newspaper office. Sure enough, that's his black short-bed truck that just parked in the lot a minute ago.

Frowning, without a word of introduction, he leads the way into an office with burlap stapled to the walls before seating himself sternly behind a gunmetal desk. The doctor studies Teresa's questionnaire in silence, motionless except every so often giving a discreet chew to the gum in his mouth. At last he speaks.

"You forgot to sign."

I look away so as not to see the effort it costs Teresa to cross the room. So much time passes, though, that I finally look back to see what's taking so long. Teresa is doubled over the shrink's desk, laboriously affixing her John Hancock in what looks like slow motion.

"You sign with your left hand?" I ask.

"Well, my right's numb, so one's as good as the other."

When she's done she takes a seat at last, sitting on a whoopie cushion named SAD COW. *Moo boo-hoo*, the cushion sobs. Teresa giggles with shame as though she'd farted.

"All right, in your own words tell me what the complaint is," Joe says.

"I'm a little discouraged because no doctor seems to figure out what's wrong with me. One says it's my weight, one says it's inflammation of the brain, another says it's a disk bangin' some nerves . . ."

On she goes, listing the missteps of the medical establishment in the years since her accident: lost records . . . dropped appointments . . . false test results. . . . I study the clock on the burlap wall, a big theatrical affair with gaudy round golden gears tucked into each other. Soon my gaze wanders to wall plaques trumpeting Joe's sideline as a dealer of prize pigs: Grand Champion Pig BUYER, they boast, as if capital letters conferred extra points. He gives another discreet chew of his gum and cuts Teresa off. "Do you know what the word *malinger* means?" he asks.

"Not . . . sure?" Teresa asks.

The doctor taps a piece of chalk on a small dusty blackboard behind him on which the word is more or less permanently written, misspelled as *malingeer.*

"*Webster* defines the word as 'to feign illness in order to avoid duty or work,'" he continues. "Of course, that's the web and you gotta take anything there with a grain a salt, but still that gets pretty close to my understanding of what the word embroils."

Wait—does he think *Webster* is part of the web, by dint of its first syllable? That *Webster* is some dodgy outdated website like Napster or Friendster? We endure the wall clock striking the hour—the golden gears wheeling open to disgorge booming noises—before he proceeds.

"'Malinger' is what the disability program wants us to separate the wheat and chaff from, as in, 'Are you, Teresa Trumbull, malingering?'"

"No?" Teresa asks, flummoxed.

The pig buyer leans back in his chair, all sinew in the neck, before allowing himself a double-chew of his gum. "I myself don't know the answer. I'm not blaming you for anything after only ten minutes, but one thing I do see is you criticizing doctors for your condition, and I don't hear one word of taking responsibility for yourself."

"But she's not responsible for her condition," I say.

"She's got a victim's mentality, is what I'm getting so far," Joe says. "She's blaming every Tom, Dick, and Harry for her situation, which ain't what I like to call a positive way to live." He turns his attention to the questionnaire before him, shaking his head.

"My take," I say before he can object, "is that Teresa is a courageous lady who tries to keep a smile on her face so her kids won't see how much she's suffering. She's in almost unendurable torment, both physical and mental, and there's not the remotest question of her malingering."

Joe lifts his head, seizing on the word. "Interesting that you yourself would use the word *malingering*," he says, tapping the blackboard again. "I myself couldn't say for sure without more evaluating. But to cut to the chase, is this young lady disabled by virtue of a mental disorder?

Not from what I've read in her workup or heard so far out of her mouth. The burden of proof is on her shoulders, not mine. Basically her mental state is solid as Theodore Roosevelt's."

"Theodore—?"

"Just pulling a name out of the hat. Maybe I shoulda said *Teddy*. I always get those two politicians mixed up."

· ·

OK, we're not getting a letter from Joe, that much is clear. But we may still have a shot with Dr. Khadir back at the clinic. Hap Hazard is still there in the waiting room, holding a tin can partway filled with expectorated tobacco juice. Across the room I'm met by the office manager, Thurma, who surprises me by silently handing me my notarization and leading the way into the office of Dr. Khadir. I was half expecting a retired military doctor from one of the Air Force bases around Alamogordo but am pleasantly surprised to find a youngish North African doctor from . . . Algiers? Tripoli? I don't find out because he doesn't seem to hear my question about where he hails from. Doesn't bother shaking hands either.

"Sit, sit," he says, scarcely looking up.

Is it silly of me to hope for some kinship with this doctor, both of us being fish out of water in southern New Mexico? But no kinship is heading my way. On the contrary, here's another doctor who seems irritated by our presence.

"Any change since our last visit?" he asks as he flips through Teresa's record.

"Comes and goes like always, only worse," Teresa says. "Vaughan can sit there poking me with a fork and I don't feel it. Sometimes it's like my body's on the other side of the room."

"Would you please stand?" he asks.

Teresa rises like a wounded animal.

"Can you bend forward?"

Maybe an inch. She's stiff as a pillar and has to hold on to the wall to make sure she doesn't topple.

"Backward?"

Not even slightly.

Dr. Khadir rolls his chair close and touches her upper back. Teresa reacts like an animal zapped by an electric prod. The doctor grimaces, but not in sympathy.

"Will you please touch your nose and then my finger?"

"What does that test for?" I ask.

He doesn't show signs of hearing me as he directs her to sit on the examining table.

"Will you please extend your left leg?"

Teresa does so, and he scrapes the bottom of her foot.

"What does that show?" I ask again.

Again he doesn't answer me. He sticks her right foot with a tooth-pick-looking device, but Teresa doesn't react. "Not sharp?" he asks.

Teresa shrugs.

"That's for what, exactly?" I ask.

The doctor is openly annoyed. "Your husband asks a lot of questions," he tells Teresa.

Her husband! So that's how well he's been understanding the dynamics here. He sees nothing incongruous in pairing us off—not our thirty-three-year age difference or anything else. He touches her middle back, and she reacts like a bull that's been gored.

He hums incongruously.

More exercises, leaning this way and that, make Teresa wince in anguish. She breathes silently through clamped teeth. Sarah keeps saying, "Just a little longer, sweetie. We're almost there." Throughout, the doctor hums what I think is "Turkey in the Straw."

"What do you think?" I ask when it's finally over.

"She's a typical person in pain," the doctor says unctuously, rinsing his hands. "I see them every day."

"Can she get better?"

"Perhaps with the right treatment. She hasn't done anything for herself in three years, is it?"

"The accident was seven years ago."

"Even longer, so. In all this time she hasn't exercised, hasn't taken supplements, lacks the right diet."

"Can you supervise in all those areas so she can get better?" I ask.

"Everyone has potential," he says dismissively. "The human body wants to come into balance."

And with that ringing endorsement he leaves the room. Teresa and Sarah look at me expectantly. For the first time I see that their ponytails are not actually black after all but dark brown, with shades of amber and even reddish highlights in them.

"In the whole interaction that just happened, did he once make eye contact with you?" I ask Teresa. "Because he sure didn't with me."

"Never yet had a one that does," she says. It's the first chance I've had to view any official write-up. Teresa is described on the first page as "a perfectly pleasant, moderately obese patient." That's accurate enough, but I'm a little offended on her behalf by the word "obese." From what I can see, the rest of the write-up consists of one slipshod error after another. It refers to a car accident that took place in 1903 instead of 2003. Maybe that's just a secretary's mistake, but it shows the general level of care. No mention anywhere of back problems, numbness, or swelling. On today's report, the one he just did, he notes, "Gait is steady." Did he not see that she is about as steady as a gored bull? I put the folder back on his desk and ready myself to cut to the chase, which I do when Dr. Khadir comes back in the door.

"So can you write a letter stating that Teresa is disabled?" I ask, reaching across the doctor's desk to pick up Teresa's medical record. The girls gasp as though I've stolen fire from the sun god before asking him to drop trou.

"What do you mean?"

"You've been seeing Teresa semiannually for years now. As you must know, she's been applying for disability benefits, which are available to all qualifying citizens under the law. But she needs a letter from an expert confirming that she's too disabled to support herself through employment. Can we get that from you?"

For the next two minutes, Dr. Khadir demonstrates every sign of resisting. Crosses his arms. Clears his throat. Blows his nose. I don't get it. Why does this have to be such a showdown? We're all here with the best of intentions; why are the doctors putting up roadblocks, as if we're trying to perpetrate a hoax? Why should they take it upon themselves to be the gatekeepers preventing Teresa from getting what she's entitled to? A terrible realization has been gnawing at me all day, but I'm still not ready to acknowledge it.

"She has any number of conflicting disorders," the doctor complains. "The bulges are swollen tissue, but others concern neurological issues. The MRI is not diagnostic for early onset MS, though there is some disk degeneration, some rheumatoid arthritis of the spine, perhaps, but nothing so bad as to account for her symptoms. We cannot figure out precisely what is her case."

"But what does it matter if you can't figure it out precisely? Can't you just report that she's too disabled to work, since that's obviously the truth?"

"But there is no textbook diagnosis I can point to."

"Can't you take in the whole picture without being specific? This is a woman in chronic pain for seven years!"

Dr. Khadir sighs heavily. "I can write her a referral to see an eye doctor for optic neuritis, but it is unlikely this will get her any closer to a solution."

"What we need is a letter for disability," I say.

"I'm afraid I will have to disappoint you in this regard—"

"Look, I'm just an outsider, but it's obvious to me that this is a patient who's falling through the cracks because you're unwilling to say that her condition is real. I mean, it may be frustrating, but it is real, is it not?"

"You are twisting my arm here," Dr. Khadir says.

"I'm certainly trying to."

"In good conscience I cannot."

Conscience! Why do people resort to the word *conscience* when compassion is in short supply? I can avoid it no longer—I finally acknowledge the realization I've been trying to keep at bay. Time to call a spade a spade. This is a class thing. If Teresa had money or education, she wouldn't be getting the runaround she's been getting for the past seven years.

It's a long way from the bottom to the top, is what I think. If this is seeing health care from the ground up, it's not a pretty sight. I never would have believed what it looked like from this vantage if I weren't seeing it through the Trumbulls' eyes: an ugly, impregnable fortress—a cardboard pyramid in the desert—and we're specks of sand beating against its base in the wind.

And I've only been dealing with it a short while. The Trumbulls have been doing battle for years. I already feel my soul being ground down; how must it be for them? If a person with ordinary middle-class resources like mine can feel disheartened this quickly, and yes, intimidated, how must people like the Trumbulls feel over the long haul? And these are the people who can least afford to keep fighting, who've had to scrape and claw their whole lives to survive, who by early middle age were all but burned out. How can they not see the medical system as the enemy?

"All set?" Sarah says, standing to leave.

"That's it, then?" I ask, incredulous. "We can't get a letter saying she's disabled?"

Dr. Khadir smiles patiently before addressing the ladies as he nods them out the door. "I think we can safely skip the next semiannual, do you agree?" he says pleasantly.

CHAPTER 24

RAZZMATAZZ FOR REAL

"**HOWDY, FRIENDS, I'M** mighty pleased to welcome you back to another episode of *Truth or Consequences*, the country's first and foremost game show . . ."

I'm slumped in the museum's church pew after hours, not paying attention to Ralph Edwards's patter turned down low. It seems like a neutral place to puzzle things out after the disaster of our medical appointments. What's our next step if all the doctors have the attitude that she's guilty until proven innocent? I honestly don't know. We've run out of options.

Cue housewife 3: "Florence, Florence, look at you wobble on up there, Florence! Hubba hubba, you're poetry in motion!"

Cue husband 2: "Jerry here is getting down to business at last! Don't let your glasses get too fogged up now, Jerry, with all those pretty girls to choose from!"

There's a phone call I'm overdue to make.

"Third base to first calling," I say. "Come in, first."

"Dan the Man?" Tony says in surprise. "My titan. Infielder to the stars."

He wants to make up. I'm good with that, but I should take the lead; it's the reason I'm calling. "I owe you an apology, Tony. I want to say I'm sorry."

"Danny Rose, chastened by time!" he exclaims. "Never thought I'd see the day. Your timing is perfect, mah brutha. You caught me on a lonely, lonely road."

"I hear you, pal. So are we all."

"No, I mean the streetlights are out in this mall parking lot. So how's the desert?"

"It's the grapes of wrath out here, Tony. Honestly, if the government didn't cook the books, I swear unemployment would prove to be as bad as during the Depression. It's like a crash course in misfortune: everyone's troubles make mine look like the wrong end of a telescope."

"Enough to make someone cry, right? And notice, please, I'm not asking specifically if you're crying, because that would be disrespectful and passive-aggressive of me. You're not the only one capable of change and growth, you know."

"That's good, Tony. I just . . . I want to ask how it's going with Hannah."

"You don't."

"Actually, this is weird, but I kind of do."

"Ouch, I hate having my reality shift from under me like this. OK, so my daughter and I Skyped. I finally got to see what she looks like. And she's beautiful, Dan—I never expected it. I may even see her in person soon. Ow, enough. I'm not ready for this schmaltz. What's your hard-luck story?"

"I've been trying to find a doctor to help us with Mary's family, but it's looking impossible." I text him a photo of Mary so he can see what she looks like. I know it's been received when I hear his slow whistle. "Fuck this hootenanny," he says. "I'm pulling over so I can take this in . . ."

I hear the squeak of his parking brake as he stops to study the photo. "Anyway," he resumes, "funny you should call me just at this moment 'cause I've been wondering: Do you think our crash was partly at least payback for us being such a couple of self-involved dickheads? I'm serious! You and I never talked about it, of course, but consider: we left our families to go gallivanting off to see the country, which wasn't that big a deal because *everyone* was gallivanting off in those days, seems like, but do you think Mary charging at us with her truck like that was revenge for our male misdeeds, in some cosmic way?"

"Deep questions, Tony, I have to admit . . ."

"Don't laugh. I'm not kidding. I know this is out of the blue for a couple of jackasses who jerk off for a living, but do you ever think shit like that? And now it maybe even seems that Vietnam, that old bugaboo, could be bringing things up to the surface again."

"Vietnam?"

"Think about it!" he says, revving his engine in neutral. "We were lucky sons-of-bitches who'd squirreled our way out of the draft while our less privileged comrades were bleeding by the boatload in 'Nam. Do you think, in hindsight, that on some subconscious level we wanted to spill some of our own blood to pay our dues a bit? Earn our red badge of courage and level the playing field somewhat?"

"Maybe you're right. I always thought we were maybe just self-destructive, but maybe more—"

"For sure, that also—but also, maybe even in an honorable way, if you can stand it, maybe we wanted to punish ourselves out of guilt? Feel a little on our skins what they were feeling on theirs? I mean, those were our playmates from the sandbox, Danny—the kids we grew up with—and there they were, carrying each other's guts out of the jungle in metal pails, while we were getting laid in the clover."

"Jesus, Tony, talk about chastened by time."

"I know, it's just . . . this separation has been hard on me, Danny. I don't like not being able to make fun of you for so long. Can we grab a preacher to renew our vows or something? Hey, what's going on in the background?"

"Nothing. Some happy horseshit from Ralph Edwards reruns."

"Ralph Edwards?"

"Remember? The goofball who started the game show—"

"Don't I know! I've been Googling, and I've gotta say he wasn't entirely the bad guy Head Shop Harry made him out to be."

"Please don't say you've been bit by the Ralph bug like everyone else out here."

"But he wasn't," Tony says. "I mean, say what you will about his motives, but his show collected five billion in today's dollars for worthy causes. He raised more money for the March of Dimes than anyone else."

"And you came by these enlightenments *how*?"

"Detective till the end, Danny! So see if you can get the big picture here. Ready? Mid-1900s. The country was in deep doo-doo—caught in a Cold War with the bomb looming overhead. Ralph managed to offer distraction to parents whose children were duck-and-covering at school. Was it so bad to provide a few laughs to ease the pain? He may have been phony as a three-dollar bill, but a three-dollar bill may have been exactly what Americans needed at that moment to assure themselves things were OK. Especially if they weren't."

"I don't know, man, you're getting too brilliant for me—"

Tony revs his engine again. "To think that the world might blow any minute, but T or C could turn into a showbiz attraction! Soap bubbles to offset the poverty. Organ chords to drown out the death rattle."

"Jesus, Tony, how much caffeine have you—?"

"I know, I'm scaring myself now too. But the counterfeit frontier spirit, wasn't that what he was selling? Dream big, pick yourself up by your bootstraps, make a better reality for yourself. American-do! Just for singing along to the game show. And didn't it work, though! Sixty years later they still trot up and down the church pews to worship the man!"

"Everyone's rooting for you, Bev, ain't that swell?" come the dulcet tones of you-know-who. "You're fulla beans, aren't you, precious! But don't faint on me yet, 'cause you just won yourself a custom-built automatic washer and dryer! *Top-loading*!"

"So you're saying I should take a page out of Ralph's playbook—"

"Precisely! Grab inspiration from the con man supreme! Buy a ticket of razzmatazz and shoot for the stars."

I'm feeling winded, not ready to take all this in or even think about how I'd go about it. And maybe Tony's feeling the same way. I can still hear him revving his Mercedes. We all need to cool down.

"Anyway, reason I called," I say, changing the subject, "I'm sorry for being such a what-cha-ma."

"Apology accepted," he says. "And me too, for being a total who's-a-what."

"Thanks."

"Thank you."

"OK, so now this is awkwardly close to being heartfelt."

"One way to take care of that."

"Right. This is first base to third, signing off."

"Over and out."

••

Slowly it sinks in. Tony's right: the get-up-and-go that Ralph embodied is something I should try to adopt. Gradually I sit up straight in my pew. My scalp tightens. Here I am stuck with the locals giving me the runaround—but what's to stop me from shooting for the top medical people in the state? Just because I'm seeing American health care from the desert floor doesn't mean I have to *stay* on the desert floor.

I shut off the TV and am relieved when the noise abates. Now I can hear that it's drizzling outside—one of the only times since I've gotten here. I go back to my pew and begin deep Googling on my phone. "New Mexico health care. Best physicians. Best hospitals." With a little cross-referencing, a few patterns begin to emerge. But man, they don't make it easy. The medical monolith protects itself under layers of deliberate obfuscation. They don't print the departments in most hospitals, for one thing. Not the specialties, much less the subspecialties. Neither the email addresses nor the phone number extensions. It all seems to be classified information.

"You'll lock the door when you leave, Dan?"

"As always, Dotty."

The more I dig, the more a single clinic keeps popping up: Protracted Pain Management Center (PPMC) in Albuquerque. As does the name of a particular doctor: Bethany Weiss, chief of the center. A medical rock star—one of the top authorities on chronic pain in the state. Complete with background information revealing key overlaps in our backgrounds.

Time for an email assault. "Dear fellow alum," I put in the subject line, referencing the college we both attended. "Kudos for the impressive work you've been doing at PPMC. I am writing with a professional favor to ask. Over the course of the past months, I've befriended a young couple from the southern part of the state who are in dire straits. They're decent people who can't catch a break. The wife, Teresa Trumbull, age twenty-seven, was in a car accident seven years ago and has been in increasing amounts of pain ever since. The local doctors are so perplexed by her symptoms that they've pretty definitively rinsed their hands of her. Could you possibly be in a position to help?"

Twenty minutes go by with no response. She's online—I can see by the tab lit up next to her name—so I email again, adding a bit more snake oil to channel my inner Ralph. "Two degrees of separation" is my next subject line, under which I lay out how much history we share without sounding like a stalker: academic honor societies, mutual friends. Did she ever know Peter Loescher in our chapter of Phi Beta Kappa?

Still no response. But I'm not leaving the museum till I've nailed this. Time to lay my cards on the table. Diligently blind-copying the King on every email to keep him in the loop, I write my next one this way: "At the risk of pressing too hard, I'll tell you why our problem is urgent. Teresa is in danger of being turned down for disability when she sees a judge in a few days, because the medical community down here is loath to say she's disabled without a specific diagnosis. What we need is someone of your stature to write a letter explaining to the judge that even without a firm diagnosis, the pain she suffers is nonetheless debilitating. My hope is that after a face-to-face with Teresa, you would be inclined to put something to that effect in writing. Time is short, so we're willing to come at a moment's notice if you could fit us in. Maybe put us on a cancellation list?"

Another twenty minutes with no word, drumming my fingers in time with the light rain on the roof. Finally on my fourth attempt I go for broke: "Final Appeal. I'm really, really sorry to badger you like this, but I need to tell you frankly that this is something you ought to do. No one is gaming the system, no one is doing anything that isn't morally correct. The judge simply needs to know that Teresa is not faking. Believe me, I'm not in the habit of throwing myself at people, and I would never be doing so for myself, but seeing this woman unable to hold her kids has cracked my heart open. Please, Bethany, for Brunonia and *Shalom aleichem* and everything else we might hold dear, please do the right thing and consent to see this poor hurting woman. Fingers crossed, Daniel."

And then, bingo. A simple ping on my phone brings the news: "Daniel, I may have a cancellation tomorrow twelve noon. Can you give my secretary Teresa's DOB and SS# so she can input her in the system? Thanks, and let me know."

Hot diggity, as Ralph Edwards might say. I carefully place my phone down, feeling ecstatic and cautious both. The rain on the roof sounds like quiet applause. We're not alone in this battle to help Teresa. At long last, we may have an ally.

A restrained response seems in order. "Much obliged, Bethany. Will send the info ASAP, and I look forward to seeing you tomorrow."

Restraint to the medical pros, but to the Trumbulls I can exult. Trembling, I tap their phone number.

"Sarah! We got it! An appointment with one of the top doctors in the state!"

Then comes something I wasn't expecting. Silence.

"Sarah, did you hear me? It was a slog, but we got it in the nick of time!"

"Scott ain't available right now," she finally replies.

What's this? Something's happened.

"Sarah, is everything OK?" I ask.

There is the sound of Sarah's hand covering the receiver, a muffled consultation in the background. The hand is removed. "Teresa's in worser pain than ever," Sarah says.

"What do you mean?"

"Her back's throbbing like her whole side's on fire. All them docs pokin' and proddin' has about done her in. The last thing she wants is another doc goin' at her some more. So we're gonna pass."

"Look, can I just swing by to explain what good news this doctor is?" I ask, but even as the words leave my mouth I can feel how badly they're being received. A miscommunication is multiplying, and I don't know how to fix it. Some faith they put in me is slipping away, and I'm surprised by how upset I'm getting.

Through the hand Sarah puts over the receiver, I hear more whispering.

"Just for a few minutes!" I yell. "To tell you about this better doctor, one of the best in the Southwest!"

But there's no need to raise my voice: Sarah is talking directly to me.

"Scott says to tell you we don't need to meet nobody else. But to thank you for tryin'."

"Wait, please," I say. I can't help feeling like I'm the enemy, adding to Teresa's pain by prodding even more. I feel guilty, as if I want this more than they do. But I also feel angry, as if I'm pushing a donkey up a hill. I feel like whacking it with a stick. I turn my anger into a plea. "Look, I'm begging you not to give up now," I say. "This could be the break we've been waiting for!"

A whispered huddle out of earshot.

"Well, Scott says to warn you the rain's picked up. But if you don't mind getting a little wet . . ."

Everything's in extra-sharp focus as I pedal: the downpour turning the dust to dirt on the sidewalks, making rivulets that quickly fill the potholes. In no time I stand in the back doorway, where the yellow porch light makes the cobwebs glisten like wet yarn. The door opens only halfway—the humidity warping the wood extra badly.

Oh yeah, things are worser, all right. The decline is visible as soon as I work my way in. The boys are ghostly pale, glued to the cartoons so intently they don't register my entrance. Across the gloom, Teresa is pushing her hillbilly wheelchair one inch at a time.

"How you doing, Scott?"

"Doing." I've never heard his voice this low before, with an edge of warning to it.

"Got a little treat for the boys," I say, offering a wet paper bag I had in my bike pouch filled with Mounds bars. I feel like a suitor from the 1920s jutting forth a box of Whitman's Samplers with a ragged ribbon.

"Sarah, can you put these on the top shelf where the boys can't get at it?" he says.

I forgot they don't let the boys eat sweets. How many missteps am I going to make?

Scott is not exactly blocking my way, but he's not moving aside either. The rain has intensified the smell of sweet gone bad. I rub the raindrops off my nose. "Sorry for the water," I say.

Scott launches right in. "I hate to say it, but these docs ain't working out so good."

"You're not kidding, Scott," I say. "I feel awful about it."

"I mean, no one's blamin' you, exactly. But Teresa's in a heap more pain than she was before the docs. Her fists are balled up; even her tongue's numb."

Teresa smiles apologetically. "Ordinarily I'm careful not to let nobody touch me. The slightest hug, even from him, makes me feel like my bones are broke. But since the docs, I grind my teeth at night something awful. If we could get me to have no pain for like ten minutes, I'd be willing to keep tryin'. But another doctor planning to jab me? No thanks. It just ain't worked out. It's like they designed the system to make you wanna give up. And we do. We give."

Whew, I can barely stand to hear this. I need to look away for a minute. The object of my gaze turns out to be the smaller boy wiping his nose on his bathing suit without blinking his attention away from the cartoons. That's wetter protoplasm than I signed up for.

I take a breath and turn to Sarah for relief. "How you doing, meantime?" I ask her.

"Oh, they're bad," Sarah says.

"What are?"

"My scabies. Didn't I tell you?"

"First I've heard," I say as brightly as possible.

"I went to the clinic for medication," Sarah continues, "but they told me I had to have a doctor before they let me see a doctor. Cats 22."

How contagious are scabies? Sorry, but it's my first thought. My second thought is, *How much of a leap can I dare to make?*

"OK, here's my angle on things," I say, for what has surely got to be my very last shot with this family. "I know you wonder why I'd make another doctor's appointment when those other docs were so terrible, but it's kind of like what you did in high school, Teresa, when your teacher wanted to flunk you for saying Japan invaded Pearl Harbor."

"Japan *did!*"

"And you were right to insist on it!" I say. "You couldn't get anywhere with your teacher, so you made an end run straight to the principal. I'm trying to follow your example: make an end run around these know-nothings and go directly to one of the principal docs in the state who'll tell us we're right, once and for all."

"Well, it *was* Japan," Teresa repeats. "I wasn't going to let her say it wasn't."

"Same here," I tell her. "That's why I want us to see this doc who's better qualified to say your pain is authentic." I pause. "So long as we can get up to Albuquerque by noon tomorrow. I know it's a long way, and every mile in a car causes you anguish—"

A chorus of groans, but not as bad as I feared. "That ain't a problem, if we thought the doc would do some good," Sarah says. "Problem is that Medivan needs three days' notice. And they wouldn't let you ride with us no way. They're strict about that. They didn't even let Scott ride just a few miles with us one time."

"Let me worry about them," I say with a smile. "I'm kind of on a roll of bulldozing people, as you can see."

This attempt at humor fails miserably. Why am I cracking wise when so much is at stake? Jesus, what is wrong with me? In the corner, the cinderblock walls glisten from a leak. I'm starting to itch. Their faces remain tighter than the sealed-in plexiglass windows against which the rain beats loudly. I have to switch tactics again or risk losing them forever.

But wait. Tactics?

All I need is to be real.

Something changes in me. I can't say what it is or why. Somehow I'm able to step down off a platform I didn't realize I was on. And to stop bullying. I've been whacking them with a donkey stick, and it's only been making them balk. I put the stick down. Immediately I feel my breathing deepen.

I take a seat on the edge of the couch and look at Scott in a new way. "I have a question for you, my friend. Were you not sure whether to trust me when I first came on the scene, back at the Cozi? I can't blame you if you were unsure, because I kind of blew into your lives with no warning. I guess I'm wondering if you had any idea where I was coming from."

Scott makes a strained face. "Now that you mention it," he says, "we did kinda wonder why you started doing all this for us. I mean, what's in it for you, since it's not like you really knew us or anything?"

"Right. You had no reason to trust me. Why should you? I was just some great-looking guy claiming to have been hit by your mom in a wreck, and suddenly I want to help your wife get better from her wreck? I mean, how crazy is that?"

"Pretty crazy," Scott says. He smiles at my "great-looking" joke, softening his lips to lower his guard a small degree.

"Tell you the truth, I can't explain it myself, really," I say, "except to say that I'm dealing with some hard stuff these days, and it makes me feel better to lend you guys a hand."

"Home life?" Scott asks, his voice sweet and high again.

"You got it."

"Wife?"

I nod. Strange, but this is the first time I've talked about myself to them. Scott looks pained to see my vulnerability, a look of concern I can only call . . . familial. "What the hay-all?" he says. "What's she thinkin'?"

"She's thinkin' she wants me out of her life, Scott."

"I knew it had to be something bad for you to be out in the desert that night, but still 'n' all, that's your family, for cripes' sake. She can't break up your family." He pops the fist of one hand into the soft palm of his other. "You seen it coming?" he asks.

"I'm starting to think no one ever sees anything coming," I admit. "All I can say is, don't go through it if you don't have to, Scott."

"Oh, I never intend to, believe me. But let me ask you this: Did it have to do with your being out here all this time?"

"Actually, my being out here is trying to fix what's wrong at home."

Scott leans forward, untightening his face like I've never seen him do before. It's obvious now that he's been wary since our first meeting at the Cozi, wondering what my motives are. His face slackens to accept me. His eyes look into mine as he sticks out his hand.

"We're here for you, buddy," he says. "Anything you need."

"I appreciate that, Scott."

"I mean it, you and your boys, you ever need to kick back for a couple weeks, my casa is your casa."

"Same goes for the car," Sarah says. "Anytime you need to borrow it, just grab it—don't even ask. The key's over the visor."

"How're your boys takin' it, meantime?" Scott asks.

"They're not really talking to me." I can't believe it, but my voice breaks a little when I confess this. I'm embarrassed and clear my throat as a way of disguising the sound, but it only makes me feel weak. Maybe weak isn't the worst thing to be right now?

"I'm so sorry," Teresa says.

"Well, I'm sorry to be pressuring you so much. It's just I'm under pressure myself."

"We get it," Sarah says. "You're tryin' to do right by this family 'cause you can't do right by your own."

I nearly gasp when she says this. Is it really so obvious, when I'm barely aware of it myself? It sounds so clear when she puts it like that, so simple yet profound. It's like one of the Zen koans that might be articulated by the genius savant Summer. Why are you trying to do right by this family? Because you ain't got no other family to do right *by*!

"But what about going to Albuquerque?" I ask, getting back on track. "I know how much it worries you, but we're truly down to the wire here."

There is an intake of breath from all three. Teresa is the first to reply.

"You sure none of this won't make the King mad? 'Cause he's our lifeline, like you said."

"I think he'll be pleased we're bolstering his case for him." I pause. "Anything else?"

"But to go 150 miles, just to get needles pushed up my legs or some such?"

"I hear you, Teresa," I say, taking her hand. "But I promise, if you don't want them to touch the spots that hurt, we'll tell them and they won't. The headline will be: Don't Do Anything Teresa Doesn't Want!"

This makes them smile, but it doesn't hide how scared and overwhelmed they are. Same goes for me. I can't help noticing how intimate it's become in this room—more intimate than I ever would have expected when I started this journey with them so many months ago. It's so strange to try to help someone: *their* need and pride, *my* need and pride, they all get knotted up together. Like Mary's bloody blond hair tangled around the steering wheel, I find myself thinking: just *you* try to get extricated from life . . .

"And I promise you, this'll be the last thing I ask of you," I say. "If this doesn't work, I'll never bother you again. I'll step out of your lives the same way I stepped in."

It's breathless in the room, to the tune of *SpongeBob*. I feel like the three of them are holding not only their future in their hands but mine too. Drops of warm rainwater roll down my back beneath my shirt, but at least I've stopped itching. Finally Scott straightens back up.

"I think we oughta give the new doc a shot, don't you?" he says. "And can someone find this man a towel, please?"

••

Next day the sun has resumed. It's so bright in Albuquerque—glare flashing off sharp-angled skyscrapers—that it hurts our eyes. In the middle seat of the Medivan, I gawk at the hurly-burly of the big city as much as Sarah and Teresa do. And the honking! It's like I've been in a sensory deprivation tank for months.

We pull into the driveway of the hospital, which appears snazzy and free of desert dust. An apprehensive Sarah helps an apprehensive Teresa into a high-end chrome wheelchair as I follow them inside, carrying the pillow and ice packs Sarah rounded up specially for the ride—the only things that made the journey tolerable for Teresa. Far from being dim green inside, like St. Ann's in T or C, this hospital is bright and airy. And so patient-friendly that some of the ceiling panels have been replaced with photos of hot air balloons, allowing patients being wheeled on stretchers to have something to look up at besides white acoustic tiles. Despite her nervousness, Teresa is trying to rally, her smile uncertain as she hears the random banter of passing people in the corridors, that breezy but crucial code of communication by which people make their connections.

"How you doin'?"

"Below average but risin'."

"Just about got it whupped."

"Any better they'd have to shovel me under."

Even the curly redhead behind the desk in Dr. Weiss's reception area engages in it. And to my astonishment, Teresa rises to the occasion like a pro. "Fatter every day," she giggles.

"Stayin' out of trouble, though?"

"Can't get into it!"

The redhead smiles warmly and extends her hand. "I'm Dr. Bethany Weiss—call me Betts. Awful glad to meet you."

"I thought you were the secretary!" I say.

"My secretary's taking lunch, so I'm giving her a hand with this pile of cow patties that's been backing up."

Very special—a highly trained specialist with a down-home manner. And she comes by it honestly, as she explains: she grew up on a cattle ranch west of Albuquerque, breaking horses before she got her medical degrees. I especially like how gentle she is, after we enter her office: always respecting Teresa's level of pain.

"All right, Miss Teresa belle," she says, fastening a blood pressure sleeve to Teresa's upper arm, "you know your body better'n I do. So you tell me if you think something's going to hurt, and I won't do it."

Nervously, Teresa casts a look my way and gets the reassuring wink she was hoping for. She puffs a little breath of relief.

"Sounds like you've been howling in the wilderness awhile," Betts says to me, pumping up the sleeve.

"Not as long as they have. They've been stonewalled for years."

Betts finishes taking Teresa's blood pressure before patting the examining table where she wants her to sit. "What you have to understand, and I don't say this to excuse anyone, but this is such an impoverished state, with so many penniless people nursing so many kinds of injuries, that health professionals are reluctant to open the floodgates. Rightly or wrongly, they tend to set themselves up as gatekeepers, holding back the tide they feel's going to overwhelm the system."

"At the cost of people like Teresa."

"I'm not disagreeing with you, but most of the doctors I deal with are decent people trying to make the system work. I'm told 5 percent of doctors create 95 percent of the malpractice." She turns her attention back to Teresa. "Let's put some drops in these eyes. You'll be like Willie Nelson: won't feel a thing."

Both Teresa and Sarah giggle a little. A trickle of water over the dam.

The doctor raises a warning finger, pretending to scold. "Though we don't want you driving after this. The police see those pupils and wonder what in heaven you been smokin'."

More water over the dam. I'm envious at how quickly the doctor has breached their defenses. It took me twice as long to get half as far.

"See, your eyes are like car headlights connected to nerves in your engine right here," Betts says, tapping her head. "How're you feeling right about now?"

"Dizzy as heck," Teresa says.

"That's your brain sending some unnecessary signals. Tell you what:

reach out and take hold of that wall to steady yourself. It'll override your brain. See that?"

Teresa's smile wavers as she touches the wall.

"How's *your* health, meanwhile?" she asks me, slipping some temporary sunglasses on Teresa so she sits there looking less like Willie Nelson than Roy Orbison. "All this barking at the moon's probably been stressful for you too."

"Me? I'm OK. Keep dreaming about cars skidding into my house."

"Like my dreams!" Teresa says.

I smile and touch her shoulder lightly. "I know, sweetie pie."

"Yeah, but knowing Dan, it was probably wishful thinkin' so he could play the hero," Sarah giggles.

A joke! At my expense! How refreshing. It's relaxed enough in here for the doctor to peer at me frankly.

"And how exactly are you related to Teresa?" she asks me.

"Just humanly," I say.

The doctor smiles to herself. "C'mon, put your chin on the chopping block," she tells Teresa. "Let's see what you got cookin' in those pretty little eyes of yours."

••

Seventy-five minutes later, we're done. Effortless and relatively pain-free. After all the trouble it's been to get Teresa here, it's almost anticlimactic how smoothly things have gone.

"The diagnosis is a tricky one," Betts sums up. "It's like a jigsaw puzzle spilled out on the floor, and people have been walking on the pieces for years. Lot of conflicting symptoms that don't add up. But I would take issue with my colleagues who say that the puzzle pieces are not real. They're real all right: you're in a great deal of distress."

"Is it my eyes, like one of the docs said?"

"You've got some beautiful colors in there, Teresa. Orange juice and reds. But they check out fine. Definitely not optic neuritis, and I apologize for the extra discomfort these false leads must have put you through. Inner ear's a good bet for the dizziness; that's the gyroscope for the entire ship—"

"So the whole thing's in my head?" Teresa asks.

"You ever get kicked in the head by a billy goat?" Betts replies. "All head injuries add up to trouble down the road. Your old accident started a whole chain of events that have only grown worse over time. Bottom line, the patient is probably not a candidate for a lunar mission. So how can I be of most help to you, exactly?"

"Can you write a letter on her behalf?" I ask.

"I can and will. Right now."

She swings to a computer whose screen lights up radiantly with the hospital's letterhead. I unfold a scrap of paper I've been carrying in my pocket since my visit with the King and dictate the precise phraseology he prescribed. The doctor volunteers a few words of her own that she thinks a disability judge might find compelling. A minute later she waves the finished document in the air, as though the ink has to dry. That one anachronistic gesture, so telling of an old-fashioned upbringing, makes me want to ask her permission to plant a righteous kiss on her lips.

But I don't. This is not my party.

"Please take good care, Miss Teresa belle," the doctor says, squeezing both of Teresa's hands in hers. "You are a most lovely young lady and deserve better luck for the rest of your days."

· ·

The sound of three locks tumbling . . .

And the door swings wide. Yes, wide! Scott must have rescrewed the hinges while we were gone. Teresa, Sarah, and I bring the party inside, flourishing our document and laughing. "We got it! The letter!"

"The letter!" scream the boys, jumping up and down on the couch.

"Can I see it?" Scott asks.

"Wash your hands first," Teresa says, lifting it from his reach. She's treating it like a royal proclamation on parchment, rolled instead of folded, but she does allow herself to bop the boys' heads with it, a playful queen bestowing blessings.

"The letter! The letter!"

The cheering is enough to fuel a pep rally. Torrents of water over the dam. The three of us from the big city have gotten the room so festive, we're drowning out the TV.

"You wouldn't believe how easy it was, after all that," I tell Scott. "We coasted back from Albuquerque in like two minutes."

Scott sniffs the air. "Smells like you brought back something good too."

"Dinner!" crows Sarah, producing three bags. "And not fast food, neither. Teresa said she wanted high off the hog . . . so Dan got the van to stop at IHOP!"

This calls for a proper sit-down, no eating from laps on the couch. Sliding Scott's computers out of the way, we pull chairs up to the pool table and parcel out sirloin steak tips, crunchy battered shrimp, and red-pepper griddle melts.

"Honestly, you should have seen your wife," I tell Scott, dishing out portions of biscuits and gravy. "She was so lucid about every detail in her medical history. If she can be half that clear before the judge, it's gotta help our case."

"Well, let's hear the letter, gurrl!"

Sarah clears her throat and wipes her hands before unfurling it. "To whom it may concern," she reads as Teresa basks shyly in the glow of words. "Mrs. Trumbull suffers from a chronic pain syndrome, which began immediately following a motor vehicle accident in 2003 when she was rear-ended. She is completely disabled by chronic pain and muscle spasms of her cervical, thoracic, and lumbar spine, along with intermittent numbness of her right arm and leg. She cannot sit or stand for more than twenty minutes at a time, nor can she lift anything more than five pounds without severe pain and worsening of her symptoms. Mrs. Trumbull cannot care for her two children without considerable help from close friends. She is unable to drive and has trouble sleeping due to her pain. In short, I can think of few better examples than Teresa Trumbull for precisely what our system of disability is for."

"Wait till the King gets a loada that," Scott says, wiping his lips. "He's gotta think it's good."

"Good enough for some Mounds bars?" I ask. "Unless you already chucked the ones I brought last night?"

This brings a slight pause to the festivities—embarrassed looks on the faces of my hosts before Teresa and Sarah bust out laughing again.

"You know what?" Teresa says. "Tonight's a happy occasion, so c'mon! Bring on the candy!"

It is indeed a happy occasion. Teresa swings her leg over the kids' safety gate to go into the kitchen—now there's an energetic move I've never seen her make before—and fetches the bag from atop the fridge. Soon all six of us are soaring with sugar highs.

"You were so funny last night holding that drippy bag in the doorway," laughs Sarah. "Like a dog being dragged to a rendezvous with a porkypine!"

"Hoo, did get pretty wet in here!" Scott laughs.

Which heightens the hilarity even more. The boys are laughing without understanding, just to be part of things. "Cowboy! Cowboy!" they shout.

"Oy, I'm a cowboy all right!" I joke in my Yiddish accent: Alfred E. Neuman with curly payot hanging below his cowboy hat. "Vot, me vorry? Straight off da vild vest!"

Feels like I haven't been this loopy in years. It's all the encouragement the boys need to slide off their chairs and start punching my thighs in merriment. "Cowboy!" they whoop before Sarah jumps up to chase them around the pool table, catching them to stuff extra Mounds in their mouths.

"Hey, Dan, ain't you gonna finish yours?"

"I'm too revved to eat," I say, pushing back from the table.

The boys spot their opening. "Read! Read!" they shout, thrusting a Pokémon comic book in my stomach and climbing aboard.

"I can do better than that," I say, taking out my phone, "if I can manage to get something off the Internet . . ."

Next thing we know I've hoisted both boys on my lap and am reading from a children's story I wrote for my kids. I'm a little bashful because it's the first time I've read *Little Charlie Tucker and His Very Noisy Nose* to anyone but Spencer and Jeremy, but my audience seems captivated—the adults as much as the kids.

"You know what?" Scott declares, when the reading is over, "I'm gonna make some cartoons for it."

"He's got the talent for it too," Teresa says.

"I'd be thrilled," I say, as Scott starts doodling on the back of the

IHOP takeout menu. The boys crowd around to see what their father is creating, and as the doodles take shape before their eyes, I dare to fantasize for the first time what disability payments could do for this family. "You know, if this letter does what I think it might, you could eat IHOP every week," I tell Scott.

"I could afford to get on stress meds," he says, drawing. "That way I could concentrate on one worry at a time."

"We could get the kids bunk beds," Teresa says.

"And you a wheelchair," Sarah says, "chromed up like the ones in Albuquerque."

"Maybe even a bike so you could exercise," Teresa tells her husband.

"Exercise, heck, I could afford to go to a gym. Maybe get a reduced rate in exchange for drawing up their brochures or something." He shoots a glance at Teresa. "Why're you lookin' at me like that, gurrl? Dan's not the only one can finagle a situation. Matter fact, I been thinking I might just fire up these ole computers one of these days and get my mail-order business started. I've checked out Dan's chops and figured if he can do it, why can't I?"

"Hey, anyone who could fix that stuck door could do anything," I say.

Teresa is wearing the closest I've seen to a blissed-out expression on her face. "I just wish we'd met Betts a long time ago," she says with a deep sigh. "I bet tomorrow morning I'll sleep till five!"

The last of the sugar highs works its magic as I take in the scene: Sarah resuming her chase of the boys around the pool table, husband and wife allowing themselves to imagine a better future for their family—real shorts for the boys instead of bathing suits, foam pillows instead of sweatshirts stuffed inside pillowcases, a proper garden for planting beans and corn like Scott's family used to do, back at the old homestead.

"Hey, Scott," I call over. "We having fun yet?"

Scott nods that slicked-back head of his. "We may just be," he says slowly. "We may just be."

CHAPTER 25

ENORMOUS SPACE IS NEAR

THIS CALLS FOR A SOAK. I'm treating myself to an extra-long time-out in the hot tank before tomorrow's appointment with the King when we get to present him with our triumphant, judge-convincing letter.

And so, behind a single-wide trailer on a double-wide street, under a sky that's giving up its fake-out blue for the day, I soak. Usually in daily life I'm plagued by the feeling that I should be doing anything but what I'm doing—exercising when I'm reading, or reading when I'm exercising—but tonight I'm allowing myself the rare contentment of doing nothing but what I'm doing: soaking in water direct from the earth's core. "This is how people heal," I murmur like a mantra. "This is how people heal."

It's just an ugly steel tank in a dirt-dumb yard, but it's from here that I have a front-row seat on the twilight. In the foreground, mourning doves align themselves exactly six inches apart atop the broken fence, their belly feathers twitching in the breeze, their necks gulping with invisible coos like a ventriloquist's trick. Closer, ants are tormenting an overturned beetle on the tank's lip. After I rescue him, the beetle makes his getaway among clods of mud as the ants jeer. In silence above, a jet streaks for the orange horizon, foaming with speed. At eye level in front of me, the surface of the water is freshly sprinkled with soft green needles of rosemary. Where'd they blow in from?

The light darkles. Such a better verb than *darkens. Darkles* has hope in it, the promise that light will come again. Colors drain away till the sky is midnight black. An owl hoots from the banks of the Rio Grande, echoed by another downriver. From time to time I slide underwater to look straight up with my eyes open. Then I sit upright again, calmly accepting my measure of peace as Geronimo must have accepted his, under the powder spray of the Milky Way. How the stars do tremble, indeed. Roy Joy back at AA may have meant it sarcastically, but he was right: they do. Meantime, the hours slip by unnoticed—two hours, three, four—while the water murmurs its softest syllables: *You're OK, you're OK, you're OK . . .*

· ·

Ping! I'm roused by a text message.

> Dad, you up?

>> OMG, ` ?

> hey

>> what r u doing up in the middle of thje night

> just want4ed to talk did I wake u

>> I must have dozed off but I'd so happy you did

> dad could you come home now nothing's working

>> what isn't sweetie

> mom and me shoeveled three feet of snow but the shovel bbroke

>> I'm trying, spenmce. maybe sooner thant you think. can you hold out a little longer

> I guess

>> maybe in the meantime we can tlak more regularly id liKE THAT sorry my capitals get setuck

> don't worry about it

>> how's the barky dog

> barky

>> good to know some things don't change

> a lot of things don't change, dad

I agree with that

its pretty sick that youi went out there tho.   ;~)

sick>? whys it sick>

sick in a good way dad back to your youyth and everything

maybe someday I can take you guys out here you'd get a kick out of it there's a dued who mnakes tye-dyed

wqhats tie-dyed

it'll be great the three of us the Rio Grande just down the street

does it have fishing

maybe   inm mean probably   I know I owe you that   I havewn't forgotten

oh aarrrgghhh jeremy just woke up how did he even know I was texting

spencve ?   spence?

hi dad this is jeremooo

hey jeremy did spence want to say goodnite

he doesnt' want to talk anhymore he was cryiung after the last time you guys spoke

im sorry to hear that

he says to say goodnite

wow but hes letting you use his phone   things must be different around ther

they are dad! you gotta see our room how mom changed it!my desk is over by the window now, and spencer's bed in the corner is that OK with you>

sure it is honey

I didn't want to do it without showing you

well its been a long time sweetie.

I;m sorryt.

nothing to be sorry abouit!! hey did you like the mounds I left you

I've been saving it to eat with you, dad

why donb't you have it now

but I want to have it togehr like the old days

were together roight now   you stil there?

yup my hands are just muhsy

Jeremy I had chocolate withj some other kids today but it wasn't the same

not mounds

yeah mounds. I'm sorry I know that's s[pecial for us

who are they?

the sons of some friends

did they like em

a lot

that's OK then, dad   even if they wwere mounds

also i just want to say   im sorry I put you in that accidenet with the shopping cart. it must have been scary for you

yeah that was dumb of you dad I still love you though

I;m glad

and I;m glad nobody got hurt

me too

that was lucky OK dad, I got to get to sleep

sleep well, honey. be sure to—

Sure to what, dad

Treat mom right, OK? better than I did

I'll try dad   love u

How bounteous is the night, suddenly, expanding in all directions. Coyotes yowl in the desert beyond, their ballads floating on a splintery breeze. The dome of the sky is so black that stars flare against it, not shooting so much as dripping slow-fast like candle drops.

Words from a poem by Rilke come to me:

> Whoever you are: some evening take a step
> out of your house, which you know so well.
> Enormous space is near

I stand to find my skin flecked with rosemary needles, towel myself dry, apply clothes, and step over another dead-coyote cardboard at the curb. I have the town to myself at this hour, walking down Broadway, feeling more complete than I knew I could. The air is cold, but buildings give off radiant heat from yesterday's sunshine. For some reason it all looks ridiculously glamorous. The broken glass signs from the 1930s, advertising hot springs, could be hanging in an art museum. A bingo sheet in the gutter—green blotches on random squares—deserves to be framed. I feel like I've cracked a code I didn't know existed. Orange traffic cones stacked on the sidewalk signify that Fiesta really is readying for its annual parade. A flyer stapled to a telephone pole announces the Miss Fiesta contest. "Contestants must have never been married, never born any children, nor have any criminal charges pending." Next to it is a photo of last year's grand marshal, and damned if it isn't Head Shop Harry, "stoned since 1971!" Harry's photo is cropped around the edges, but it's obvious from his grin that just out of range he's giving the camera the finger.

I'm walking other streets now, where people live. Coughing comes through open windows from the darkness within. Only one of the windows flickers with color, and out of it tinkles a tune from long ago: *Boop-boop-de-doop-oop!* It's Summer's bedroom. I peek in his window and see glossy color photos of Betty Boop signed in the same vivid red as her lipstick. But no sign of Summer himself, so I continue walking past the windows of snowbirds and square dancers and wood carvers, past the spectral ruins of what may have been saloons or whorehouses back in the day. If I squint, I can just about make out catchy names like Silver Slipper and Muffy's Lounge still legible on the rain-stained wood fronts. I can practically hear the catcalls and cocking of guns.

Speaking of which, is that a pretend gunfighter approaching from his end of the street, walking in the middle as I am? Are we going to have a mock shoot-out? I curl my arms so it looks like I'm getting ready to draw. Disappointingly, he doesn't do the same. As we get closer, I see it's Summer, alone on patrol. He walks past without noticing me, chewing his tongue.

"The most unprecedented action ever taken by a city anywhere. . . ." The words of the newspaper article announcing the town's name change come back to me as I walk to the base of the water tower overlooking the town. I shake my head at the hubris, but maybe that's the hubris it took to keep T or C kicking the past hundred years. I gaze down over the slumbering streets, shamed by how little I understood about this place and its people, as oblivious as the six thousand people blasting by on the interstate every day, more than two million each year. How many of them give this town more than a passing glance? How many see the drunk-driving billboards and think that's kinda cute or they tee-hee at the town's name and wonder if there's a Ye Olde Souvenyre Shoppe worth stopping for, never dreaming that there are people here who sometimes find it as hard to stand up straight as they do?

Donkeys bray from an unknown distance, signaling daybreak on its way. Before long dawn finds me picking up litter in the Jornada, patiently extracting remnants of someone's red taillight from under a cactus. A foggy plastic applesauce container. I make an executive decision that rusty beer cans so old as to have triangles punched in their tops have earned the right to stay. After a certain number of decades, litter becomes landscape. Likewise, I'm content to leave the shreds of Walmart bags I can't reach nesting on thorns, this town's version of Tibetan prayer flags. They'll disintegrate soon enough. I'm half hoping to find a stray cavalry bullet casing in the sand, but never mind; it's enough to experience myself being more steadfast and meticulous than ever before. Attention this deep feels devotional—a trash meditation.

As daylight spreads above the empty road, I get the sense that I'm being watched. Is it the skinny long-eared hare sitting sideways, breathing with his body as he pretends not to stare? I perk my ears at an almost inaudible sound—the chuck wagon bell of Assholes Anonymous, a call to dawn breakfast carried on a breeze all the miles out here. My stomach gurgles at the thought of grub. "Let go of the reins," Clay from the Assholes had advised me. Am I destined to remember that for the rest of my life whenever my stomach rumbles?

As I make my way down the road, I pass the spot where I lay on my back in the sand, hoping to be struck by lightning. There is the imprint of my torso all these months later, battered by the elements but still visible. But how minuscule it is! Barely the size of a bath mat. From my shoulders to my waist, it's nothing but a dimple in the sand mixed in with gray pebbles, pieces of truck tire, clotted cactus quills. I feel like a lifetime of dog gunk has been removed from my eyes; I can see farther than ever before. Before long I spy what's either a mirage or a vehicle of some sort far down the road. Turns out it's a gleaming black Land Cruiser, latest model. When it stops beside me, the window slides down to reveal an expansive black leather interior and a driver wearing a visor. "You a convict?" he says, seeing my shirt poached with sweat. "You know they used to make chain gangs do what you're doing. Or is yours more like a personal penance–type deal? Mind I ask what you did wrong?"

"Lots," I say, plucking a thorn from my thumb with my teeth. "Mostly against the opposite sex."

"Hell, we'd all be out here if that was a punishable offense," he says. In the back seat, a sleeping man groans as he resprawls himself across the leather.

"Hey, is that Ted Turner?" I ask. "His spread's not far from here, right?"

"No comment," the driver says. "But I will say we don't spend more than a few days here at a time. Which is fine with me." He pauses, then asks the question he's been aiming to ask the whole time. "No offense, but how can you stand to live in a shithole like this?"

"It may be a shithole," I say, rapping his roof goodbye. "But it's Tuscany to me."

CHAPTER 26

SCAREFUL OF ACCIDENTS

THAT AFTERNOON WE'RE sitting in the office of Western kitsch—Teresa, Sarah, and me—all smiles as we eagerly await the King's arrival. So it's a shock when he explodes through the doorway and kicks my legs out of the way before dropping two legal boxes on the floor in front of us. "And get your damn notepad off my desk!" he yells before collapsing into his throne.

"Are you . . . OK?" I ask, taken aback.

"I assure you I am not OK, Mr. Nosey," he says, wiping his face that is sweaty with agitation. "Not OK in the least."

"What's the matter?"

"The matter," he says, reaching for a Big Gulp and trying to take a sip, but the straw seems to be clogged, "is that I do not take kindly to being bulldozed!"

The gurrls have adopted the expression of schoolchildren being scolded.

"What are you talking about?" I stutter.

"I'm talking about you have used up my patience, for starters, cluttering my in-box with copies of every damn email you see fit to send, like I got nothing better to do than follow all your precious progress reports!"

Is he joking? "I've just been trying to keep you in the loop," I say, "seeing doctors like you said last time, when you were so helpful."

The King draws himself up magisterially, so furious his voice starts doing a singsong thing. "That was before you-uuuuuuu started embarrassing me-eeeeeee . . ."

"I was just doing what you advised—"

"No, no, you don't know," he roars, nearly incoherent with rage. "You don't know because you're not a lawyer, because I've been a lawyer for years and I know how I want this case to go. I'm steering the ship, not you. I run the show—"

"Of course you run the show. I was just—"

"You were just. You were just. That's your problem right there! Why you gotta just? I'm head honcho here! Do I tell you how to run your business? Do I? Do I?"

"No, of course you don't tell me how to run—"

"That's what I'm sayin'! So what gives you the right . . . the god-damned attitude . . . to go shoot your mouth all over town asking this question and that question—"

"Only did what you—"

"What you only did was make people in town think I haven't been doing my job, is what you only did. And going all the way up to Albuquerque, that's just rubbing my face in it, boy."

My face is sweaty now too. I'm unbearably hot. Doesn't the man believe in air-conditioning? But I see it's going full blast. "You told me to get as much medical support as I could—"

"Did I tell you to go to the state capital for it? You went way outside my comfort zone on that one, pal. And now here I'm getting calls from all over hell's kitchen and back—"

Head honcho. Head honcho. Where have I heard that phrase before? But I have no time to pursue it, feeling rage of my own starting to rise. "With all due respect," I say, "it's not *you* who should be getting upset here. It's Teresa, who's been waiting seven long years in absolute torment to get any kind of action on this—"

I glance over to see the ladies watching me with expressions of horror. *Dan, no, don't—*

"Because you *haven't* been doing your job!" I continue, ignoring them. "The truth is, you *don't* give a hoot about these people! You finally secured a court date after seven years only because I've been breathing down your neck!"

The gurrls reach out their arms to me. *Stop, Dan, stop before—*

The King pushes back his throne with a squeal.

"You're right, I don't give a hoot!" he shouts. "You ever hear of a little thing in this country called the disability industrial complex? Fourteen million Americans, the number doubling every fifteen years? Quarter of a trillion dollars per year on disability, which is more than we spend on welfare and food stamps combined? You have any idea how many people in this town I put on disability? Half of 'em don't deserve a dime of it—"

"But this one does! She can't even pick up a gallon of milk to pour into her kids' breakfast cereal!"

"You know what I'm gonna say about that? You know what I'm gonna do? See these boxes here?" He pushes them forward with the tip of his ostrich boot, spilling legal forms and medical CDs. "My assistant spent the better part of the weekend xeroxing your records for you, and now you can have 'em back. They're all yours."

"What are you talking about?"

The King mops his face a final time and reassembles his composure. It's suddenly quiet enough to hear "the singing cowboy" Gene Autry tape on its loop in the reception area. "I'm talking about you messed up big time," he says in a voice of well-modulated victory. "You thought you could come out here and put on a desperado hat and pick up this case like it's all about *you-uuuuuuu*. Well, I got news for you, my friend. We all got lives of our own before you came, and we'll have 'em long after you go and never give this place a second thought."

I want to stave off what he's going to say next, but can't find the words to stop him. I feel the blood rush to my face—

"Yeah, it's sinking in now, isn't it, big shot?" he says, with a slow wide smile. "You see what all your arrogance has brought you. You have fucked it up royally for these people, Nosey-Rosey. How you like them marbles? Because of your being such a big shot, I'm closing the books on it. I'm withdrawing from the case. As of today, I'm no longer her lawyer."

My stomach plummets. Instinctively I pat my pocket for my home keys, as though they could help even if I could find them. "Wait," I stammer, "you can't do that."

"Oh yes I can. I can and I am."

"But we've got a court appearance tomorrow!"

His face can't help but betray how much he is actively relishing this moment.

"I want to take this opportunity to wish you good luck with that, boys and girls," he says, dusting his palms clean, "because I am no longer counsel of record."

Panic is smearing my vision. I can't see the expression on Teresa's face. I can't even bear to look.

"You're quitting the day before the court appearance?"

"I am no longer interested in the case! Plain and simple enough for you? As of this moment you're on your own. But I'm sure there are plenty of other lawyers who would be delighted to work with such an enterprising adviser as you."

"We're not going to find another lawyer at this late date."

"Not my problem, Rosey! But you have finished pushing your weight around here, I can tell you that. So next time you might want to think twice about bargin' in someplace with all your six shooters blazing, thinking you could light a fire under our lazy asses. 'Cause that fire done backfired, right here and right now."

"Please," I find myself begging. "You haven't even seen our letter from the doctor . . ."

"You think one letter is the shit that turns the toilet bowl white?" the King laughs. "You're still so far from the finish line it ain't funny! Hell, you ain't hardly begun. I'm only sorry I won't be there tomorrow to see that good ole Texas judge eat you alive."

Teresa and Sarah are finally out of their chairs, pulling on my arms to get me to stand as his secretary enters the room with a tailor's tape measure.

"So you may kindly leave my office now and take the lovely former grocery clerk Ms. Trumbull with you. She of the dainty constitution and mysterious ailments. Maybe you could even enlist her to help carry a few boxes with you. A little exercise wouldn't kill her. As for me," he says, unsnapping his cowboy shirt in one rip to bare his barrel chest. "I'm gonna get fitted for my Fiesta costume. The parade deserves a handsome devil to be grand marshal!"

CHAPTER 27

THE BIG BEYOND

SARAH AND I may not actually be limping the way Teresa is, but it feels like we are. Teresa herself shakes her head, unable to form a sentence, but I know what that headshake means: *Dan, this is exactly what we were afraid of.*

In the parking lot the gurrls collapse against their car while I drop the files into the back seat. Preparing to go our separate ways, we're too defeated to even discuss future plans. I pick up Flower Power. But it has a flat. I push it along the sidewalk, old and heavy.

Grand marshal. Grand marshal. My mortified brain plays the phrase over and over. Of course the King is the grand marshal, not Harry. It must have been someone's idea of a joke to staple Harry's face to the Fiesta poster. Or I was in some alternative mind space and imagined it. Roy Joy was right. My head's been up my ass so long I think the view is the Grand Canyon. It's why I lost my wife. It's why I lose everything.

Head honcho. Head honcho. Where have I heard that phrase before? Wasn't that how Frank the drunk described the "hot-shit lawyer" whose wife ran over his fiancée? My mind makes a leap. Did the King ever drive a Cadillac before he got his Hummer? With a human foot stuck to its grill? I don't pursue the thought; I'm not in my right mind. But could he or his wife have been the ones who purchased Frank's silence with $900 in hush money? And yet for all I know, the King is also the anonymous donor who pays for Summer's nightly coffee with ice cream at the Sunset Grille. I don't know anything about anyone. Everyone's a hopeless mix of good and bad I can't begin to figure out. *Grille? Grill?*

Growwl . . . The rottweilers behind the King's fence gnash at me as I round the corner, but also they don't. Everything startles me and doesn't. The sight of a brother and sister kicking around a brand-new soccer ball, wearing matching black T-shirts that read, Bad Ass Towing.

The gurrls come up behind me in their piece-a-shit automobile. "Climb in, Dan."

I lay my bike against the fence and crawl over the boxes in the back seat. I know it's shamefully presumptuous to ask, especially after ruining their case for them, but presumptuous is apparently who I am and what I do. "Would you mind if I borrowed your car for a bit? There's something I've gotta do."

We travel in abject silence a few blocks to their brown cinderblock house so they can get out. I can't bear to go inside with them and see the expression on Scott's face. It's enough to picture him sitting there in defeat, his head down, the boys not knowing what's wrong, their hands on his shoulder as they softly ask, *Dad? Daddy?*

Teresa and Sarah go inside and leave me to the car. I climb in the front that's in even worse shape than the back. Like in Tony's old Land Cruiser, I can see the road through gaps in the floorboard, despite the clutter of crap from Sarah's old carnival job: whistles and whirligigs, booby prizes a couple of rungs below McDonald's toys. The radio is busted with a screwdriver sticking out of its middle.

Taking the driver's seat feels momentous—operating a motor vehicle for pretty much the first time since the shopping-cart incident with Jeremy. But this is a drive I must take. I'm paralyzed at first, my hands trembling on the wheel. But slowly I ease the car forward a foot, and before I know it I'm on the highway driving south. In half an hour I'm there, in Hatch, looking at the graveyard that's surrounded by more chain-link. Scott's words come back to me from the night we met at the Cozi. *Fourth row under two big cedar trees.* I step out and in a minute am standing before Mary's grave.

It's the closest I've been to her since our crash. I'm glad to see it's a proper grave beside her mother's, not an unmarked grave with rocks on top to keep the coyotes out. But that's not what I'm here to say. What I'm here to say is, *I'm sorry. I fucked up and I'm sorry. I came all the way across the country on some half-assed mission, and all I've managed to accomplish is to wreck your family's chance at getting a fair shake from the system. God knows they didn't have much of a shake to begin with, but I made sure they had none at all. I should have gone into the King's*

office with hat meekly in hand, but I had to be Daniel, thinking I knew
best and me-eee, me-eee, me-eee . . .

Here's the worst part, only fully sinking in now as the pages of a
Walmart leaflet twirl around the gravestones in the rising wind. I must
have somehow felt that if I could save the Trumbulls' home life, I could
also save whatever was savable in mine. But what arrogant reckless-
ness! I'm as reckless as I was forty years ago. More so, because back
then it was only my own life I was reckless about, but here I've been
reckless with a family of innocent bystanders who have to live with the
consequences the rest of their lives. I'll be ready to leave at some point
and go my merry or not-so-merry way, but the Trumbulls are stuck in
this life, forced to salvage whatever fragments are left.

Preparing to depart Mary's grave, it's the moment when I either
touch her headstone or not. It feels like a life-size decision.

I touch. Skin to stone.

"Forgive me, Mary."

A speck of granite falls loose under my fingertips.

• •

The air winkles like lightning in the afternoon sunshine. A pinch of
desert sand pelts me, like the speck of gravestone granite, but more of
them now, scores of them swirling. I don't realize how hard the wind
is picking up until I open the car door and it swings out of my control.
There are at least a dozen houseflies inside—maybe they're taking
refuge from the storm that's about to hit? Because that's what the radio
is saying. Guess it isn't busted after all. A voice on an emergency air-
wave is issuing a warning:

> Weather alert! Dust storm advisory for this afternoon.
> Zero visibility is possible, with damaging winds in excess
> of sixty miles per hour. If you are outside, seek emergency
> shelter at once.

The radio voice is half-familiar as I wave the flies out and head for
the highway. But then there's another radio warning that makes me do
a U-turn before I reach the entrance ramp:

I-25 is shut down due to emergency conditions. Nickel-
sized hail and lightning strikes are possible. Everyone off
the roads! Everyone off the roads!

It sounds like Summer speaking in his broadcast weatherman
voice. But the warnings are valid: conditions are deteriorating by the
minute. The sun is engulfed by churning sand, obscuring the roadway.
The car is being buffeted by dust blowing from all sides as I inch along,
seeking a secondary route north. A coyote family races across the road
in alarm. A roadrunner sprints from the underbrush. Nature's in panic
as the weather comes roaring in.

Have I entered the realm of the supernatural? Has karma always
made for such a crappy ride? Because things are getting more out of
hand. In between static, the radio gives me snippets of voices from near
and far. Or so it seems. Is that Farwell growling about the dark side and
Head Shop Harry ranting about the vortex grabbing hold? A new sound
emerges, but it's not the radio. It's my cell phone—with Tony crying.

"Dan. Dan. My daughter came to visit. Hannah."

"Tony, that's great!" I shout, trying to stay on the road I can barely
see. "That's nothing to cry about!"

"You don't get it," he says, his voice blubbery. "She has breast cancer!
She's—"

His voice cuts in and out. "—not supposed to happen, Danny! To find
my long-lost daughter, only to have her facing the possibility of, of—"

"Tony, is this really you? I've never heard you like this before. But a
lot of freaky—"

"What are you talking about, Dan? How could this not be me? She's
got stage two, undergoing chemo—"

Wind pummels the car. A tumbleweed skips across the road and
explodes against my windshield. Dry lightning momentarily turns the
landscape into a negative of itself: black where it should be white and
white where it should be black.

"Tony, I want to hear about Hannah. But right now—"

"There's some weird shit at work there, Dan. That's what I called to
say. We both got in too deep—"

All hell is breaking loose as I drive. It's a twister filled with choking
desert silt, lashing the car every which way, even spiraling up through

the gaps in the floorboard like gritty gray smoke blowing in my face, blurring my vision.

"Check out the photo of Mary you sent me," Tony is saying. "Can you zoom in? Look at her smile. Can you see? She's got the same chip in her tooth that you do. It's like you're different versions of the same person!"

I don't need to look because I noticed it weeks ago without really noticing it: the same chip in her left front tooth.

"It's what I've been trying to figure out this whole time, Dan. Don't you see what's been happening? Everyone's identities have crisscrossed over time. We keep flying in and out of each other's lives like a motherfucker. We're not just Danny Rose and Tony Wilson, but I'm you and you're me, Dan-Tony, or Tony-Dan, or some freaky blend of both, and right now it's all about to come crash—"

But now I've lost him. Or rather, replaced him with a visual: Tony floating outside my window, frantically mouthing the words: "Get out while you can!" Then Tony's replaced by an image of Judi the newspaper editor, holding up a front-page headline: "Crash Dummy Back for Another Crack at Death." I twist the radio screwdriver to get an update on the storm but only succeed in activating more havoc. *Boop-boop-de-doop-oop!*

The interior of a dust storm is a place of hallucinations, evidently. Or its opposite—truth visions. As I approach T or C from the distance, I make out the water tower and recall the graffiti near its base: "S&T 4ever." I suffer a terrible thought. Did S&T stand for Scott and Teresa? But how could they have reached that high? In the center of the storm I allow myself to think the unthinkable. Could it be that Teresa isn't quite as physically impaired as she makes herself out to be? That her disability case is a scam? Didn't I once see her lift her leg over the kitchen gate to get to the Mounds bars I brought them? *Was* she malingering? Were the medical and legal establishments right to deny her so long?

Having fun yet?

Lightning detonates to reveal the silhouette of a buzzard on the sharpest branch of a barren tree. I swerve at the T or C turnoff to avoid being hit by a family-style station wagon speeding the wrong way with a yellow scarf flapping behind. No, I'm imagining that. Maybe I'm imagining everything. In the wake of her speedy passage, there's a whirlwind of rosemary leaves. Then lightning again, seeming as radioactively bright as the bomb lit here so many years ago, fusing pebbles together and charring the air. I sense something about to come crashing in on my right, or my left, or where? How can anyone tell where anything is coming from, or when, or why? We're all so vulnerable every moment of our lives—

"Tony, she's not stopping!"

And just like that, the dust clears. The wind dies. I'm back at the Crash Site of forty years ago—but unlike forty years ago, this time I'm somehow able to watch the proceedings unfold clearly. It's a sunny, unclouded morning . . . as confirmed by the weather report, broadcasting placidly from the radio:

"Hot and dry this Saturday morning, the fifth of September, 1970. Accident taking place at the intersection of Broadway and Austin, brought to you in bright slow motion . . ."

And it *is* in bright slow motion. With a clarity I wasn't privy to last time, I watch the miracle crash unravelling before my eyes. The intersection laid out in front of me is like a film clip from some lost region of my brain I haven't been able to access in forty years. A pickup is gunning it in slo-mo out of a dirt gulch to my right. Then suddenly I'm out—*bang!*—the warm air lofting me away. I almost remember—no, I, *do* remember—paddling slowly through the air, an undignified position that drops me in the middle of the roadway, blacking out. But because I have an overview this time, clarity instead of confusion, I realize the truth of what Tony was saying a few minutes ago. We do indeed keep flying in and out of each other's lives like a motherfucker. Why else would Sarah's car be a Plymouth, probably the same kind the cops drove to our crash in 1970? Why else would Teresa, the daughter-in-law of the woman who hit me with a truck, get hit by a truck herself; would Head Shop Harry and Tony seem like doppelgangers of each other; would Tony end up crying when he always teases me for crying; would I have chipped my front tooth exactly where Mary chipped hers? On and on. One minute I'm on a stretcher trying to convince the emergency doctor I'm not a pill-pushing criminal; the next minute it's he who turns out to be the pill-pushing criminal. One minute I'm resting my head in Mary's lap, relieved I still have a head; next thing it's her head that's gone, quite literally—courtesy of her last husband. We're constantly slipping in and out of ourselves as though none of us permanently inhabits the role we think we do. Given enough time, the identities that are so precious to us get swapped out with the precious identities of everyone else on the planet. No part of us is set in stone; every molecule is in motion. We think we own this experience of being who we are, but really we're just borrowing each other for a short while, jiggering and rejiggering ourselves till we're all jumbled together in endless bounty.

We are all . . .

In the hospital, coming back to consciousness I find myself in the old grade school classroom; I see the clock hands from sixth grade again, hastening around the dial to reveal a secret whose precise words are coming into focus, at first only three, then five, then fully seven—*over time . . . we are all . . . each other*—words so simple, so surpassingly obvious, that I fight off the perverse impulse to lose them again as soon as possible, to blink them back into oblivion. But this final time I won't let the words sift off into the sunlight. I clutch them tight as I am bequeathed one final vision.

My wife. My goodly wife, weeping quietly to herself, because she's been in a car crash too—the car crash of her marriage that unfolded slowly over sixteen years. Not all of it was bad by any means, but she suffered too much and too long, pining for a partner who was off in his own world. The awful truth amounts to another kind of revelation, one I'm long overdue to have: being with me made her lonely. How could I have been so blind? She tried telling me, but I didn't hear. She tried showing me, but I didn't feel. Now I do, the vision of her knows that I do, and this woman whose smile always melted me is smiling to me through her tears, nodding like I got it, I finally got it—even though there's nothing I can do to make it up to her now except, as Scott says, to be as good to her for as long as I can be till the end of my days, even if it's too late to do so as her husband.

The present time returns. I sit quietly alone with my revelations in Sarah's car at the Crash Site, the air so clear it's as if the sky's been sandblasted, revealing its inner nature at last, neither guilty nor innocent but a blue of blue blueness, nothing more, nothing less. In a minute the air winkles again like lightning in sunshine, signaling the division between all the dark that came beforehand and all the whatever that will come henceforth. I cruise down Scott's street toward the house of brown cinderblocks straight ahead. Sarah's car and I are back to normal life from wherever we were, and it's with a sense of deliverance that I hear the radio playing the trusty jingle:

Trucks! Truck! Trucks! We got 'em!
Cars! Cars! Cars! We got 'em!

Time to face the music.

··

I stand in Scott's doorway, a stricken man, ready to take my medicine.

After a deep breath, I knock. While waiting I notice for the first time that the cement stoop has horseshoe prints around the border. A sadly decorative touch. I knock again. No one comes to the door. I understand. If I were them, I'd put in extra locks to make sure I never darkened their doorway again.

I'm about to leave when the door opens. But it's not a pretty sight inside. A seated Scott does indeed have his head down, but not with despair, as I feared. The kids do indeed have their hands on his shoulder, softly asking, "Dad? Daddy?"

But that's only because they're working together to untangle some old contraption from an old McDonald's toy.

"Oh hey, Dan, good to see you," Scott says cheerfully as he finishes his task, tossing keys to the boys, who race with them across the room. "How goes the old grind?"

"I've had better days," I say.

"Why? What's the matter?"

"The matter? The King quitting! The case good as gone! Didn't you hear?"

"Oh, heck, we're used to that," he says in that genial tone of his. "Nuthin' we ain't seed before."

To my astonishment, the gurrls are nodding, Sarah placidly braiding Teresa's hair as though there's nothing amiss. But she's also flinching with a spasm somewhere. One glance at her erases the vision I had in the storm that there might be any kind of scam going on. This is a woman in anguish.

"These are the keys to the jail," the bigger boy is saying to the smaller one by the pool table. "I'm your parole officer, and you're under arrest."

Scott takes note of the expression on my face and decides to elaborate. "It's no big surprise, Dan. People like us, we never expected to win. Not really, deep down."

"But didn't you hear how badly I blew it with the King?"

"Know what I think? That was bull he slung at you back there," he says, as the gurrls nod agreement. "It wasn't that you were swampin' him with emails or whatever else he said you did or didn't do. It was just him coverin' his butt 'cause he knew he had a weak case. We figured that out easy enough. He was lookin' for an excuse to get out of it 'cause he didn't do his homework, so he's throwing out a smokescreen so he can say it ain't his fault. Plus of course he wants to drive a wedge between you and us, which ain't gonna happen."

"Yeah, but I antagonized the one person who was your lifeline!"

"Naw, man, he was a bull scam artist. You called his bluff, and I say good for you."

"But if I hadn't shot my mouth off—"

"Don't get me wrong," Scott says, cutting me off. "It would have been nice to win some money. I won't lie. We were hoping for a miracle. But you know what? I don't give a hoot about the money. I've been poor before, and it ain't so bad. We grew up without shoes, had to heat water on the stove to take showers, so I don't even care about the money. Heck, if it was between Teresa getting well and getting the money? No contest. I just want her well."

"But with money you could have afforded better health care."

"You don't get it, Dan. None a that matters. You tried, that's what matters. You cared enough to go to bat for us. No one ever did that for us before. You gave it your all. That's what means the world."

"But I ruined it for you, Scott."

Scott bangs his forehead with exasperation. "You apologize one more time, I'll have to kneecap you. Man, no wonder people keep smackin' you sideways. You don't know when to shut up!"

I smile. Scott smiles too.

"I hear what you're sayin'," he says. "One time I tried to get a tick offa Teresa and ended up leaving his head in, which only made him madder than he would a been if I'd just let him be in the first place."

"Which reminds me of something else I may have screwed up," I say. "I think maybe I was the one who brought scabies into your home."

He peers at me with that gift of his, that nonjudgmental way of looking at things. "How you figure?"

"That night you found me in the desert, I'd been in Candy's bar not long before. If any place would have scabies, it'd be that one. I never got them myself but I might have been a carrier, sitting in the taxi next to you."

"Dan, you gotta take a chill pill. Why d'you keep thinking you did this and you did that when it ain't even about you in the first place, and never was! It was just our little problems we had to deal with whether you happened to show up or not."

I peer at him, trying to believe he means what he says. "So you don't hate me?"

"What I gotta do?" he cries. "Get a two-by-four and knock you between the earlobes? You could come here in the middle of the night and eat us outa house and home, and still we couldn't hate you!"

Scott keeps his hands in a "what I gotta do?" gesture.

"How could I hate you, after all you done? I never knew my mother sang. That she knew her Bible. All I used to know was that she—well, you know what I used to know. But you came in here not knowing me from a hole in the wall, and look what you done. You gave me back my mother, is what you done. You gave me back my history: where I come from and who my mother was. She cooked and wrote letters and took pictures. She loved me! She loved me, Dan! Do you know what that means to me? And even if I never see those uncles you're always bugging me about, just being reminded they're around, that's something."

Teresa and Sarah are nodding, their eyes sparkling.

"That's why I say: You always have a home here. If you ever need us. I meant it when I said my casa is your casa. You ever need food, just come in and raid the fridge, man. Don't even bother to knock. What more can I tell you? You're family now. And we won't never throw you out, neither."

SpongeBob music is playing. I love *SpongeBob* music.

"So would you allow me to take Teresa to El Paso tomorrow?" I ask. "We already have the appointment anyway."

"Why the heck not. Let her testify. And add your two cents to the judge, if you like. We don't expect nuthin', but if you wanna see it through—"

"And if it doesn't work tomorrow, may I keep trying from wherever I land, interviewing new lawyers and such?"

"You leavin' us?"

"I thought I'd fly back from El Paso tomorrow, after court."

Scott inhales sharply through his nose. "See, that reminds me," he says. "Truth is, crap always happens to the nicest people. That's what it comes down to. Here you are, nice as can be, and the crap you're going through being without your boys? I see you suffering without 'em. You don't talk about it, but I see it. I can't even imagine. If someone tried to put some daylight between my boys and me? Don't even ask. And the crap happening to Teresa? I tell you, we got three seventeen-year-old girls at the Cozi on disability; they're running up and down the stairs. And Teresa, who wouldn't hurt a flea—she can't get squat. And sick as she is, still all she can think of is other people. She says, 'Put me in a home, I don't want to be a burden.' I say, 'Hush your mouth. Ain't no one putting you nowhere.'"

From their corner, the boys are shaking their keys. "C'mon with me to jail, I'm lockin' you up."

"You know what she told me this morning?" Scott goes on. "She said, 'Scott, what's the worst that could happen? We don't get no money, so what? That comes and that goes, nothin' you can depend on. If I can't afford a wheelchair, heck, there are women all over the world worser off'n me, and they ain't got no wheelchairs. I got two wonderful boys, a loving husband, and the best Sarah that ever could be, so what the heck am I complainin' about?' That's what she said, word verbatim."

"Word verbatim," Sarah confirms. "I heard her too."

"And I don't hold no ill will against the King, neither," Teresa adds. "He's not a bad man. Just stretched probably too thin, is all. He didn't have to take us on in the first place. It was never like he was gonna make a fortune off us."

"You're generous to let him off the hook," I say.

"Heck, you gotta be nice to everybody, 'cause you never know who's gonna be standing on your air hose someday."

A joke from Teresa! And not a bad one either. But Scott has fixed me with a serious look.

"No, but for real?" he says. "This is our one shot at life, you know? And it goes by too quick to add to each other's burdens. You could be in a pile-up tomorrow, and you missed your chance to be good to someone. Know what I'm saying? There's more pain out there than you can shake a stick at. So we all gotta throttle back and just try to be kind to each other."

"Damn, Scott," I say. "How'd you manage to learn that by age thirty?"

Scott doesn't blink. "By having the crap kicked out of me more times than I can count."

I flash on something. You know how they say you grow new synapses in your brain when you do crossword puzzles or mental games that challenge your brain? These few words with the Trumbulls—they give me synapses of the soul, sprouting up all over. Maybe I'm not too old for this crap, after all.

"Lockin' you up and throwin' away the keys," the boys are saying. And then I see: Those keys aren't part of an old McDonald's toy. They're . . . no, they're not. Could they be? My key chain? My home keys?

"Really—yours?" Scott says. "How do you like that? Sarah said she found 'em under the car seat a few days ago mixed with all the old carnival junk. Maybe you dropped 'em when you helped out at the gas station."

I'm holding them in my hand, all these months later. The #1 Dad! key chain! With a color drawing of my sons and me fishing. The keys to the jail. Not that T or C was jail, exactly. But it was someplace I couldn't bust out of until, until—

"What's that on your shirt front?" Scott asks, plucking off a rosemary needle to examine. "Where'd that come from?"

"Huh, Rose and Mary," Teresa says. "Dan Rose and Mary Green. Like the two of you mashed up together in one word."

"OK, I'm outa here—that's too much for me," I say.

"For me, too," Scott says. "This whole business—I gotta go give my head a rest."

CHAPTER 28

GOODBYE, EVERYBODY!

A BRIGHT-PINK COLANDER. That's what a policeman wears on his head as he directs traffic along Main Street early next morning. Yes, it's Fiasco time—sorry, Fiesta—and everyone's in high spirits. The May celebration, held annually since 1950, doesn't officially kick off till later with a grand-slam parade, but this being T or C, folks are getting in the spirit ahead of time. In Ralph Edwards Park, Porta-Johns are being hauled into place, bunting is being hung on fortune-telling booths, and Head Shop Harry is doing a brisk trade selling tie-dyed yarmulkes. Bringing up the rear is what looks like a contingent of mini-Geronimo warriors on snare drums. Velma the office receptionist seems to have a special dose of Fiesta fever, leading her Brownie troop through some ambitious baton-twirling routine. The Brownies are dropping their batons a lot, but Vel is a pro!

It's not even 7 a.m. but warm already.

"Gonna be a hot one."

"Could light a match off it, um-hum."

That's communication, is what that is.

Freshly shaven of my Wyatt Earp mustache, I'm listening to Tony on the phone with me as I inflate Flower Power's tire at the gas station where I first met Teresa. "My point is, you've got a big day ahead and it's natural to feel conflicted," he's saying. "On the one hand you're hopeful about showing Teresa's medical letter to the judge, but on the other hand you're worried how court's gonna play out without a lawyer. Then after you fly back, what will the reception be like with your family? It's the picture of paradox: a festive atmosphere, but danger everywhere. Be scareful!"

I shift the backpack on my shoulders, light with the few things I'm taking with me, and blow dirt out of the air valve. "What about you, Tony? Your daughter—"

"I'm glad to take that one off your mind. The cancer's a little less invasive than they thought. Matter fact, I'm flying down to Tampa this weekend to be with her for the resumption of her chemo."

"That's, terrific, Tony!"

"I'm trying not to get my hopes up too much," Tony says, releasing a shy half yawn to change the subject. "So here's my final point, maybe the biggest of them all. After all these years, you're finally starting to realize you took the exact wrong lesson from our crash. The fact that you survived made you think you were bulletproof, when in actual fact all you were was fuck-a-duck lucky. It should have been a wake-up call to how much you were the *opposite* of invincible—"

"Well, I'm feeling vincible now, I can tell you."

"Humble pie, how refreshing. So do me one last favor, please? As you wrap things up, don't go around romanticizing the place, making T or C out to be some Miracle-Gro spirituality center or something."

"Miracle-Gro?"

"You know, some epic growing things or whatever. I'm the one who got you out there, so I'm the one who can tell you."

"Tell me what?" I ask, though I feel it coming days before he says it.

"That you could have gone anywhere, these past many months. Fact is, it's just a scrappy little town with a few nut jobs and a pretentious name, that's all. The point was just to get you out of the sunporch, but you could have gone to Ass-Scratch, Alaska, and it would have been the same. So don't go making out how this is your amazing home away from home, the community you've been seeking your whole life, blah blah. You know as well as I do you'll be forgotten the minute you leave, if you haven't been already."

As if to underscore his words, the bikers I met at this gas station roar by without a sidelong glance. And as close as the next pump over, Freckles the hundred-year-old is pumping his own gas with no sign of ever having met me. Mercifully, Mitchell the chiropractor waves as he drives by in his very own Land Cruiser.

"I'm not sure either of us believes that about Alaska, Tony."

"Actually, I was just trying it out to hear how it sounded," he confesses. "Tell you the truth, I'm not sure what I believe in anymore. Did I tell you I Googled Hotcha Hinton, just to see what she was up to?" We do our ritual bow to the stripper, who turns out to have been a female impersonator all these years. What does that mean, that our first nude lady was a man? I'm so confused. Did we get everything wrong? Did we never even make that triple play back in Little League? Maybe the newspaper article about our crash was nothing but an illusion. I just wish we'd found some solid scrap of evidence at Farwell's junkyard to prove it was real. Didn't even have to be our scrap, just a piece of anyone's to prove we didn't dream up the whole enchilada."

This time it's me who yawns, appreciatively, though I'd be hard-pressed to say precisely what it is I'm appreciating.

"Anyway, Anthony, for what it's worth," I say, screwing the cap back on the air valve and straightening up, "thank you. I'm glad I didn't stay home cleaning the dog gunk."

"You're welcome, for what it's worth," Tony says. "And I'm sure you'll keep them to yourself, those guts I spilled." He executes a final *whaaang* on his ukulele to mark the pronouncement. "So good luck with the rest of your life. Say hi to the boys for me."

"Will do. And me to Hannah."

"First base to third for the out."

"And the game."

"OK, who's next?" Jose the barber asks, pocketing his tip as the freshly shorn lama bows and takes his leave. "Anyone else got last words for Daniel here before he heads back to where he hails from?"

The motorcycle momma Dayna steps forth to get her buzz cut renewed, bringing a weight to the proceedings even greater than the lama's. She acknowledges me with a curt nod, silencing the room as she steps into the chair.

"I been thinkin'," she says, clearing her throat. "I come through town often enough to hear the talk, and people got all sorts of theories. Some say Dan and Mary met on an astral plane before either of 'em were born, made a pact for her to crash into him so he'd come back years later to help her family in their hour of need. Others say it happened on accounta the water he sipped from the iron spigot just before his crash. The magic water and all that. I don't make a judgment on these matters. All I say is you'd be a damn fool to shut your eyes and not notice that something's going on, everywhere and every day, and it's a heap bigger than we are. A god thing? It is what it is. Karma, whatever. If it's true, it don't need me or anyone else to believe in it anyway. Maybe all we have to do is say thank you and leave it at that."

No one speaks. The only sound is Jose's scissors, snipping so quietly we can hear an empty cardboard twelve-pack outside, stuck against the back tire of a passing truck. *Fwup-fwup-fwup! Fwup.*

"Well, I hear the talk too," he says, working on Dayna's sideburns. "Most of it's too rich for my blood. I'm not qualified to put words on it. Maybe it's wrong for us to put words on it anyway, or try to bend it to our logic. We don't know, is the end-all and be-all. We don't know. All we know for sure," he says, and here he stops snipping for a second, "is that Mary sure picked the right fellas to hit."

Murmurs of approval ripple through the barbershop. A gentleman in back lowers the newspaper from in front of his face.

"That about gives me goose bumps," Kenny says.

We share a handshake. It's a good one this time.

· ·

A warm breeze blows through the open door of a brown cinderblock house. The Trumbulls are expecting me.

"Hey, beautiful!" I say to Teresa. Because she is. And Sarah too. They've spruced themselves up for El Paso with lipstick and powder, looking shiny and good.

"How you?" Sarah asks, semiflirty.

"Just about got it whupped," I say, semiflirty back.

"What happened to the 'stache?" Scott calls over from his seat at the pool table where he's working on a jumbo computer. "Shaved it for the judge?"

"You got it," I say, ruffling the boys' hair. "Hey, cowboys!"

But both boys are sleepy on their father's lap. "Yeah, the monkeys didn't hardly catch a wink all night so they could see Mommy off this morning."

Putting a barrette in her hair, Teresa is rehearsing the speech she's going to give later this morning. "Hello, your honor, my name is Teresa Trumbull. I was rear-ended by a truck seven years ago. I cannot pick up a plate without breaking it. I cannot lift a gallon of milk. I cannot . . ."

I've been muttering in the same manner all morning. "Hello, your honor. In the short time I've known Teresa Trumbull, I've come to believe that she is exactly the sort of person disability laws were designed to protect. She and the other Teresas of the world . . ."

Without disturbing the boys on his lap, Scott is tapping softly on the keyboard of one of the computers.

"I've been doing a little research," Scott says, "and it's true about Texas judges. Apparently the Fifth Circuit is the most conservative court in the country, and Judge Smith's the most conservative one they got. But the good news is I've been going through Teresa's medical CDs." He runs the cursor down the screen adeptly, cross-checking with the King's files at his feet. "It says right here she shows 'classic symptoms of DDD'—degenerative disc disease. Heck, we could make a case right from that alone."

"Who wrote that?"

"One of the Social Security docs we saw years ago. And they're supposed to be the toughest of all. It's buried down in the paperwork but plain as can be. So even if today's judge flunks her, seems to me we still got a shot at an appeal." He starts copying things down off the screen. "Medium-sized disc extension which appears to touch the left S1 nerve . . ."

"I'm leaving my bike in your shed, for anyone who wants to give it a spin," I say. But no one seems to hear in the general hubbub as we make our way to the car outside.

"You mind drivin'?" Sarah asks me as she snugs Teresa in the back seat, encasing her in freezer packs for the ride. I shoot her a look like, *You trust me to?*—which Sarah deems not worth answering. "I can drive Teresa back home afterward, but mornings are bad for my sciatica."

"Since when have you had sciatica?" I ask but am gently laughed at. Don't ask.

Time for taking leave of Scott. I put out my hand, trying to decide whether I should show him the way his uncle Sandy shakes, one hand enclosing the other's, or the way his distant relative the Apache elder Eddie Montoya does, one loose palm pressed against the other. But Scott beats me to it, handing the boys to Sarah and engulfing me in a full-frontal hug, no male spacer needed. The embrace contains an extra charge I wasn't expecting, packed with another person's sorrow in a three-way. Mary may be invisible, but her sadness feels locked in with us, along with our cautious hope. Breaking away, Scott passes me a handmade cassette tape. "For the ride," he says, waving the floppy boys' arms goodbye.

Festivities are warming up as we navigate downtown on our way to the interstate. Cars are streaming into town from miles around, from Roswell and Alamogordo and even as far as Santa Fe and Phoenix and Las Vegas. Gridlock is worsened by the fact that traffic is confined to one lane: orange cones cordon off half the length of Main Street. But hey, good for T or C! We managed to get half the job done.

"The most unprecedented action ever taken by a city anywhere. . . ."

It's getting to be quite a party. Old-school hippie chicks off the desert communes are dancing free-form on the hoods of monster trucks. A clarinet squeaks as stray members of the high school marching band practice their scales. Other high school kids, self-conscious in ROTC uniforms, plant brand-new flags to line the sidewalk, crisp and colorful.

In the passenger seat, Sarah pops open a bag of Chocolate Turtle Chex Mix as we try to escape the traffic jam by turning left past Assholes Anonymous. But, uh-oh, there's Roy Joy blocking the road in his wheel-chair, brandishing a baseball bat.

"Where you think you're going, cock munch?" he thunders.

I look at my passengers. What kind of danger are we in for this time?

"Just toyin' with ya!" he says, wheeling around the side window to gallantly kiss Teresa's hand and wink salaciously at me. "Done all right for yourself, Brother Dan! Double your pleasure zones!"

Clay from Assholes Anonymous lopes down off the porch, followed by Hap Hazard and Bird Brain. Clay spies my key chain and takes in the situation at once.

"And so #1 Dad! sits tall in the saddle, ready to head homeward," he says.

"Right. *Home sweet home* as opposed to *homebound*," I agree. "'Cause it may be too late for that."

"Carry it on your back, can't never lose it," Clay says.

He assesses me, squinting against the ashes from his hand-rolled, flittering off in the breeze. "Looks to me you got yourself another soft landing," he says. "A little worse for wear, but nothing you need an X-ray for." He flips the butt away. "So d'you get the story you come for?"

"Enough to know it was never really mine to begin with. I just got whacked by a piece of it."

"That's how it is, old son. We think we're the star of our little show. Come to find out we are too. But then so is everyone else the star of theirs."

We fist bump. Bird Brain swats the windshield with his flyswatter.

"I'm gonna miss this town," I tell Clay.

"Just keep growing that goodliness of yours. And don't forget to duck!"

As I pull away, Summer stands on the corner, fervently squeezing his eyes shut as he clutches Raggedy Ann to his chest with both arms. "Bye, Dan-Rose-going-back-to-his-boys!"

I try to honk, but the horn's busted.

..

I'm driving out of town with the gurrls when the notion of a detour comes to me—a short side run that should still give us time to make our appointment in El Paso, two hours away. I steer us through the mountain pass and emerge on the other side where Tony and I first met Farwell sitting with his ghost dogs. But that time it was nearing sunset; this time it's early morning and the sun is casting an opposite light on things. As I stop near the old sandblasted signs, for the first time I can make out dunes and drifts in the sand like a half-buried dinosaur graveyard: the shank of a fender poking out amid a few other fossilized auto parts that escaped being crushed and carted to Las Cruces, among nuggets of windshield glass glittering in the morning sun. If they're not the remnants of our old wreck in particular, it doesn't matter—they're those of a hundred others whose tales will never be told: of desperate husbands driving into the base of the dam and despondent wives steering off the cliff curves, of teen boys showing off for their girlfriends and grandmothers faced with the loss of life partners. May they rest in peace.

With that thought—*flash!*—I'm blinded by the sun reflected in a half-buried rearview mirror. Still parked overlooking the junkyard, but 'remembering forward,' in the words of the medicine man, I am able in another moment of crazy clairvoyance to witness the fate of Teresa and her family being decided two hours hence in an El Paso courtroom, the Honorable Judge Smith presiding.

··

Judge Smith (in white crew cut): All right, before I start I want to know, Who is that man with you in the courtroom today?

Teresa: That's my moral support, Dan Rose.

Judge: Uh-huh. And let me ask you this. When you say "moral support," does he come moseyin' round your precious home or just talk you up on the phone?

Teresa: Both, Your Honor.

Judge: And how often does he do this?

Teresa: Do what?

Judge: Mosey into your private home, and be aware that this is officially on the record and this testimony may be used against you.

Teresa: Maybe three times a week, Your Honor. He checks up on me and my husband and our two boys.

Judge: And tell me this: Is your husband present when this man comes over to mosey?

Teresa: I don't understand the question, Your Honor.

Judge: I'm askin', Is your lawfully wedded husband on the premises, or is he conveniently away at work on those occasions?

Teresa: Most of the time he tries to be home, Your Honor. He's a little protective with me around other men.

Judge: Uh-huh, and tell me this: Is he especially protective around this man?

Teresa: He used to be, but then Dan here gained his confidence.

Judge: Oh, he did, did he? I just bet he did. All right, I've got enough to make my ruling. You'll be notified in four to six months.

Dan Rose: But, Your Honor, we—

Judge: I said I've heard enough outa you!

Dan Rose: But, Judge, we have important new evidence we'd like to introduce—

Judge: I would most soberly advise you to hold your tongue lest there be unfriendly repercussions.

Dan Rose: We lost our counsel—

Judge: I said I've got enough. Please leave at once.

Dan Rose: We have a letter from one of the best doctors—

Judge: Someone eject this man from the room—

• •

The sun moves on, closing the glimpse of the future in the rearview mirror of Farwell's vanished junkyard. But I've seen enough to imagine the rest: that the judge's ruling six months later will be unfavorable, and over the course of the next two years the Trumbulls and I will weed our way through a total of eleven lawyers from all over the state who will decline to take us on, before we land on one named Victor Blake, who will believe in our appeal and will proceed to final victory in an Albuquerque courtroom.

I myself will decide not to accompany Teresa to court that second time for two reasons: my presence hadn't exactly been helpful at the first court appearance, and also I sense it is important for the Trumbulls to handle it themselves.

It isn't, I'm trying to say, about me.

So let Teresa tell what went down in this new venue, as she gushed it to me over the phone an hour after the new verdict was pronounced.

"I liked this new judge—he was very nice and gentle. I didn't know what he meant at first when he said he was granting our claim, but once we got in the hallway my lawyer turned to me and said, 'You won it all!' He said he never seen this judge give a decision on the spot like that before, but the evidence was so strong he overruled the Texas judge then and there. Seven years back payments and full disability going forward, for the rest of my life. That's the Powerball to us, is what it is. Just in time, too, 'cause we are down to our last few nickels; Scott was on his hands and knees yesterday checking the couch cushions for coins. Didn't find none, neither.

"I'm still in shock, tell you the truth," Teresa goes on. "My chest is still pounding. My body don't know how to react to good news. Scott, too—when I called him at home he said he needed to sit down. Not me. I've been sittin' too long. I would be jumpin' up and down, but I'll let the kids do the jumpin' for me. We're taking them to the movie theater tonight to celebrate. See us some toons!

"See, that was part of my depression," she continues. "That I'm useless. Can't cook. Can't clean. But now I can do things! I can pay the bills! Know what I'd like to do most of all? I'd like to make a big sign saying, 'We won!' and shake it in front of that asshole's face, the King. And I know I shouldn't use language like that, but in this case that's what he was. Calling me a grocery clerk that time? I weren't never no grocery clerk! I was a bagger! I had to lift heavy objects daily before I got hurt, which weren't my fault! Him and that ole crew-cut judge! So screw them 'cause we won! We won! We won!"

But all that, as I say, is two years down the line. For now we are still in Sarah's piece-a-shit vehicle overlooking Farwell's junkyard. The sun has moved on, releasing us from remembering forward. The gurrls pass their Chex Mix between them while I watch the veneer of sand shifting in the morning breeze, covering and uncovering more auto fragments from the undulating hills. In the distance I see the traces of a tar road being broken up by weeds, returning to desert. I remember Farwell saying that the entire Southwest was once covered in lush ponderosa pine forests, the puzzle pieces of their bark smelling of vanilla, and that it may revert to being that way again, given enough time. He said it with a smile, like it was a comforting thought, somehow—the hills steaming into mist, the pines rearing up and dissolving away and rearing up again. "Tony, she's not stopping!"—I said once, years ago, and I was right. She wasn't. Nothing stops. For better or worse, everything's in motion, forever.

Us too. Flying in and out of each other's lives like a motherfucker.

F R WE L, says the sign closest to us, and as the three of us pull back onto the roadway, we plug in the tape cassette, twist the screwdriver, and there is Scott's voice accompanying us on our ride:

> Go down, go down, you Hard Knocks girl
> With the dark and roving eyes
> Go down, go down, you Hard Knocks girl
> You can never be my bride.

A beautiful tenor—he has his mother's voice!—sweetly singing the violent words, as out on the road we go, past a bright new sign:

ADOPT-A-HIGHWAY
LITTER CONTROL

with two names proudly rejiggered inside out for all the world to see:

TONY ROSE
AND
DANNY WILSON

TWO YEARS LATER

CATTAIL POLLEN

"HELLO, DANIEL, THIS is sad news from T or C," began the email I received from Mary's brother Sandy, champion bingo player from the Moose Lodge, two years later. "Porter, the cop who I believe helped out in your crash, passed away recently. He was sick a long time on that porch of his, so it wasn't much of a shock. But when I called the paper to ask for details, I was told that his old sidekick Kenny also died suddenly from a massive heart attack. Doc Studds, too, I believe you met him? The surgeon who sewed up your friend in the emergency room back in 1970? Gone just like that."

"Boy, this is getting scary," I thought aloud. "I wonder what will hurry up next, as they sometimes say out there."

So I went back. To see what would happen next. At age sixty-two, freshly divorced, I returned with my two boys. Scott's family had remained a strong, calm unit in the interim. Mine, I'm sorry to report, had flown too far to save. My wife and I wiped each other's tears and signed those terrible papers. But my boys and I were closer than ever before, and here I was again, back in town after all this time.

Spencer with his proud new learner's permit drove into the Trumbulls' driveway to the new house they'd bought with part of their disability payout. Enclosed within a shiny chain-link fence all around, the Trumbulls' yard was adjacent to property that ran down to the edge of the Rio Grande. The house itself, situated only a few blocks from the iron spigot where I first splashed myself with water that morning back in 1970, was flooded with sunlight. Festive red-pepper lights ran around large windows, an antidote to the gloom and doom of their old house. A spacious corridor ran down the middle with shiny bedrooms on both sides. You know what it looked like, especially compared to their previous place? A desert castle. Not the one Tony had in mind, maybe, but a desert castle just the same.

"We got curtains, bunk beds, forty-eight-inch flat-screen TV—we're all set up," Teresa said, still gushing as she showed me around. "Best of all, we own it free and clear, so it's something the boys can't never get kicked out of."

Sarah nudged her. "Tell him the other thing, Teresa."

"I got my first ever professional teeth cleaning!" Teresa said, swiveling across the gleaming floor tiles in her chrome wheelchair. "That dental floss, though, my gums didn't take kindly to that!"

But this wasn't the most pressing development Sarah wanted Teresa to tell me. It was left for Scott to say what that was.

"I'm going to college," he said modestly. "Graphic arts, with my aim to go into media art and animation. Got a 94 percent average so far, mostly A's except one B when Draike caught the flu. It's all online so I can stay home and help with the kids. Plus we've had a mail-order business up and running for what, three months now?"

"Three months, two weeks," Sarah answered smartly. "Called Shilouette. Not silhouette: Shilouette. Just the coolest name we could think of."

Down the hall Sarah opened the door to the home office where I got a peek of scanners and laptops. On the website screen were pictures of "cowboy collectables"—miniaturized bronze buffaloes and rustic wood picture frames ornamented with tiny Colt .45 pistols—all the Fake Wild West schlock they must have admired in the King's office. Proving once again that you don't have to like someone to borrow some of their attributes. In and out of each other's lives like a motherfucker.

"Here's the thing that kinda eased me into it," Scott said, handing me a laminated booklet with computer-generated cartoons. *Little Charlie Tucker and His Very Noisy Nose*. Complete with a mean rain cloud and Charlie wearing a winsome expression like he's half expecting good things and half expecting bad. Like Scott himself. Worriedly hopeful.

Charlie's winsome expression. Drawing by Ernest Pierce.

"The monkeys' favorite book," Scott told me. "But that there top copy's for you."

"Speaking of the monkeys, where'd they all get off to?" I asked with rising alarm. "They didn't go down to the river by themselves, did they? The current's pretty strong this time of year."

"No worries, Dan," Scott said, leading me into the yard where Proto and Plasm—correction, Draike Vaughan and Vaughan Draike—were down at the river's edge with Spencer and Jeremy, all four of them safely fishing on the banks of the Rio Grande where we two #1 Dads! joined them for a spell, talking about the future.

"That's where we're planning us a garden," Scott told me, pointing out a grassy patch by the river bank. "Teach the boys how to grow things like what my grandparents grew. Beans, corn. Maybe even pecans to make cake with, what they're eating now."

"How is it?" I asked the boys, who were stuffing their faces. "Good as Mounds bars?"

"Mm-hmm," Jeremy said.

"Mm-hmm, *mm-hmm!*" Spencer agreed.

"Onliest thing I'm worried about is over there," Scott said, pointing with his chin to a run-down camper trailer across the river. "I'm too spooked to go over, but sure looks like a crack house right across from where my kids play."

"Mind if you watch the boys and I'll take a quick look?" I asked. I located a half-sunk tree trunk upstream and crossed over. The trailer was long deserted: the rusty door scraped off its hinge as I opened it. Inside I could see where rainwater had come through two broken windows and soaked a broken black cowboy hat. A pair of granny sunglasses with gray paint speckles lay bent amid a pile of empty vermouth bottles.

"Fate and fate and fate," I said to myself. "How's a person supposed to carry his home on his back if he falls off the wagon?"

··

Other developments from the past two years:

Kenny the Cop: Dead, as already noted, but bears repeating. Made like smoke and blew away.

Doc Studds: Also dead, and also bears repeating. The defrocked doctor was said to have no shortage of women snuffling into hankies at his funeral.

Barker-the-Barker: *Bark bark bark!*

John Porter, the Babe, the big cop dying small on his porch: May I pay my respects to him again, too, one last time? It feels like a point of honor, for some reason. RIP, good sir.

Rocky, the cabdriver: Dead. T-boned in a crash not dissimilar to ours, hit by a driver who didn't see him coming despite full visibility in broad daylight. Forcing Scott to learn to drive himself, which he discovered wasn't half as scary as he'd always thought.

Summer: Dead. Making T or C infinitely lonelier than it was, without its Raggedy Ann–toting sentry. His death paradoxically gave new life to the rumor that it was the King who for years had paid for Summer's daily coffee with a single scoop of vanilla ice cream.

Farwell the junkyard owner: Sadly, neither dead nor alive but stroked out, unable to speak or whittle. Still waiting for the day when someone takes his ashes up the hills and scatters 'em out with the wild goats.

The boys, Proto and Plasm: "Ornery as heck!"

Fred "Freckles" Pitch, the hundred-year-old from the barber shop: I'd love to report that he was still licking his finger to see which way the wind was blowing before jitterbugging across the street. But he died in his sleep the next year at age 101. Here's his obituary with his real name: http://www.legacy.com/obituaries/lcsun-news/obituary.aspx?pid=147156224.

Head Shop Harry: Not dead! In fact, I continue to send him license plates from time to time for him to nail to his ceiling. A feature on him in the *El Paso Times* (using his real name) ended with this quote of his: "Look at me. Dressed the way I am in the middle of the day, would you stop and talk to me if you had never seen me before? Probably not. Normal is just a setting on the dryer, and who wants to be that?"

Tammy / Doctor Tom: Didn't make it. Had his sex change the first winter, got depressed, took himself out to Ralph Edwards Park one night and shot himself in the head.

The Vietnam War: Not totally forgotten.

Frank the drunk from Candy's bar: Rumored to have sobered up enough to become the town's new driver's ed teacher, but I find that most unlikely. Assistant teacher, maybe? Shop instructor? Whatever the truth is, he was said to have wed his "humble" from the bar in a ceremony quiet and tasteful.

Cactus: Dead—lots of it, anyway. "Global warnin'?" Anyone's guess. The winter after I left, the temp dropped to seven below. For two days people couldn't heat their living spaces higher than fifty degrees, and they took to their beds under all the blankets they could find. Fixing all the burst pipes kept the town's five plumbers backed up for months.

Water, the magic water of T or C: Still attracting and repelling travelers from near and far, even if they stop only long enough to splash a handful of rusty water on their faces.

Half-buried junkyard auto parts: Continue to rise and sink in the fluid tectonics of the desert, so that every now and then, when the sun is right, you may still be able to glimpse the future in a rearview mirror, or in the words of the medicine man Eddie Montoya: "remember forward." In any case, auto fragments continue to spin and turn slowly in the flowing desert sands, eventually earning their right to be considered part of the landscape.

As for my world, not much more to report. With so much evidence that the globe's in almost symphonic flux, I've come to grasp a bit of what the town elders taught me: that time is the real head honcho in this drama, conducting the microseconds of a car crash and rejiggering the planets. In fact I had only the tiniest grace period in which to capture this story before it disappeared for good. Forty years after the crash, if I'd come back only a few months later, I never would have been able to meet half the principal players before they'd passed away. The story would have been lost to the sand grains of forever.

All of which leaves me feeling precarious, like I was kept alive only to tell this story, and there's no more reason for the air to loft me much longer. It may happen that I live to a grand old age ("a hunret!" as Freckles the centenarian would boast), in which case the laugh's on me. But as of right now, I have an odd, close-up feeling, not unlike the rank breath of death roaring up from the canyon floors below, but more like the dark perfume of—

Never mind. Time will count the hours. Meanwhile, the sand urgency in my throat is gone, at least for the time being. I've become a ridiculously cautious driver, always bracing myself against vehicles lunging at me from every direction at once. And yes, I'm being the best ex-husband I can be. Not perfect, but whenever a question arises as to which path I could take, I try to choose the best ex-husband path.

As for the orange-yellow, truth-telling, cattail pollen applied to my lips that afternoon in the ghost town by the medicine man Montoya: I can still taste the memory. I can! I do!

And, finally, the Louvin Brothers, who recorded "Knoxville Girl" when Mary was a girl of eight. According to their biography, Ira Louvin survived being shot six times with a .22 caliber pistol by his third wife after trying to strangle her with a telephone cord. He himself was killed two years later by a driver who was nine times over the legal limit for drunkenness while Ira himself was wanted on a DUI warrant. His beloved mandolin was reportedly the only thing not smashed to smithereens. Younger brother Charlie Louvin lived to the age of eighty-three and died only a few months after the events described in this book. Classified as a murder ballad, "Knoxville Girl" was meant to be sung as a warning against everlasting sin.

· END ·

Two Injured Wh

Saturday when these
reets.